EXMOUTH AT WAR

LIFE ON THE HOME FRONT IN DEVON DURING WORLD WAR II

ARTHUR COOK

HALSGROVE

DEDICATION
To Lesley

First published in Great Britain in 2010

British Library Cataloguing-in-Publication Data
A CIP record for this title is available from the British Library

ISBN 978 0 85704 071 8

HALSGROVE
Halsgrove House,
Ryelands Industrial Estate,
Bagley Road, Wellington, Somerset TA21 9PZ
Tel: 01823 653777   Fax: 01823 216796
email: sales@halsgrove.com

Part of the Halsgrove group of companies
Information on all Halsgrove titles is available at: www.halsgrove.com

Printed and bound by SRP Ltd, Exeter

Contents

BOOK
PRODUCTION
WAR ECONOMY
STANDARD

THIS BOOK IS PRODUCED IN
COMPLETE CONFORMITY
WITH THE AUTHORIZED
ECONOMY STANDARDS

Abbreviations

A.C.	All Clear	L.B.V.	Landing Barge Vehicle
A.F.	Auxiliary Fireman	L.C.I.	Landing Craft Infantry
A.F.S.	Auxiliary Fire Service	L.C.M.	Landing Craft Mechanised
A.R.P.	Air Raid Precautions	Me (109)	Messerschmitt
A.S.R.U.	Air Sea Rescue Unit	N.C.O.	Non Commissioned Officer
A.T.C.	Air Training Corps	N.F.S.	National Fire Service
B.E.M.	British Empire Medal	O.C.	Observer Corps
C.D.	Civil Defence	R.A.	Raiders Approaching
D.U.K.W.	(Duck) Amphibious G.M.C. Truck	R.A.F.	Royal Air Force
F.A.P.	First Aid Party	R.M.	Royal Marine
F.W. 190	Focke Wulf 190	R.O.C.	Royal Observer Corps
G.I.	Government Issue	S.C.	Sprengbombe Cylindrishe (High Explosive Bomb)
G.M.C.	General Motors Corporation	T.E.D.	Time Exposed to Danger
G.T.C.	Girls Training Corps	U.D.C.	Urban District Council
H.E.	High Explosive	U.S.	United States
H.G.	Home Guard	V.A.D.	Voluntary Aid Detachment (Red Cross)
H.Q.	Headquarters	W.I.	Women's Institute
H.M.S.	His Majesties Ship	W.L.A.	Women's Land Army
H.T.	High Tension	W.R.N.S.	Women's Royal Naval Service
I.T.M.A.	It's That Man Again, Tommy Handley's popular radio show	W.V.S.	Women's Voluntary Service
Jabo	Jagd Bomber (Hunter Bomber)		

Introduction

Everybody likes a story including me. I have spent many years listening to people's stories of their lives in WWI and WWII, always fascinated how ordinary people can become embroiled in situations which are beyond their control and which are often extremely dangerous and traumatic. Many servicemen I have talked to over the years, remained haunted by their experiences for all their lives, due to their involvement in fighting in the battles of the 20th Century's conflicts on land, sea and air, which eventually won us the freedom of thought, deed and expression that we enjoy today.

Many of these servicemen and women, although witnessing some terrible things, also looked back fondly on the comradeship and sense of purpose experienced whilst serving, and profoundly missed the situations and sometimes humorous circumstances they found themselves in, caused by the privations of war.

Having recently moved to Exmouth four years ago and also having previously worked for Exmouth Town Council as the Organiser of their Arts Festival for two years, I took advantage of my connections made with the people of Exmouth and started to pursue my interest in WWII more vigorously, talking to people about their experiences on the home front.

As the stories and facts started to unfold, I decided to write up my findings in this book.

It seemed to me that most people of all generations had a story to tell about Exmouth during the war. Some could have been easily cast aside and put down to urban myth, while some incidents and aspects which were undoubtedly true, seemed almost unbelievable. Some people, from later generations, also seemed to think that nothing at all had happened in Exmouth during the war and also, some who served overseas or were children in the town at the time were unclear of events, times and dates. My primary focus has not been to destroy our local stories, but to put them into context with what was happening elsewhere in the world at this time.

Exmothians such as Bill Sleeman and Geoff Perriam had already started research and collected evidence and newspaper cuttings from the war years. Some are available to see in Exmouth Museum. In the post war years the local newspapers, such as the *Exmouth Journal* and the *Express and Echo* contained reports and articles from other well know Exmothians such as George Pridmore and Bill Gorfin. These reflective and nostalgic editorials were published on anniversaries and these events from people's memories proved very useful in laying the foundations for further investigation.

It became clear to me at this point that the task was quite a large one and if possible I should try and piece together the story as best I could from the following sources.

Primary sources: Eyewitness accounts, reports, period photographs and paperwork. Some held in private collections and others in local Libraries, Museums, Records Offices and reports in wartime newspapers, bearing in mind these were heavily censored at the time.

Secondary sources: Relatives testimonies, photographs presumed to be from Exmouth but were inconclusively labelled, and local hearsay which gave me some incredible leads into finding out what really happened.

I decided the "leaving no stone unturned" was the best approach and I have tried my best to get everything as accurate as possible under the circumstances and apologise in advance for any omissions or mistakes.

The next stage for my research was to use the local shop keeper's community spirit to put up 200 posters in shops and Town Council notice-boards for a period of nearly a year, which brought in people for me to interview. This was further helped by the *Exmouth Journal* and *Express and Echo* who published articles on my behalf advising the local population of what I was doing and urged them to get in touch with me. I cannot thank the papers enough for the role they played in my research. Newspapers play an important role in society and feed quality information to the community with limited resources and increasing competition with other media sources. They should not be underestimated in projects such as these and need support to secure their future.

Gradually, I was able to interview around 100 people locally, which was great fun and I enjoyed meeting so many new people, some of which tolerated my questioning on more that one occasion and I have now become good friends with most of these people. I am always amazed when talking with older people by the wealth of wisdom and knowledge they possess which unfortunately gets overlooked these days.

During the course of the interviews I wouldn't let on what I already knew for two main reasons. Firstly I did not want to put words into people's mouths so they would only tell me what I wanted to hear. Secondly with very careful questioning, I was consciously looking for three pointers from three different eyewitness accounts to confirm the events as they happened and in what sequence and over what time scale they occurred.

For instance when I interviewed Mike Heard, who is sadly deceased now, it was apparent to me that he had an incredible eye for detail and an incredible memory. He described to me the way the Hart's bus to Budleigh had looked when he cycled through The Strand after the raid on 26th February 1943 and said that "the bus was a dirty red colour and looked as if someone had lent on the back of it with a giant hand". It was almost a year before I eventually found a photograph (in the Bill Sleeman Photographic Collection) and sure enough, that's what it looked like.

One point that should be noted is that I have used women interviewee's maiden names, if they were not married at the time or their married name if they were. Hopefully this will make peoples lives easier when researching local families many years from now.

After reading around 600 war time copies of the *Exmouth Journal & Chronicle* held at Exmouth Library (boy, they must have got fed up with me!), and keeping careful notes on my computer, I was then able to start cross referencing my findings with eyewitness accounts, times and dates etc. and began to get a feel for the wartime censorship laws and began to read between the lines as certain phrases came up time and again.

Newspaper and private photographs, which were difficult to evidence when and where the events depicted in them happened, became a lot easier to decipher as I photographed, in tiny detail, the remaining buildings in the town and compared the architectural similarities of them now with photographs taken at the time. By showing "then and now" photographs this will hopefully give an indication to future generations that things did happen in Exmouth during the war. The face of the town is changing so rapidly at present. Some of these events were in fact terrible as you will see later.

I have also tried to include local landmarks in the photographs wherever possible, including things like war time post boxes and jubilee telephone kiosks which are gradually disappearing from our streets.

I must thank the people who generously let me make digital copies of their personal photographs. I was able to repair the damaged ones using new computer programmes in order to preserve them for the future.

The final results of my research and writing up resulted in nearly 3,000 pages of text. This was much more than I had anticipated. As you can imagine editing the information I had gained into one volume which every one could enjoy and understand became the next task. Thankfully I have had a lot of support from a good publishing company and their guidance has been much appreciated.

I hope you enjoy this book and thank you for buying it. Please try and go through it with you children and grandchildren on a wet Sunday afternoon or take a walk and look at the photos and the buildings in existence now and try and imagine what it was like during the raids.

Weights and measures I have recorded in kilograms and litres etc. to make it easier for children to understand, but the prices of wartime goods and postage etc I have left in £.S.D. so you can work it out for yourselves as our currency changes in the years to come.

My plans for the future include continuing to interview and collect information from this period in Exmouth's history and I am always looking for more information. Please feel free to contact me at the numbers and addresses given at the back of this book if there is something that you think would help my research.

Thank You.

Arthur Cook
Exmouth 2010

Chapter 1
Pre-war Exmouth

The Exmouth Presentation Tank

Exmouth had a Mk IV tank donated to the town on Tuesday 9 September 1919, as a gift in recognition for the services the town had made to aid the war effort in WWI. The aid was in the form of National War Savings contributions donated to purchase weapons of war. It was displayed on the seafront next to the old lifeboat station with its front facing towards Orcombe Point.

Aubrey Sleeman
'As kids we used to play on the old tank on the seafront, we used to lift the gun barrels up to their highest elevation and let them drop. They had no breech blocks on the back so they always fell back down with a big "Bang!" and to us that was the sound of the guns firing.'

John Pascoe-Watson
'We used to climb all over the tank on the seafront as children. It was good fun. Inside the tank there were partitions. It was very cramped and dark inside. I couldn't stand up easily inside the tank. It was painted a battleship grey colour at the time, but was pretty faded as it had been left to the elements. We used to play on top of it and ran up and down the tracks. I think the tank was taken away at the same time that all the railings were removed from the town, which was at the time of the Dunkirk evacuations around June-July 1940.'

In the inter-war period people were sick and tired of WWI and the misery it had brought to many local families. Many people also considered the tank an unsightly and inappropriate reminder of bad times.

Finally the town council decided to scrap the tank for the war effort in July 1940, in response to Lord Beaverbrook's appeal for aluminium and metal for munitions.

Mike Heard
'As children we used to spend our time down on Shelly Beach in the summer. We'd also ride to Woodbury on our bikes in the autumn sometimes to

The WWI Mk IV Male Tank

gather chestnuts. We used to play Stanley and Dr. Livingstone, pretending to be explorers out in the woods, during our early years. We'd ride our bikes round to Budleigh and spend hours playing with the pebbles throwing them into the sea. We also threw bricks into the slaked lime pits at brickworks to make big clouds of dust, just for fun. Not exactly safe!'

If you lived in Exeter, coming to the seaside was a real treat.

Jim Dyer
'Once in a while, before the war, we had a school trip or Sunday School trip to Exmouth. We used to travel to Exmouth in a hired charabanc; it was like an open bus with no suspension. We went to the lifeboat station area. There was a café behind and we would sit and have a cream tea or round buns with jam and cream on them.'

Fred Butler
'We used to go to Sandy Bay beach before the war. The beach access was down an old iron ladder. We used to have a lovely time playing and swimming. After spending the day on the beach we went to have tea with a Mrs. Tooze. A family friend.'

Exmouth Beach

Devon Seaside resorts were very busy as usual on the eve of WWII, as the weather had been good for the

Left to right: *Joy Penwarden enjoying a donkey ride; Mandy Bryant plays on the beach; Derek Rowsell and his family in their boat on Shelley Beach August 1939.*

most part during the summer season. Exmouth was bustling with summer tourists and day-trippers on Saturday 2nd September 1939. The beach was reported as busy and the town was full of visitors some coming to shop or enjoy a film at the Savoy Cinema or dance at one of Exmouth's renowned dance halls.

Donkeys on the Beach

The Donkey Rides were owned and worked by Mr. William John Richards prior to the Second World War. The donkeys' paddock was at Foxholes then and they were walked down to the beach every day for children to ride on. At the start of the war the donkeys had to stop working the beach, to prepare for anti invasion obstacles.

Mary Ashleigh
"The Donkeys near the Octagon petrified me for some reason!"

Bernard Greenaway
'The beach huts were actually placed on the sand before the war. They were placed on the beach on

John Pascoe Watson looks towards his future

April 1st every year and removed again on September 29th. They were positioned right on the sand on the seaward side of the sea wall at the time. From the old lifeboat station to the rocks.'

John Pascoe-Watson
'I was taken for a ride by my father in a de Havilland Rapide aircraft which landed at a field near Clyst Honiton to give pleasure flights. I was scared stiff to go at first, but loved it so much I decided that was what I wanted to do, be a pilot.'

Bernard Greenaway
'Before the war the only sign of any Military activity was when the Territorial Army (4th Battalion of the Devonshire Regiment) took over a large field near St Johns in the Wood Church. The trainees were taught to ride horses and jump, and military drills etc. We used to go to watch these displays with my father Harry. Other than this, there was very little military involvement in Exmouth before the war.'

There was still a general feeling in some areas of Britain that war could be avoided through the rapidly closing political channels and some of the less informed remained blissfully unaware of any real threat from Germany locally and nationally.

On Saturday 2nd September 1939 at 11 o'clock the B.B.C. announced that war was imminent.

4th Battalion the Devonshire Regiment Cap Badge and Devonshire Regiment pre-war shoulder titles

Chapter 2
War with Germany

11.00 a.m. Sunday 3 September 1939

It was a sunny, September sunday, when the news that Britain had declared war on Germany was broadcast. Where possible people had either stayed in to listen to the impending news on their wireless (radio) sets, or gone to their neighbours to listen to the Prime Minister Neville Chamberlain's fateful speech to the nation. Some Exmouth people can remember exactly where they were and what they were doing when war was declared.

Bill Sleeman

'I was on route to Woodbury Common on a cycling trip with friends at the time. We stopped at a house which had the neighbouring families leaning in through open windows listening to the wireless.'

Ivor Pike

'I can remember Neville Chamberlain's declaration of war speech, on the Sunday morning; I was six at the time. The family were gathered round the wireless listening quietly. Amy Davis the milk lady who used a horse and cart to deliver her milk, which she ladled out into jugs, was with us.'

Ron Lee

'I was in Exmouth on duty in uniform. At the police station in Victoria Road we heard the news on the wireless. Sergeant Buckingham and other constables were there listening very intently to the news'

'We had sealed instructions which were delivered some weeks before the war and other information in envelopes, which we had to open if war was declared. The first job we then had to do was put sand bags outside the door of the Victoria Road Police Station, in case of bombing raids.'

Exmouth was initially considered a low risk area of attack from an aggressor, as it was thought it had no real military or strategic importance and so it was deemed as a "safe" area to send evacuees from London and some of the larger cities in the event of a war.

Operation Pied Piper

In September 1938, the Government had published its initial plans for evacuating children from London and other large cities. This date was one full year before the start of WWII. By May 1939 the registration of names of those who wished their children to be evacuated, to escape the threat of bombing or invasion in the event of a war had already started

Since 1937 the British had realised that the Germans policy of "Blitzkrieg" (lightning war), with the aid of the Luftwaffe (German Air force) could raze to the ground any city they chose. One such city was Guernica, which was virtually destroyed by the Spanish Nationalists and the Luftwaffe on 27th April 1937 during the Spanish Civil War.

More recently Warsaw had been subjected to similar treatment and the British were secure in the knowledge that they would have the same tactics used against them in a "Total War" with Germany. Civil Defence plans and policies were starting to be adopted all over Britain by 1938 and one of the most important of these was the evacuation of children from metropolitan areas deemed at risk from German air raids.

By August 1939 the full evacuation plans had already been in place for several months and children, some with parents, or just mothers and others to be evacuated on their own, were ready to travel in the event of the outbreak of war to escape the threat of bombing or invasion.

THE
OUTBREAK OF WAR
2nd AUGUST   1st SEPTEMBER
1939

MINISTRY OF INFORMATION
LONDON

Ministry of Information Outbreak of War *pamphlet*

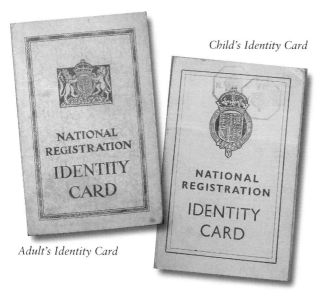

Child's Identity Card

Adult's Identity Card

On Friday September 1st 1939, the first 776 evacuees arrived at Exmouth Station. It was the beginning of an operation code named "Pied Piper", the British Government's evacuation of over three million children thought to be at risk from German bombing in London and other high-risk areas. In the first two days alone 1.5 million children between the ages of 4 and 14 were evacuated and the efficiency of this operation was mainly helped by the rehearsals which had been organised in July and August.

Children had to report to their schools at 6 o'clock in the morning with one small case and their respirators. Identity cards and address labels with numbers were tied on their coats. All Metropolitan cities Glasgow, Manchester, Liverpool and even Plymouth had evacuations some of the children were billeted in Exmouth.

In Exmouth well-organised local people had already volunteered the use of their cars to drive women and children to the Evacuation Centre and after registration, to temporary new homes.

Exmouth's Women's Voluntary Service (W.V.S.), the Salvation Army and the Y.M.C.A. all helped with organising the evacuation and also supplied mobile kitchens and canteens to help feed the evacuees.

All were busy making plans on Friday 1st and Saturday 2nd of September organising an evacuation centre at the Pavilion on the seafront. From here the evacuees would then be sent to local community halls, where people could go and choose the young children and families that they would be prepared to billet. At this time the evacuees were already on route, from London Paddington and Waterloo stations.

Whilst the Government plans were set in motion, private evacuations of a further 2 million people had started. Whole families had uprooted and gone to set up home in a place far away from the reaches of the total war that other central European countries had already been subjected to. There were soon new groups of evacuees arriving every week, most people had every room in the house filled and some people had to be coerced by harder means to help.

Ron Lee a Policeman in Exmouth at the time remembers the complicated arrangements which had to be organised in very little time.

Ron Lee
'On 1st September 1939, two days before the declaration of war, the first evacuation scheme from London started and evacuees began to arrive at Exmouth railway station. After a few days, I was given the job of assisting the billeting officer with placing them. Exmouth people turned up with their cars to take women and children to their new homes. It was the local families that were asked to put them up. Families who had at least one spare room.'

'These evacuees were all from London and its surrounding areas and were mostly just the children,

Evacuees' suitcases

Evacuees' labels

W.V.S. Civil Defence hat

W.V.S. Civil Defence badge

Exmouth W.V.S. Tea Van

Evacuees at the Exmouth Pavilion

there were hundreds. Every week another group arrived and soon every spare room was occupied. Not everyone was happy with the arrangement and some had to be persuaded to take in their share.'

The 1940 London Blitz saw the second wave of evacuations and Exmouth once again took on its share of evacuated children.

In October 150 Women and Children arrived from the East End of London within 12 hours notice and 400 more were expected the following day. Marpool Hall in Phear Park (now demolished) was requisitioned by the council and the new evacuees were housed here for a while. The Red Cross V.A.D. and W.V.S. helped with organising the accommodation of this group and begged and borrowed bedding and cooking utensils from wherever they could. The Pavilion was also used on later occasions to home approx 400 new evacuees at a time until more permanent accommodation could be secured for them.

John Pascoe-Watson
'It was quite sad really, a bit like a Roman slave auction; they would bring a child forward and say who wants this one. Sometimes no hands would go up and they would have to find another way to find a home for a child.'

There were soon new groups of evacuees arriving every week, most people had every room in the house filled and some people had to be coerced by harder means to help. Initially some of the local children took a dislike to the new arrivals, as they were having a lot of attention paid to them.

Ivor Pike
'Some of the evacuees smelt pretty bad and others had nits and lice. We couldn't understand why some were so dirty and poor and their clothes were in tatters. Local people rallied round and gave them second hand shoes, clothes and blankets.'

'The evacuees fitted in well after a while. There were some squabbles naturally and fights, but it all turned out alright, I think the locals got a bit jealous of them. It didn't help that the mums were saying," poor little mites!" and making a fuss of them.

I didn't like the injustice when some evacuees were bullied or picked on. So I befriended an evacuee called William Pask and stuck up for him, we became really good friends. I've got a far better understanding of what they had to go through now and would have hated to be in their position.'

Roy Hole
'The alley-way from the Colonies to the Town Centre

Became known as the Lambeth Walk, mainly because a lot of the first evacuees came from Lambeth. The song was very popular here too, at the time. The route of this alley went across someone's private property and the owner of the land would try and charge 1d for every one who wanted to go through it!'

Just after D-Day, in June 1944 the third wave of evacuations started, prompted by the V1 and V2 attacks on London. By 1942 only 27 of the millions of children evacuated to other areas of Britain had been killed in German air raids.

Mike Heard
'Some evacuees from London were billeted in Council run hostels. Some of the bigger houses in the Avenues were requisitioned by the council and the evacuees that were too rough to be housed with local families ended up there. Ironically, they took over some of the best houses! A lot of the evacuees from London had never seen the sea before; they loved it here in Exmouth.'

Brian Baker
'I moved to Exmouth when I was six. The war had started in 1939 and we were living in Croydon. The area was badly bombed in 1940 and my Father thought it best that we moved away to a safer area of Britain.' My whole family came down with me, we had nine children and we were known locally as the Horrible Baker Brothers. We lived at Number 23 New North Road during the war and I went to Exeter Road School.'

I met wartime evacuees the Collin's sisters Jean, Maureen and Rose in the Cavendish Hotel on one of their holiday's to the town. Sally Stocker arranged the introduction for me.

Jean Collins
'We were evacuated from the Oratory school in Chelsea, at the beginning of the war. We had no idea where we going to live. All we knew is they would be complete strangers to us. Me and my three sisters, Maureen, Rose and Anne, left home with a label round our neck and a parcel tied up with string containing some clothes and a gas mask.'

'When we got to Exmouth, we couldn't write to our parents, phone them, or contact them in any way to start with. We were treated very well by the locals generally, but the first woman we lived with was terrible. After a time we were split up, Rose and Maureen went to one house and Anne and I went to another. These new people treated us really nicely.'

'Things turned out alright in the end for us when our Mum moved down to be with us. We had a lovely time then. We made some really good friends. We've

come back to Exmouth on regular holiday's ever since and still love it here.'

Jack Humphries

'Some of the evacuees were a bit rough, occasional fights and disagreements would happen but generally speaking everyone mucked in together at school and at play. A lot of the evacuees found it hard being away from home and were always waiting for a letter from their folks, but some didn't receive any letters at all during the course of the war due to problems with literacy. Some just didn't hear a thing!'

By the end of 1944 most evacuees had been returned to their homes. However a lot of children did not want to go back home after the war. Marriages were wrecked due to separation. Parents had been killed and some did not want their children to return as they could not be bothered with them. Some had no houses and homes to return to as they had been destroyed.

Twenty-six children for one reason or another were never claimed.

Refugees

Jack Humphries

'Louis Bloomfield was a Jewish refugee from Germany, who had settled with his family in London and was then evacuated from London. His family had been persecuted in Germany but luckily they managed to get out just before the war. His name was changed from Blumenfeld to Bloomfield, to make sure they were not persecuted again in Britain for having a German name during a war with Germany.'

Peggy Gibbins

'When I was at Exeter Road School, we had some Jewish girls arrive who had escaped from Germany just before the war had started. They were very nice girls who lodged with Miss Sweet on Salterton Road. They were beautiful girls, blonde haired and blue eyed, really pretty. They were called Beatrice and May Schloss their parents had been arrested by the Germans and they had been smuggled out of Germany and ended up in Exmouth.

There were quite a few others too later on, all really nice girls. We got on well with them. There were two girls called Mari Goldstein and Lea Lavenstein, aged about 11 and 13. Every weekend they went to special religious services in Torquay.'

Joe Radgick

'As the Channel Islands fell, the army set up a defensive Lewis gun position on the docks. The Army and Police were notified that a launch was coming in full of evacuees from The Channel Islands. They first held them off at gunpoint and then let them land, where they were interrogated for two days by the Police and local authorities in case they were German spies or 5th columnist's '

Jack Humphries, Louis and friends in the Church School Christmas pantomime1939

Winifred Gliddon

'I left Jersey when I was 6, we just escaped the German occupation. I remember mother was crying because the Germans were making their way to the Islands in ships ready to invade. Boats took the people from the Channel Islands, who wanted to, or could leave across to England.

It was a ferry service from Jersey that took me, my father, mother and brother; I was wearing an Astrakhan coat and stood on deck next to the railings looking at the sea. We left at the last very last minute. My father had been thinking of taking mother to Exeter as she needed an operation, just before the threat of invasion and so we came to Devon and she went into hospital.'

'We moved to my mother's home town of Exmouth and stayed at first with my Gran and Grandad, who lived at Pound Street. Grandad was the care-taker of the Exeter Road School during the war. His name was Mr. Collins. After a short time we managed to rent a house in Fore Street and moved the family in there.'

The Phoney War

Elizabeth Maycock

'There was a lull after war had been announced and nothing seemed to happen, I was expecting to find German soldiers around every corner and always thought that they were on the way!.'

A few months after the first evacuations, Britain entered a period know as the "Phoney War". The Country was technically at war with Germany, but they were not engaging the German's in land battles. The war at sea had already begun and Exmouth had already lost men in an engagement at sea where H.M.S. *Courageous* was sunk killing four local men, just two weeks after the declaration of war.

Air engagements between enemy aircraft and planes of the R.A.F. were few and most encounters were with German reconnaissance planes, which had over flown most parts of the British Isles to take photographs of military or strategic targets, bridges, industrial areas and potential landing grounds.

Civil defence welfare shoulder badge.

Residents Ask For Imprisonment

Fines Imposed For Alleged Refusal To Billet Evacuees

ALL DAY SITTING AT EXMOUTH COURT

The first cases brought before Exmouth Magistrates for alleged failure to comply with the requirements of billeting notices, were heard at the Police Court on Monday. Of the nine cases eight residents were fined and one dismissed. Two of those fined declared their intention of going to prison for 14 days, the alternatile to the fines imposed. The Bench was composed of Mr. G. E. Mackmurdo (Chairman), Col. M. G. D. Rowlandson, Mr. W. Bardens and Mrs. D. A. Roberts.

Chapter 3
Exmouth's Defences

Beach Defences

After 3 September 1939 the Army quickly took control of the beach and removed everything, kiosks, boats and small businesses, deckchairs, donkeys and boat trips had to cease trading from the beach area. Initially the beach was cut off completely from the area around Coast Guard House and the Lifeboat Station to Orcombe point. The pier was also closed and the wooden boards taken up to make landing from boats more difficult for the enemy.

Although the seafront was generally closed for business, impromptu concerts were set up by various brass bands and singing groups. Walking along the seafront was still a popular pastime during the war.

Mary Ashleigh
'During the war, barbed wire cut off the beach areas. Sometimes we used the beach area near the Stuart Line Cruises ticket office. At the pier we used to climb the slope to get "pop" bottles and get the deposit back! I always wanted to be a Salvation Army "Sunbeam" with their grey and yellow uniforms, who played and sang on Sunday afternoons near where the Harbour View café is now.'

Joy Penwarden
'My Friend Dianne and I used to ride our bikes all the time, from Bradham Lane all the way down to the seafront. There was barbed wire all along the sea wall, I was walking along it with my aunt and uncle one day, and I fell against it and cut my leg.'

Geoff Perriam
'Early in the war the Army used the beach for .22 live firing practises. They fired at anything they could see on the beach and from a health a safety point of view, any amount of the public could have been killed by misplaced shots and ricochets.'

The beach huts were removed at the threat of invasion June1940. Geoff remembers the general feeling of gloom in Exmouth when it was thought that the Germans were about to invade, he listened to the wireless regularly and could tell by the tone of the broadcasts that things were going badly.

Bernard Greenaway
'When it was thought that invasion was imminent the beach huts had to be removed from the beach so as to give a clear field of fire to the defending troops.'

Beach Obstacles

Ivor Pike
'I used to got to Sunday school in the afternoon and then for a family walk across the cliff tops to Budleigh. You couldn't go down on the beach because of rolls of barbed wire and scaffolding.'

'I recall the frustration of seeing the sea on our walks, or after school and not being able to get to it for these great rolls of barbed wire. You could just about get your feet wet if it was a very high tide, enough for the sea to just creep under the barbed wire.'

Barbed wire and scaffolding obstacles were put in place and existing ones continually strengthened and improved. They stretched from the Pier at the Docks to Orcombe point. They were made from steel scaffolding poles and barbed wire, around 15-20ft in height. Some were positioned so they sat just below the water at high tide. From Maer rocks to Orcombe Point sea mines were laid by the Royal Navy. These were kept for a time in the Buoy Store near the dock. There were approx 20 mines and they could be detonated by remote control during an invasion, by a Royal Naval unit housed in the Harbour View on the seafront.

Jim Shapter
'I was a schoolboy when war broke out. We used to swim out to the scaffolding defences and climb all over them when we were children; they were great fun to play on. The army didn't like us to go on them and told us to clear off!'

Robert Knowling
'I remember the beach defences having an effigy of Hitler put on them. He had a swastika flag which he held in his hand. It was situated between the lifeboat slipway and the bottom of Carlton Hill. I was about six at the time so I think it must have been around 1944, just prior to D-Day.'

Family photograph amongst the beach defences

There was a ban on photographing beach defences and military establishments during the war the penalties were extremely severe and the accused could be charged with spying or treason both capital offences, for which the maximum penalty was hanging. Because of this there are very few photographs available of the beach during WWII.

Machine gun emplacements (pill boxes) were positioned at vulnerable points along the seafront and 4.7" ex naval guns positioned at foxholes on the landward side of the Queens Drive.

An Allen-Williams steel turret, now displayed on the seafront, which housed a Lewis gun was placed at the mouth of the docks, which gave a good field of fire over the estuary and some protection against aerial attack.

Exmouth Warren

Exmouth Warren opposite the pier had around 30 small holiday homes and a tea room on it before the

The Allen-Williams Turret

war. People would stay on the Warren during the summer months and relax, sunbathe and fish for mackerel in small boats. On August 11th 1939 a 7'5" shark weighing 102lb was caught with a rod and line, which was a highly unusual occurrence.

No one was allowed to take photographs on any accessible part of the beach. After sunset, especially on the Warren, the situation was even more perilous. The fear of being wrongly identified as invaders and causing an unnecessary alert, may have resulted in being shot as enemy agents by the Home Guard. On July 5th 1940 just after the evacuation of Dunkirk, It was decided that the Army should also take over what was left of Exmouth Warren.

Due to gale-force winds, high tides and rough seas, a large section of Exmouth Warren was washed away on February 16th 1941. Some of the bungalows had collapsed into the sea destroying people's homes and possessions. Further storms on the 3rd March finally sealed its fate. Finally the remains of the small dwellings were demolished by the military to make way for barbed wire and anti-aircraft guns as the threat of invasion grew.

There was a scaffolding boom from the bottom of the Belsher slipway across to the Warren. It could be opened and closed by a chain and steel hawser with

Pre-war Exmouth Warren

WARNING
1940

THE PUBLIC are warned that between the hours of 10 p.m. and 6 a.m. inclusive, the Beaches from SPRAY POINT TO WARREN POINT are closed. This Order comes into operation from and including tonight, 8th July, 1940.

Resident Occupiers of Bungalows etc., situate on the seaward side of the Great Western Railway at Dawlish Warren must remain in their Bungalows during the hours stated.

Persons disregarding this Order do so at their own risk and will be detained by the Military for investigation.

C. J. BIDDLESTONE
Clerk to the Council.

A warning to residents of Exmouth Warren

'The Kennel' was washed into the sea after the storms of 1941

floats attached to it. This could be raised and lowered by the men of the Royal Naval Patrol Service, during the day. It was left in fixed in place during the night with the Home Guard keeping watch over it. It was supposed to prevent ships and landing craft being able to enter the river estuary in the event of an invasion. How successful it would have been is debatable.

The swing-bridge at the docks was also immobilised every night and concrete tank blocks moved in front of the approaches to it. Once again the Home Guard patrolled it nightly, also staffing the pillar mounts for Lewis guns, which were placed by the swing-bridge. Exmouth gradually became a fortress and the population went about their everyday business, trying their best to put on a brave face and put the war out of their minds.

Tank Blocks and Defensive Lines

Joe Radgick

'Mamhead slipway had tank traps placed on it, it was laughable really 2'6" high concrete pyramid traps with a piece of railway track inserted into the top, to stop panzers, one is still there down by Shelley Beach, in the sand.'

In June 1940 tank blocks appeared on the dock slipways, at major road junctions and on the approach roads to the town, as were the approaches to the railway bridge over Exeter Road and the railway line.

Roy Penberthy

'There were two guns pointing out to sea, inside concrete caissons, one near the lifeboat station and

The 4.7" Naval Guns and observation post by foxholes car park

the other at Foxholes car park. There were searchlights up on the cliff face you could get to them by climbing up the cliff walk.'

John Pascoe-Watson

'There was a rectangular, pill box next to the Belsher slipway, right at the end of the groins on the right hand side. It was for housing Lewis guns and was staffed by the Home Guard.'

Joe Radgick

'At the top of the steps for the ferry to Starcross, is a rectangular concrete gun emplacement with rectangular firing slots. This was camouflaged to look like a workman's hut; it was covered in wooden slats.'

Roy Penberthy

'A London film studios scenery department, were sent to do the camouflaging on the concrete structures. They were also involved in building decoy and deception camouflage in the docks and the estuary for protection against reconnaissance planes and air raids.'

John Middleton

'There was a Bofors guns on a Mound facing the estuary, between Carters Avenue and Mudbank we used to go and have a look at it. There were more Bofors guns on top of the cliffs at Orcombe point.'

Brian Baker

'I had just learned to ride a bike. My father was holding on to the back and then he let go, he kept shouting encouragement to me. I was cycling a circuit up Salisbury Road up Church Road then back down Halsdon Road again. On the second circuit he shouted "Go on! Keep on going." just after that the was a terrific noise from a plane which was flying down the estuary. The Bofors guns at Mudbank opened up and the noise was deafening, I was virtually blown off my bike. It frightened me to death and I ran home pushing my bike.'

There were around 20 Bofors 40mm anti-aircraft guns placed at various points on the seafront, the Warren, the estuary, the cliffs and at sites further inland. These were staffed by the Royal Artillery Light Anti Aircraft batteries initially.

Roy Hatten

'I was at the town dump where the rugby ground is now, next to the estuary. Me and my friends used to play there, at the weekends and talk to the men of the R.A.F. Regiment who manned the anti-aircraft guns. There was one 20mm anti-aircraft gun there, a single barrelled Polsten gun.'

Ray Challis

'An anti-aircraft gun was mounted on the railway bank, an Oerlikon cannon (Polsten gun). There were two more mounted on the viaduct, we used to take the troops tea. Mrs. Muggeridge would make the tea and we would pull it up to them with a rope and bucket with the mugs in.'

There were Polsten gun sites all over Exmouth eventually. The increase was mainly due to the "hit and run" raids by German single engine fighter bombers, which were in progress from early 1942.

Bren-Gun Carriers

"Universal" Bren gun carriers with Bren's mounted on anti-aircraft tripods were at the entrance to Phear Park, the Maer Golf Course and patrolled the seafront. For a while these provided a flexible system of "moveable" light anti-aircraft gun platforms put in place in mid 1942 as part of a temporary solution to the "hit and run" raids.

Z Rocket Batteries

At least one battery was present in Exmouth consisting of 80 U.P. (Unrotated Projectile) 2" rockets positioned in prime locations from Foxholes car park to the docks. These were staffed by the Royal Artillery at first. The positions were covered by camouflaged nets and tree branches and made them very difficult to spot from the air or sea.

"Q" Decoy sites

"Q" decoy sites were set up on Woodbury Common, Clyst St Mary and Aylesbeare, these could be set on fire in the event a large force of raiders were discovered approaching Exeter. The sites were used during the Exeter blitz 3-4 May 1942 to good effect.

Tony Smith

'Woodbury Common area had a decoy aerodrome when I was at the camp. It was designed to be set alight to encourage German pilots to drop their bombloads short of Exeter and R.A.F. Exeter.'

Chapter 4
The Home Guard

The Formation of the Local Defence Volunteers (L.D.V.)

At around 9.15 p.m. on Tuesday 14 May 1940, just after the 9 o'clock news, the Minister for War, Anthony Eden appealed to the nation for the formation of the Local Defence Volunteers. The L.D.V. as it became known would constitute a part-time, defensive Army, to be trained by the Regular Army, which would train to defend Britain's shores against a German Invasion. Candidates were asked to enrol at their local Police station, which in Exmouth was situated at Victoria Road.

No enrolment forms were available because of the rushed nature of the need for volunteers. The Police were instructed by the Chief Constable to register the

L.D.V. and Home Guard Equipment

names and addresses only, of those who came forward. It was clearly stated that the organisation and control of this new part time Army would be the responsibility of the regular Army. The Police were however obliged to ask the following questions.

1. Are you familiar with firearms?
2. What is your occupation?
3. What military experience, if any have you?
4. Are you prepared to serve away from home?

Bill Sleeman

Bill Sleeman was a well known character and helped his father run a popular quality tailoring business in Exmouth. The business was started by his father in 1907 and still continues under family ownership to this day. Unfortunately Bill passed away when this book was being written, so although he had a chance to see what his own entries and inclusions would entail, in our meetings at his shop, he didn't get the chance to see it in context with the whole body of work. This is a great shame, because he clearly had very fond memories of his time in the Home Guard.

Bill described himself as *"A founder member of the Exmouth Home Guard"*, joining at the Police Station Victoria Road at 11 o'clock on the morning of Wednesday 15th May 1940 after hearing and responding to Anthony Eden's announcement on the B.B.C. on Tuesday 14th May 1940.

Bill was 18 years old at the time and was not alone in his desire to defend his country. Bill Gorfin was purported to be, in his own words:

'The first man, to register for the Exmouth Local Defence Volunteers.'

In his position as the editor of the *Exmouth Journal* newspaper he was aware of the Government's planned Home Defence initiative in an advanced press notice, the night before the radio announcement. This notice was to be published in the local paper in the next available publication and so he registered his name at the Victoria Road Police Station before the national radio announcement was even made.

Volunteers

The National target figure that the Government had hoped for within the first few months was 175,000 volunteers and were surprised to find that 250,000 men between the ages of 17 and 65 (not being in the fighting services already), had come forward in the first 24 hours to sign on the dotted line. Some lied about their age, young and old, and during the course of the war it was found that some were as young as 14 years old and others as old as 80 when they had volunteered to serve the colours.

Although this huge number of volunteers created an administrative nightmare for the local Police, by the time the British Expeditionary Force was being evacuated from the beaches at Dunkirk in the little ships, 400,000 men had volunteered. By the end of June 1940 the L.D.V. had an astonishing million and a half men under its command. The same size as Britain's pre-war Regular Army.

The Potential German Threat to Exmouth

Bill Sleeman

'It was feared that paratroops may land on Woodbury Common or some act of sabotage may occur, from the enemy landing on the coast at night. We were instructed only to watch and report back to our H.Q. After

Dunkirk however, everybody thought that was the end of it. Most of us expected and invasion of some sort.'

When asked if he was prepared to kill an enemy invader, as he was so young at the time, Bill thought for a while and said:

'Yes, I suppose so because that's what they trained us to do!'

The principal tasks of the L.D.V. were to guard Britain's potential coastal landing and airborne invasion sites, by setting up regular patrols. Woodbury Common was believed to be a probable site for airborne invasion, as was Exmoor which due to its immense size was equipped with a Home Guard horse patrol, as was Dartmoor.

Amongst other priority tasks for the L.D.V. was the need to defend Britain's railway, docks and inland waterway infrastructures against potential attack, or sabotage by clandestine "5th Columnists" (traitors and saboteurs) which may have existed in Britain at the time.

It is well known that the German intelligence services had maps and had gathered information about possible invasion sites and landing grounds from agents working in Britain before the war. Military

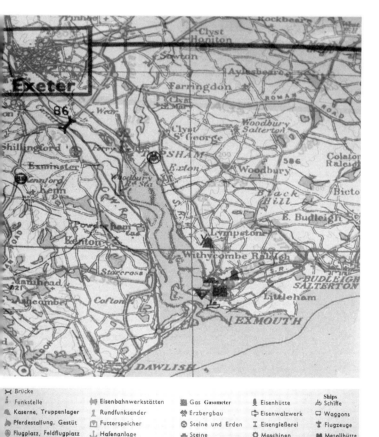

Above: *Beating the Invader leaflet, delivered to every household in Britain in 1940*

Left: *German converted Ordnance Survey map section and key*

targets were marked in red and strategic ones in purple on these maps.

It is interesting to note that the gasometer and Hospital amongst other targets are marked in purple as strategic targets, on the 1940 dated German maps held by the West Country Studies Library in Exeter. There is no doubt in my mind that the threat to the local populace of Exmouth during wartime was very real.

Early L.D.V. armband

The Volunteers

Bill Sleeman

'The initial meetings of the L.D.V. were held at the Grammar School at Gypsy lane. All of our initial training was done here under the instruction of their old School Master, Mr. Heath. After the taking of registers etc the basic training and drill instruction was using broom handles for drill, as rifles were not yet available.'

'No-one was really sure of what was expected of them initially and everything, although very primitive at the time, was taken very seriously, not at all like the impression given by the programme "Dad's Army". The threat of invasion was very real and a coastal town with a large estuary and two and a half miles of beach and potential landing grounds to defend, meant that Exmouth could have easily been a target.'

Civilian respirator with metal cylinder case

Most Exmouth L.D.V. men were in employment or ran local shops and businesses, this meant that most men were occupied during the daylight hours and could only spare 6-8 hours a week volunteering. It was quickly decided that the main function of this new force would not be to engage the enemy, (for lack of weapons), but to mount patrols and watches, reporting back information regarding any enemy activity so that the Regular Army Home Defence Battalions, could be called in to counter any threat.

Nicknames

The L.D.V. was subjected to some gentle mockery in the early days of their development. They earned the nickname of "The Broomstick Army" from the regular soldiers. Which was an irony in itself, as a large proportion of the regulars in the B.E. F. had thrown their rifles into the sea understandably to prevent them falling in to enemy hands: This act had seriously contributed to the lack of arms available for the L.D.V. and later the Home Guard. It must be remembered though, that at a time of international emergency these men volunteered to fight and defend their homeland, even with the prospect of having no real weapons yet!

The nickname "Look, Duck and Vanish", was widely used throughout Britain, but upon the change of the name to the Home Guard, the more affectionate nickname, "Dad's Army" came into being, due to the amount of WWI veterans which had now swelled the ranks. The older members in Exmouth in turn had then christened the 17 year olds, who were joining up in droves, prior to receiving their "Call Up" papers, the "Battle Patrol."

As uniforms were not originally issued it was desirable to have at least some type of uniform and a lot of the early L.D.V.'s chose work uniforms or smart practical clothing.

Bill Sleeman

'We wore our own clothes at first and were soon supplied with armbands with L.D.V. written on them, which were made locally.'

These armbands became obsolete at the renaming of the L.D.V. as the Home Guard in Late July 1940. The L.D.V. used their civilian gas masks initially and were issued with a special metal case to withstand the knocks on duty. Later military style service respirators were supplied.

Shotguns and Personal Weapons

Gun owners with official licences could use their own weapons. During these early days, Bill Sleeman said that they had managed to acquire some shotguns. As Devon was a large farming county, a higher percentage of the population had them. Bill had his own .410 shotgun which in peacetime he used to shoot rabbits on a relative's land.

Bill Sleeman

'If you had your own weapon you were considered to be elite, rifles were in such short supply nationally'.

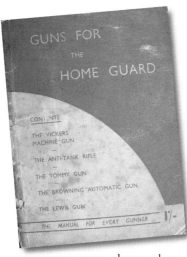

Personal knives and daggers, home-made knuckle dusters, iron bars, crowbars cudgels, hammers, jam-tin bombs and jar bombs were all experimented with locally.

The original concept of the Local Defence Volunteers was to train men to become fighting "savages" with what ever was to hand. Later when the name was changed to the Home Guard and equipment, uniforms and supplies became more easily available. It is clear through talking to Home Guard members over the years that they were definitely "up for it!"

Molotov Cocktail Training

Exmouth Home Guardsman practised with their Molotov Cocktails and jam tin bombs on Woodbury Common and Orcombe Point. By the end of 1941 all home made bombs and weapons were banned from use by the Government, mainly due to injuries sustained to Home Guard personnel during their manufacture and use in training. The Molotov cocktail was still kept in use, however, provided it was ignited with a striking fuse commercially produced for military use.

Mike Heard

'At the Drill Hall on the seafront, they had supplies of Molotov cocktails ready made in boxes. These were buried underground for safety reasons. In the event of an invasion they would have been ready to use. They came in wooden crates with a screw off top ready made, you just used to had to light the rag and throw them, then duck down to avoid getting hurt!'

The Invasion Alarm

In July 1940 after the fall of Dunkirk, the risk of invasion was very high and the Government decided that the best way of informing the population that an invasion was underway, was to ring the church bells. Church bells could not be rung for church gatherings or weddings at the time, as this may signify invasion

Top: *Home made lead-filled cudgel and ex M.P. truncheon*
Above: *Home Guard's Mk II steel helmet with camouflage net*
Left: *Bill Sleeman in his new Home Guard uniform*

Exmouth 447 Royal Artillery Coastal Battery Home Guard at stand-down. The Imperial Hotel 24th September 1944. See Appendix II page 154 for key to named individuals.

Mk II Steel helmet, 38 pattern Battle Dress, armbands and equipment of the 2nd "Clyst" Battalion Exmouth Home Guard; Home Guard officer's hat; Home Guard woven shoulder titles.

From left to right: *H.G. Members lapel badge; 2nd "Clyst" Battalion shoulder distinctions; The Devonshire Regiment cap badge worn by Home Guard members; Women's Home Guard Auxiliary, plastic cap badge.*

From left to right: *Bombardier Harry Long, 477 Royal Artillery Coastal Battery Home Guard; Donald Bradford 2nd "Clyst" Battalion Exmouth Home Guard; The bell tent look-out post on the Beacon October 1940.*

so the bells would only be rung in the event of an invasion proper and around the 25th of July it was decided that this job would be executed by the Home Guard.

Chris Long

'My Father was Harry Long. He was called up to the join the Army, but it was decided that he had a job which qualified him for a reserve occupation. He was a miller at my Grandfather's, Henry Long's Mill, at Withycombe, and would need to return to Exmouth. He did return, against his will, as he was enjoying himself away from home and had made good friends in the Army.'

'After he had returned he resumed his job at the mill and joined the Exmouth Home Guard. His Brother

Stanley Long had also joined the Home Guard, as he had a reserve occupation as a farmer. He owned Lower Halsdon Farm, a 200 acre farm during the war and this was crucial for growing food during the war years.'

Hazel Bradford

'My Brother joined the Home Guard when he was 17 years old. One of Donald's best friends was Mike Heard, they used to be seen around together a lot and would meet at the Drill Hall on the Home Guard nights. The Home Guard's meetings were held at the Imperial Road Drill Hall. It was round the side of the night club, the entrance was just before you get to the Manor Gardens.'

'The Home Guard had a tent erected on the Beacon, out side the Royal Beacon Hotel. They used it as a look-out to keep watch over the mouth of the river.'

Above: *Home Guard H.Q. The Sailors' Rest in Imperial Road*

Left: *N.C.O.'s of Exmouth Company 2nd (Clyst) Battalion Home Guard. See Appendix II page 154 for key to named individuals.*

Above left: *Exmouth Company No. 4 Platoon photographed in Manor Garden's behind the Drill Hall*

Chapter 5
Daily Life and Work

Exmouth Urban District Council. 1941

The Men and Women members of Exmouth Urban District Council, had a tough job to do during the war, making sure everyone was provided for and protected, either from gas, bombing or impending invasion. In 1940-41 Exmouth had a population of around 18,000 people, an unknown amount of British servicemen and Women, over 13,500 evacuees in varying concentrations over the five year period, plus a further 3,500 American Servicemen from 1943. According to the views of the 100 people I interviewed it seems they did a very good job; there were very few complaints.

Exmouth U.D.C. behind the Imperial Hotel 1943
Below: U.D.C. offices sign now held at Exmouth Museum

The morale of the town was generally good, people felt like they had a common enemy and a common aim. Although they had very little to eat and most of the men had been sent overseas, they made the most of a bad lot. Positive propaganda posters appeared on any available wall-space, encouraging people to think carefully and act wisely.

Removal of Railway Station and Road Signs

This was carried out after May 31 1940. In the event of an invasion it was hoped that this act would cause confusion for the invading enemy and slow up their advance.

Double Summer Time

It started in the first week of April to the first week in October. The clocks were brought forward 2 hours instead of the usual 1 hour. This was intended to make the most productive use of the daylight working hours.

Board and Lodging Costs

Board and lodgings in Exmouth for a family of three all in including heating and three meals a day, was approximately £2.00 per week. A billeting allowance for Evacuee's was available from the Exmouth Council at 17 shillings a week.

The General Post Office

It was situated at the top of Rolle Street on the left where it meets Bicton Street.

Postal Deliveries

Monday-Saturday. 7.30. a.m. and 2.30. p.m.
Sundays. No Deliveries.

A lot of wartime post boxes are still in use today. See if you can spot them. Look for the GRVI ciphers and the King's Crown. I have chosen to photograph the post boxes which are near to the scenes of wartime bombings. They stand as silent witnesses to the events and mark the locations should you want to go and see how the areas look now.

Exmouth's Post Women. Doll Stone, Kath Evans, Joyce Pengelly and Violet Hanger

From left to right: *The Beacon / Louisa Terrace pillar box; The pillar box opposite Harbour View.*
Below: *Small envelope sent from the Sailors' Rest, Home Guard Headquarters.*

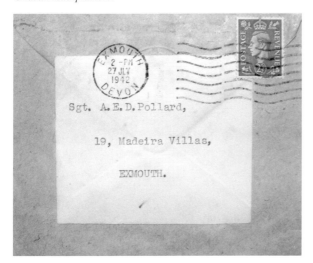

Letter Post

Letters and packets, not exceeding 2oz in weight; one and a half-pence; For every additional 2oz, or fraction thereof, an additional one half-penny.

Letters Home from the Armed Forces

Postal Services were also available to serving members of His Majesties Armed Forces, Army, Navy or Royal Air Force, stationed at home or abroad.

The Post Office organised the collection of books for the troops and mail to be forwarded to Prisoners of War via the Red Cross.

The Army Censorship Office was worried about the whereabouts of troops and their units and this was reflected in the way that all letters sent home had to be read by the censors.

Some people did try and get information back as to their whereabouts, but most just succumbed and tolerated the intrusion on their privacy. At one point in the war the Censorship Office was worried about the amount of "kisses" marked with an "X" at the bottom of letters and these were allowed as long as they were not arranged in rows or patterns which may have constituted a dangerous secret code!

Popular Acronyms like S.W.A.L.K. "Sealed With A Loving Kiss" and H.O.L.L.A.N.D. (which was another source of concern for the censors at the time of the airborne assault on Arnhem), but innocently meant "Hope Our Love Lasts And Never Dies", were also popular.

Anonymous
'There was what we called, the "Abode of love", under the wall on the beach near Temple Steps. This is where all the courting couples went, also opposite the swimming baths.'

Telephones

Exmouth had 1,250 telephones installed in buildings by 1939. A new electronic exchange was also installed in 1939. It was introduced to service the increased demand for private telecommunications and to be used by the Civil Defence in the event of a war.

The type 332 Telephone was introduced in 1936 and was typical of the type of phone used British emergency services and in homes during WWII.

Pay phones were situated all over the town housed in "Jubilee" Kiosks designed in 1936 and some are still in use today. The one photographed stands near Hulham Road shops, one of the few survivors in the town of this great British icon.

Type 332 "Cheese Tray" telephone

The Jubilee Kiosk No. 6 one of the very few left in Exmouth

The Working Week

The Government provided training courses for school leavers who had left school at the age of 14 (which, was most children at the time). Compulsory enrolment for manageable jobs for the disabled were initiated. Everyone had to register and it was decided by a local body who would be able to work and who

couldn't and this dictated what style of work they would have to undertake.

Pearl Cawse

'I had an Uncle with a withered arm and leg who couldn't work, but he was determined to do something. He had a wheel barrow in which he carried cases for people coming off the train. He enjoyed it and it gave him his independence. He was called Fred Sanson. He had a difficult start in life, as he had epilepsy as well, but he was extremely bright and likable. I have very fond memories of him.'

Men and women had their call-up papers on their 18th Birthday. They joined H.M. Armed Forces. Hundreds of Exmouth men and women served in the Armed Forces all over the world.

R.A.S.C. Driver John Whatmore's Army paybook

Harry Lawes in his 1938 pattern battledress

Lionel Bradford in his Merchant Navy Uniform

Ron Lavis

'My Father was Harry Lavis and Grandfather Charles Henry Lavis, who was still working at the boatyard during the war.

In the early stages of the war, the boatyard was taken over by the Admiralty, they built sailing dinghies first, then they started building Admiral's barges, liberty boats, small tugs and lifeboats all approx 30 foot and under.'

Mike Heard

'I had a reserved occupation and worked 48 hours a week as a boat builder at Lavis's boatyard. This included Saturdays as well. I also had 12 hours a week patrolling and training with the Home Guard, where I was also called up regularly for emergencies, U.X.B. cordons, invasion alerts and exercises and in my spare time. I was a launcher for the Exmouth lifeboat.'

Joe Radgick

'Part of Exmouth's contribution to the industrial war effort was Dixon's and Lavis's boatyards. Dixon's had two boatyards. One was behind 124 St Andrews Road the Other was on the dockside which had it own slipway. They specialised in manufacturing 8 metre long motor cutters. These were used ship to shore by the Royal Navy as tenders. They also made 5 metre long rowing boats and 12 metre long harbour launches, which were also used by the Royal Navy in

a ship to shore role. It was a labour-intensive boatyard and they employed 30-40 boat-builders who had reserve occupation status.'

Joe Radgick remained on a reserve occupation as a boat-builder throughout the war, and sometimes felt embarrassed because of his reserve occupation, feeling he would have rather have been serving in the forces.

Peggy Gibbins

'No one took proper holidays during the war. No one could afford the time away from work and there was nowhere to go really."

Mike Heard

'We had a happy time at work. Nobody had much money and everyone mucked in and helped each other out.'

Transport

People's primary source of transport was walking. Those who had them, used push bikes and they were at a premium. Friends would lend them to one another knowing that they would be returned. A small percentage of the population had motorcycles and very few had cars. Only people who had a special permit to use a car could do so, even then the petrol was rationed, and so journeys were only made when absolutely necessary.

Post Woman Kath Evans with Exmouth's most popular form of transport

which was operated by Mr and Mrs Hart of Budleigh Salterton. They ran a very popular and successful bus service, in their small 30-seat single-decker country buses, to Budleigh.

These buses also went from Otterton to Exmouth with a return fare of 5d (2p) for the under-14s and 10d (4p) for adults. The driver would deliver parcels too, for 2d (1p) or 4d (2p).

Trains

The trains ran regularly: the Southern Region line to Exeter and the branch line across the viaduct to Budleigh. The trains were very popular with the locals who could afford to use them and essential for the movement of military personnel.

Peggy Gibbins
'The steam trains to Exeter left at 8.10 in the morning. They had separate compartments in the carriages which held approximately eight people. At Exmouth station at really busy times, the W.V.S. ran out of proper cups and so used clean jam jars and tins even to make sure everyone could get a cup of tea. When the Americans were here there were soldiers and airman of all nationalities coming and going from the station. It really did get very busy sometimes.'

Devon General Driver's Greatcoat

The Bus Services

There were two main bus companies in Exmouth the main Devon General routes to Exeter and the larger towns and the privately-owned Hart's bus service

The Media

Newspapers
Exmouth had two well run newspapers locally. The *Exmouth Journal*, which is still in business today and the *Exmouth Chronicle*. The newspaper was the main way in which people could find out about what was

W.H. Smith Exmouth Station

happening locally. Topics always on the agenda were dog fouling, teenage crime, burglaries and the more topical subjects of, ignoring the blackout and refusing to billet evacuees. On a more positive note these newspapers had a wonderful balance about them, still finding plenty of space for humour and poetry amongst the adverts for local businesses and serious journalism.

Peggy Gibbins

'I left school when I was 14 I started work at Delderfield's, the printers of the Exmouth Chronicle *newspaper, on Chapel Hill. I was trained in printing, compositing, distributing, typesetting and using the Heidelberg press to print newspapers and a platen press which was used to print ration cards etc for Exton Camp. If we went to a party or dance with the soldiers, we used to print off a few extra coupons and give them to the British soldiers, as we felt so sorry for them. We also used to print the tickets for dances and always print a few extra for friends, so we could go to the Pavilion, very naughty! I was only 15 at the time, but it was great fun!'*

Wireless (Radio)

Prices

Pye Baby "Q".	£8 18s 6d
Phillips.	£9 15s 0d
Ever-Ready.	£8 10s 0d
Roberts.	£9 9s 0d
Ultra.	£10 10s 0d

The wireless was the main way in which people kept up to date with national news and topical subjects. During the war years the B.B.C. was broadcasting day and night in 46 different languages worldwide to an audience of 200 million people.

Tommy Handley broadcast his famous show "Its That Man Again" (I.T.M.A.) a popular comedy show, the title of which poked fun at the acronym's in common use during the war. Bebe Daniels interviewed American servicemen and women and the World Service's ubiquitous strap line, "This is London Calling the World" could be heard literally all over the world.

The B.B.C. employed 54 wartime announcers, who presented not only popular music shows but programmes like "Freedom Forum" a political chat show, broadcast to show that Britain and the Commonwealth still had freedom of speech and "The Brains Trust" who were adept at solving everyday wartime problems, giving out the solutions to listener's letters.

Lord Haw Haw

Joy Penwarden

'I Remember Lord Haw Haw, on the wireless, everyone hated him.'

William Joyce had been an English Radio presenter, who sympathised with the Nazi cause. His broadcasts could be heard nightly on the wireless and it was not illegal to listen to his reports in Britain, as it was illegal to listen to the B.B.C. in any part of Germany or the Greater Reich. He was one of the most hated, characters of the war. He used a specific catch phrase to identify his programme and it was common for Exmouth people to mimic the sound of his dull voice and make up their own jokes and fake bulletins about him.

'Germany Calling, Germany Calling, Germany Calling. Here are the Reich's Station Centrum, Deutsch Station Bremen and station D.X.B. on the 31 metre band. You are about to hear the news in English.'

One night he continued; 'Tonight we are planning to burn Exeter to the ground.' On another, 'Tonight the Luftwaffe carried out a successful raid on Exmouth Docks.' After the war, William Joyce was tried and found guilty of being a traitor at the Nuremberg Trials and executed.

Chapter 6
Wartime Entertainment

Free entertainment for the servicemen and women, was put on weekly in town by Toc H. and the Y.M.C.A. at their hall in Imperial Road. In the Manor Gardens, dancing to dance bands and brass band concerts, were twice daily at 2.30 p.m. and 7.30 p.m. when the weather was good. On Sunday afternoons military parades connected to various war collections could often be seen marching up Rolle Street and around The Parade and The Strand.

The Pavilion

The Queen's Regiment held boxing tournaments in the Pavilion, Oscar Rabin's Embassy Band, would play regularly and people could dance and even roller skate to their music. The Pavilion rota for roller skating was from October to June two sessions daily at 2.30 p.m. and 7.p.m. The admission charge of one shilling included skates.

On January 9th, 10th and 11th 1945, the yearly pantomime was staged at the Pavilion. The production was Aladdin and proved very popular, selling out on all three nights.

Music and Dancing

Performing live bands and dances were held every night at the Pavilion. It was a good release from the privations of the war and presented an opportunity for romance. The admission charges in 1943 were as follows:

Roll on to ... — VICTORY
At the PAVILION
ROLLER SKATING DAILY at
2.30 to 5 and 7 to 10 p.m.
Admission : Adults 1/-   Children 6d.   (including Skates).
" WATCH FOR SPECIAL NOVEL ATTRACTIONS ! "

Roll on to Victory, skating at the Pavilion

The Wings for Victory Parade enters The Parade June 1943

The cast of the Aladdin pantomime at the Pavilion 1945

Admission Charges

Weekdays.   2/-

Saturdays.   2/- 6d

Servicemen in Uniform.

Weekdays.   9d

Saturdays.   1/- 9d

On Saturday August 8th 1943 the final of the "Miss Devon" beauty contest was held at the Pavilion. Heats throughout the week were held at a number of dances at the Pavilion. Officers of the Royal Navy, Army and Royal Airforce were competition Judges.

The winner was a dark-haired lovely, Miss Jean Stanley, a Lancashire girl but at the time living in Dawlish. The runner up was Miss Vera Howe a W.A.A.F. from Exeter.

Mike Heard
'The American bands started coming over to Britain and some made their way down to Exmouth. They brought over the swing music and I really liked the "Lindy hopping" and "jitterbug" dancing, it gave us an introduction to the girls. The girls liked the Americans best. They had more money, better uniforms and could get things that we couldn't, from their P.X.'

'The American U.S. Navy Big Band used to play at the Pavilion on some nights, Sam Donahue was the band leader. He was from Artie Shaw's pre-war Big Band. I loved the swing music. The Americans played it brilliantly. Dances were held at the Pavilion every night of the week except Thursdays, from 8-11.'

'It was 2 shillings to go in, with no bar and no bouncers, but you had to get in the venue by 10.00 p.m. All nationalities were there, Poles, Czech's, Royal Marines, South African's, Australians and Yanks after 1942. The British Blacks and Whites were allowed to mix, but girls were boycotted by us if they danced with the Black Men.'

Pearl Cawse
'Entertainment was organised to raise money for the war effort. Concerts were organised on Church Road in the Colonies, in a house beside a piece of waste ground. We used to go to the variety concerts and concert party's there. There was always a lot of singing. The organisers used to wheel our piano over to play the concerts. It was really good fun.'

The Cinema

There were five cinemas in Exmouth during the war. It was one of the most popular pastimes for adults and children alike. It offered the opportunity to escape from the war's privations and also kept people up to date with current affairs. The names of the cinemas were the Carlton, the Savoy, the Regal, the Forum and the Grand.

Roy Hole
'It was 6d or 9d upstairs for a child to go to the Cinema during the war. We used to go on Saturday mornings. We usually called the Cinema "the pictures" or "the flicks" some people called it "the movies".'

Joy Penwarden
'In the "The Flea Pit", the Grand Cinema on Exeter Road, we used to go to Saturday morning pictures. Some boy's were misbehaving one day and spilled ink, all over my dress.'

Table tennis tournaments proved popular in Exmouth

Chapter 7
British Forces in Exmouth

The Army

Elements of the British Army moved to Exmouth soon after war was declared in September 1939. At different periods different units moved into the area to help defend the town and to train for specific jobs, manly relating to the D-Day landings.

Ray Challis

'I heard the declaration of war announcement on the radio. The first troops I remember seeing was just a few days after this announcement. They were billeted in the Church Hall, where Every's Solicitors is now, on Church Street. There was a soldier on guard duty outside here at the time, dressed in khaki.'

The 70th Battalion of the Queen's Royal Regiment (West Surreys) affectionately nicknamed the "Mutton Lancers" locally, were moved to Exmouth in the early stages of 1940. "E" Company were stationed in Exmouth and billeted in the Wesleyan Chapel attached to Tower Street Methodist Church. The Company H.Q. was in offices over Burtons the "50 Shilling Tailors" in Exeter Road. Route marches were regular training exercises for them and they could often be seen around the town at incidents working hard with the Rescue Services to clear the bombed buildings.

Off Duty

Men of the West Surreys regularly frequented the Pilot Inn for drinks. The Royal Marines liked the Volunteer and the Imperial Hotel bar. Local inter-unit team games were organised and were attended by the local population as well as the servicemen.

Joy Thorn

'Some evenings I worked at the Kit Bag Canteen in Little Bicton Place, it was held at the Congregational Chapel. We mostly made cheese sandwiches for the troops and served cups of tea; anyone could use it. Another Exmouth girl, my friend Phyllis Frume, worked there too.'

Peter Mattholie was in the Royal Navy serving on an L.B.V. waiting to sail to Omaha Beach on D-Day. He used to enjoy going to the pub with the American Rangers.

Peter Mattholie

'The American Rangers would train at Orcombe Point. They were shinning up ropes and ladders to the top of the cliffs. We went to Orcombe Point one Sunday, when we had a day off and somebody photographed us in our uniforms. We never did see

70th Battalion of the Queen's Royal Regiment (West Surreys) cap badge

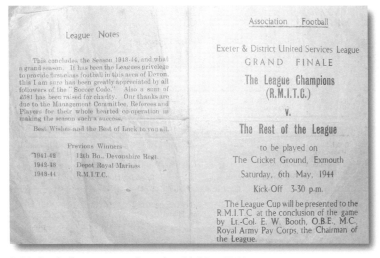

R.M. football programme Saturday 6th May 1944

Royal Marines Training at Dalditch Camp

The R.A.F. march past Lloyds Bank in The Strand during Salute the Soldier Week

the photo. We used to go drinking with them in the Ship Inn or sometimes the Pilot. The Rangers' medics used to take a small bottle of pure alcohol from their first aid kits to the pub and put it in their beer. They used to get so drunk and very cheaply. Occasionally fights broke out between rival units when the pub was drunk dry. The Ship Inn had navy badges from all nationalities and souvenirs from the sailors and combined ops men that drank in the pub. They were all over the walls and behind the bar.'

Some servicemen obtained travel permits occasionally but most stayed in the town.

* * *

Royal Marines at Dalditch Camp 1944

Dalditch Camp

Tony Smith

'We were very hard pressed training recruits up at Dalditch Camp and at the end of each course I normally took the train from Exmouth to Waterloo via Exeter on Friday evening, spent the weekend with my girlfriend and then back on the 1 a.m. train from Waterloo to Exeter, then on to Exmouth, a quick change and wash and then on parade addressing my new recruits, at 8am- phew!'

'The weekends that I stayed in Exmouth, we drank at the Feathers in Budleigh, at the Imperial Hotel in Exmouth (very dull in those days), the Beacon and other pubs in Exmouth. There seemed very few girls about in Exmouth to my recollection. Perhaps the Exmouth mothers were very wise.'

Chapter 8
The Police

The Exmouth Police Force was a section of "D" Division Whose Headquarters were at Honiton. Under the supervision of Superintendent J. Marshall. The Exmouth Police Station was in Victoria Road.

Police whistle dated 1939

Police Constable Ron Lee

Victoria Road Police Station

Ron Lee Joined the Exmouth Force in 1938. He was called "the baby" by his colleagues. The youngest Policeman in the force at the time. They would say "Look out! The baby's coming". He had come to Exmouth from the Midlands as a regular constable and was 19 years old by this time.

Ron Lee

'Life was so good and very little was stolen. We knew everyone and their families and generally trusted people. The uniform was well respected and also the man if he was a good man. We knew the people on a very personal level and this grew even more as the bombings and hardships started.'

' During shifts, every shop doorway was checked by the patrolling constables during the night and if premises had been broken in to, you would be woken first thing in the morning to be asked what time you checked it. The answer to this was that you checked all of them at the last possible moment on your shift.'

'There seemed to be hardly any trouble during this period and what there was mainly due to the visitors to the town. There was no traffic like there is today but there were plenty of push bikes. If someone found their bike was missing, it would be brought back in a few minutes and it was usually found that a friend had borrowed it'

Exmouth's War Reserve Constables 1943. See Appendix IV page 156 for key to named individuals.

Policeman's MKII steel helmet

Police truncheon dated 1938

Crime and Punishment

The type of petty crime which took place in Exmouth during WWII remain pretty much the same today. I compared several issues of today's *Exmouth Journal* to the wartime editions of similar dates and apart from infringements of the wartime Emergency Regulations, the frequency of crimes and types of crimes were very similar.

Mr. H. Downs ('Porky' Downs the Butcher) was fined £1 for breaching the blackout.

When he left his premises in a rush one night to attend an emergency. A Mr. Skelly and his girlfriend were fined 5/- for riding a bicycle with the girl sitting on the cross bar.

One thing was completely different though. The penalties for certain types of crime were far higher during wartime. Three men who stole two sides of bacon locally were told in court by the judge at the start of their hearing that the maximum penalty for their crime was death, as it was a "hanging offence", for stealing food during times of war. The Magistrate however was lenient and fined one man £7.00 and the other £2.00. The accomplices to the crime were also fined £5.00 each.

Birching was the punishment for boys over the age of 14 for crimes such as cruelty to animals, arson or theft. You needed a licence to keep a dog during the war and fines were imposed if you were caught without one. Statutory fines of 10/- were issued for late payment of car licences.

Chapter 9
The Black-out

The Blackout

The blackout was ordered by the British Government on the Friday 1 September 1939. The Pavements, trees in pedestrian areas and other hazards all had white stripes painted on them, as did motor vehicles of all types, usually on the mudguards to give some indication of the size of vehicle and it's extremities and these served to reflect what little natural light was available as a warning to pedestrians and other road users.

People were reminded to walk facing the traffic, so their faces could be seen by the oncoming traffic. People were virtually invisible from the rear when walking with the direction of the traffic on dark nights, so they were asked to leave their shirt tails out or even carry a newspaper if nothing else could be found in order to make themselves visible to traffic.

Roy Pemberthy

'You had to have 150 mm of white paint on the back mudguard and a red reflector. I had a dynamo hub on the back wheel of my bike and another one pressing against the tyre. When you stopped riding the lights would go out, which could be quite dangerous when stopped at junctions.'

Roy Hole

'If you had a car or a bike and wanted to ride it at night, you had to have the headlights shielded. A lot of people made these covers and hoods from old cans, as they were difficult to get hold of and quite expensive. Instructions were given in the newspapers. You cut a slot in the bottom of the can, where you cut the slot; you left one edge uncut and bent the piece up. Making car headlight covers and hoods'

Every building had to have black out curtains or shutters fitted and these had to be closed after dark. Initially black-out cloth was hard to come by locally and so a great deal of improvisation took place in the early days. After dark A.R.P. Wardens on patrol on the streets enforced the blackout stringently. Heavy fines were imposed for breaking this law.

Ivor Pike

'We had blackout screens made from a thick black material stretched over a wooden frame. We had to lift them in at blackout time and then removed them again when it became light. The windows had criss-cross tape over them, to prevent the broken glass from flying about when a bomb went off.'

BLACK-OUT TIMES		
	Ends	Begins
To-day	5.27 a.m.	11.11 p.m.
Sunday	5.28 ,,	11.11 ,,
Monday	5.29 ,,	11.10 ,,
Tuesday	5.30 ,,	11. 9 ,,
Wednesday	5.31 ,,	11. 8 ,,
Thursday	5.32 ,,	11. 7 ,,
Friday	5.34 ,,	11. 6 ,,
Saturday	'5.35 ,,	11. 5 ,,

Blackout times for the 10th July 1942

Ron Lee's girlfriend Aimee on his Ardie motorcycle, complete with lamp blackout covers

Peggy Gibbins
'In the blackout, you couldn't see your hand in front of your face. I always carried a torch at night.'

Specialist blackout torches were manufactured for the Armed Services and the A.R.P. Services. Pedestrians were advised by the A.R.P. to buy and carry these A.R.P.-approved hooded torches using 1 x 1.5 volt battery.

Roy Pemberthy
'We had gas lighting in the Colonies, in the house and the street lighting. Someone had to light the gas lights using a ladder, they were there till the early sixties, I'm sure, but not used during the war due to the black out. Green paper blinds light and blast proof were available from ironmonger's shops.'

Geoff Perriam
'The blackout was extremely dark, I remember walking along the top of North Street and then along Danby Terrace with one foot in the gutter keeping it pressed against the side of the kerb so I could follow the line of the road. The one good thing about the blackout was, you could see the stars on a clear night, which seems unbelievable now, but it really was so dark!'

On 17 September 1944 the black out ended officially as the threat of bombings was thought to be over.

A.R.P. hooded blackout torch

Chapter 10
Children

School

The schools in Exmouth had to accommodate the usual amount of children, plus the evacuees which were billeted in the town. Overcrowding became a serious issue initially with teachers having to cope with up to 50 children in a class. This situation was slowly rectified by the local children attending school in the morning and the evacuees attending in the afternoon.

John Pascoe Watson

'I was top of the class before the evacuees arrived. I won a school prize, a book, which was a book about the Royal Air Force. Then Peter Blanks, an evacuee arrived from London. He was very clever and went to stay with Mr D'Arcy. I lost a bit of impetus after that and fell into bad company with a lad called Jim Perriam, we were constantly playing tricks on teachers and being bad; I was about 13 at the time.'

Above left: *Kathleen and Sydney Bryant with their new baby Mandy, outside their home in Lyndhurst Road in 1940*

Above right: *Proud mum Kathleen, with new baby and new pram 1940*

"Deeds not words" the motto of Exmouth Grammar School

Derek, Brian and Peter "Spud" Rowsell

Sheila Lovering

'I went to Exeter Road School. The evacuees were treated quite badly by some of the kids and their mothers. They thought they were dirty which some obviously were because of the circumstances. Some evacuees and locals alike had ringworm and were painted with gentian violet ointment. Also iodine was used for scrapes abrasions or sores. All children got nits and lice. But it was a good school and a lot of fun. I have good memories of my school.'

As penicillin was not available at the beginning of the war cuts and abrasions had to be dealt with immediately against risk of infections such as blood poisoning.

Sheila Lovering

'We were told, if we were in school and there was a raid, we had to get under the desks. If we were on the way to school but nearer home we had to go home, and nearer to the school we had to go to the school shelters.

Peggy Gibbins

'I was about 13 years old I was at Branksome Park School for Girls at Green Close, which is now the Secondary Modern School. At around this time air

Exmouth Secondary Modern School staff 1945

Fancy dress for Exmouth Carnival 1943. Cossack Rita Pannell, Red Indian Jeff Pannell, Bo-Peep Winifred Gliddon

Exmouth Secondary Modern School girls, summer 1945

raid shelters were built all over our school site 4 or 5 shelters in all, made from brick and concrete. When we heard the siren go we had to go into the shelters as quickly as possible. The shelter I had to go to was outside the Headmistress's office. There were wooden benches to sit on inside. You had to file out very quickly, taking your gas mask if the siren went off in a lesson and stay in there until all clear.'

John Middleton
'As far as I can remember we had to carry our gas masks with us right to the end of the war in Europe, or at least until the threat of an attack by gas bombs had become unlikely, some time after D-Day.'

Winifred Gliddon just managed to escape the German occupation of Jersey with her family on Saturday June 29th 1940, the day before the Channel Islands were invaded.

Winifred and her family's status was that of refugees in their own country, rather than evacuees, as the Channel Islands was the only part of the British Isles to be occupied by the Germans in WWII.

Winnifred Gliddon
'I didn't speak English until I was eight and later about the age of nine when I could speak English. I was in a school play with one of the Mason boys, the play was called "Jenny Wren". I was Jenny and Ronald Mason was my pretend husband and we were married on stage.'

'In Market Street, there was a lady who lived there called "Winnie" Madge; she was in the St Johns Ambulance Brigade. Winifred's Mother had a second-hand shop in Market Street and she was good fun. She used to dress all the children up in fancy dress and take them to the carnival or parades in the town. We had a lovely time.'

Dressing up and pageants were a popular way of dispelling the blues in wartime. If there was any excuse people would make fancy costumes from scrap and waste material and swap costumes with each other. Exmouth still has a keen interest in fancy dress, as anyone who has been out on the town on a New Year's Eve will tell you.

Playing on Bomb Sites
Barry Clarke
'As young children during the war and after the war we used to play on the bomb sites, Wilson's store basement was a favourite and a house in Windsor Square. Wilson's store frequently flooded and we used to go paddling, wading and even swimming when it was really bad.'

Collecting Shrapnel

Ray Challis

'Not only did shrapnel come from exploding German bombs it fell back to earth from our own anti-aircraft shells. That's why every one had to wear a steel helmet that worked outside during raids. We used to collect every piece we could lay our hands on.'

'At Pitts Farm on the Exeter Road there was a raid of incendiary bombs in the cornfields. The incendiary bombs had gone right into the earth with just the tails sticking out in some cases; we knew not to touch the live ones. But the ones which were burnt out completely or partially burnt we would pick up, you could see where the ground was burnt and we used to dig round them with our hands or a stick and then pull them out. Children used to take shrapnel to school and swap it or exchange it for money or sweets if they could get them.'

In April 1944 strips of aluminium foil called "Window" was found in the streets of Exmouth. It was caught up in trees and bushes and all over the streets. It was designed to be dropped en-masse from British bombers as a diversionary tactic, when it would show up on German radar equipment and appear like a bomber formation to them. As there were very few toys available during the war in the war children collected it eagerly.

The Danger from Unexploded Munitions

During the war large areas of the country were turned over to the Ministry of Defence for use by the army to train troops for the liberation of mainland Europe. One of these areas was Woodbury Common. Soldiers carried out live firing training exercises frequently in the area.

They used a great variety of weapons, including mortars, hand grenades and land mines (for practising mine detection). The Army was extremely careful in the way it trained it's personnel in the safe handling of these weapons, but due to the overgrown nature of the terrain some unexploded or "blind rounds" went missing and remained potentially dangerous concealed in the under growth. The live firing ranges on Woodbury Common and Straight Point were fenced off with barbed wired and warning signs were visible at all points where it was considered access to these ranges could be forced. The severity of the warnings was quite clear:

Unexploded Ordnance Keep Out.
Danger Keep Out.
Danger Mines.
Keep Away From The Coast.

German 1kg incendiary bomb tails

Richard Tarr's childhood collection of shrapnel from Exmouth Beach

Rounds found on Exmouth Beach and at Woodbury common

.50 calibre casing found on Dawlish Warren

Some people chose to ignore these warnings at their peril. Two soldiers were killed on a coastal cliff path near Orcombe Point when they went through the barbed wire and down to a secluded part of the beach. A mine exploded and killed them both. There was an enquiry, with the verdict of accidental death.

Exmouth had another tragic fatality, when local boys couldn't resist the temptation of collecting what they thought were spent mortar rounds.

From The *Exmouth Journal* Saturday March 28 1942

EXMOUTH BOY KILLED BY BOMB EXPLOSION

A Fatal Plaything

NINE BOMBS COLLECTED AS SOUVENIRS.

12 year old Kenneth Edward Norton died instantly as a result of a mortar bomb explosion in the back garden of his house on Wednesday 24th March 1942. Mr. Albert Frederick Wood his next door neighbour had been working in his garden and had seen Kenneth playing in the garden with something but had not realised what it was. He heard an explosion which he thought must have been made by a plane circling nearby but when he looked over the fence saw the remains of Kenneth.

Kenneth, his 15 year old Brother, William George Norton and two other friends (Peter Collins and Arthur Hodge) had picked up the mortar bomb along with 8 others from a practice range at Woodbury Common on Sunday 22nd March. When they returned home that evening they hid the bombs on the route home from Woodbury Common, William and Arthur returning on the Wednesday, later in the week to retrieve the bombs and bring them back home to Exmouth in a bag.

William hung the bag with the bombs on the back of the kitchen door. When Kenneth took the bag down from the back of the door four of the bombs fell out on to the floor and his mother told him to take them all out into the back garden in case there was any danger from them. William then heard his brother knocking something with a stone and then an explosion. He ran and told his mother what had happened.

At the inquest William said that they had not seen any barbed wire or warning signs at the practice range on the common until they came out of the range. A staff captain who later inspected the range said that barbed wire and warning signs had been erected and were all

2" Mortar bomb tail found on Woodbury Common dated 1942

in position and had said that it was always possible to find unexploded mortar rounds in the undergrowth as they could be difficult to find by the troops in the undergrowth.

P.C. Fogwill had been to the school previously to warn the Headmaster of the dangers of children playing on the firing ranges and had returned since the incident to issue more warnings.

On the Sunday the bombs were found Inspector Abrahams had seen the boys making off with the bombs and it was after this that William had decided to hide them. He had told the court inquest that this was the first time he had realised the bombs were dangerous, before that they had thought they were "Duds" (inactive). He then told the court that he had returned on the Wednesday to collect the bombs from the hiding place, as his younger brother Kenneth, wanted them as souvenirs.

The Coroner pronounced that the death was caused by multiple injuries sustained by the explosion of the bomb he was handling and that the cause of Kenneth's death was accidental.

Children's Punishments

Mary Ashleigh

'Mr. Marcombe the Headmaster gave me the cane when I took all my mum's jewellery to school and gave it out to my class mates as they had none. It fell out of their school knickers' pockets during keep fit!'

Jack Humphries

'Children were hit liberally with rulers in junior classes and canes in secondary school, on the hands or the bottom. People were always getting hit! The birch was also a punishment for public offences.'

Bed Time and Bombs

Bedtime was 7.p.m. even during double summer time for some children. This meant it was still light at around 11.30 because of double summer time. Most parents and children slept when they could and didn't stick to a regimented pattern as everyone was deprived of sleep because of air raids, sirens sounding and overcrowding.

Mary Ashleigh

'Children often slept top to tail four in a small bed because of lack of room.'

Joy Penwarden

'My dad was at the A.F.S. Fire Station at night, on duty. When the siren went off, mother and I rushed to get our navy blue siren suits and dashed downstairs to sit under the dining room table. We didn't have an air raid shelter.'

Robert Knowling

'We hid under our dining room table and under the stairs on the nights of the Plymouth and Exeter blitzes. Later when we had a look, we could see the sky was ablaze from the large incendiary raid on Plymouth.'

John Pascoe-Watson

'We were regularly woken up in the middle of the night to hear German bombers overhead.'

John Middleton

'We were living in Halsdon Road at the time of the Chapel Street bombing. I was lying in bed and we heard the bombs go off. They were great big bangs!'

Jack Humphries

'We were always listening for aircraft noises. The enemy planes had a very distinctive sound and we

John Pascoe Watson in his A.T.C. Uniform, at home by Shelley Beach

Dennis Pratt in 299 Exmouth A.T.C. Uniform

would only get worried when we heard them. We could tell the difference easily between our planes and the enemies.'

Exmouth's Youth and Children's Organisations

The A.T.C.

John Pascoe-Watson

'I joined the Exmouth 299 A.T.C. Squadron when I was 16. My cadet number was 115. At times in the

Above: *Salute the Soldier parade. The A.T.C. band march along the seafront*

Left: *Wings for Victory newspaper advert*

Right: *John Pascoe-Watson's boyhood dreams come to fruition, as a fighter pilot, seen here post-war with his Spitfire Mk XVI*

Below: *The A.T.C. band marching past Lloyds Bank in The Strand*

A.T.C. *were detailed to fill up sand bags from the Maer to put round gun emplacements and to protect sensitive buildings in the town.'*

The Squadrons unofficial motto was "Second To None" and it provided an excellent training facility offering some wonderful experiences for Exmouth's youth.

John Pascoe-Watson
'*Whilst I was in the A.T.C. we were taken to Exeter Aerodrome regularly to help out, or learn how to handle aircraft. I had a fantastic time with all the different types of aircraft coming and going. We were often taken up in aircraft. I sat in the ball gun turret in the back of a Boulton Paul Defiant which was on a flight once. I also flew in a Swordfish, an Albacore, a Fulmar and an Avro Anson amongst many other planes. We were occasionally allowed to get the feel of the controls and this was a truly fantastic experience for a sixteen year old boy. It would never be allowed these days.'*

'*When I was about 16 a pilot asked me if I'd like to go on a night time flight to Plymouth. I said "yes" and when I got to the plane on a beautiful moonlit night I found a W.A.A.F. sitting in the co-pilot's seat and thought I'll never get a chance to fly the plane. After flying for a short while the pilot asked me if I would like to try the controls. The W.A.A.F. then sat on the pilot's lap and proceeded to kiss and cuddle, while I flew the plane on to Plymouth.'*

'*Later I became a Flight Sergeant in the A.T.C. and then joined the R.A.F. three days before D-Day and was accepted as aircrew.'*

During "Wings for Victory" week in 1943 five squadrons of the A.T.C. Paraded in Exmouth Town Centre. They were from Exmouth, Budleigh Salterton, Sidmouth, Honiton and Exeter.

John has written a fantastic book about his experiences in the R.A.F. as a pilot titled *Laughter Silvered Wings*. It is available from local bookshops.

The Scouts and Wolf Cubs

Roy Hole
'*I was a member of the Cubs first and then the 3rd Exmouth Scouts. Later on at the age of around 12-13 I joined the newly formed Air Scouts towards the end of the war, but it didn't last very long. We went on camp three times during the war to Chagford, Moreton-hampstead, and then to Buckfastleigh. We were taken there in the back of a lorry with all our camping gear, and stayed a fortnight each year. After the Air Scouts I joined the Air Training Corps, because I like aircraft so much. Later on after the war I joined the R.A.F.'*

The W.R.N.S. and Sea Rangers marching through The Strand

The Sea Cadets marching through The Strand during the Salute the Soldier parade

Jean Acton
'*We went round with the Guides and did duties at the Y.M.C.A. We had to follow a route and collect unwanted packaging and cardboard. Whilst collecting cardboard I used to visit Clapp's Café I was given off-cuts of cake by the owner. The route consisted of mainly businesses and some private homes. We collected scrap paper and card and newspapers every Saturday, we even collected the cardboard milk bottle tops. Some we kept for ourselves, then cut a hole in the middle and made pom-poms by winding brightly coloured scrap wool around them.'*

The Sea Scouts

Roy Hatten
'*I was in the Sea Scouts when I was around 14 years old. We met at St Andrews Church Hall and would learn how to row and sail small boats and tie knots amongst other things. Dickie Burwood was a great friend of mine, an evacuee from London. We had a "gang" and got up to all sorts of mischief, we would sit on the old piano in the church hall and take it in turns pushing each other along and racing around on*

it. One day when we were playing this game someone knocked the piano over. The keyboard landed on my toe and broke it.'

The Army Cadets

John Middleton

'I joined the Army Cadets. We used to meet at the Drill Hall. Charlie Levers, a school teacher and the Captain of the Boys Brigade, was also the Captain of the Army Cadets.'

'The Home Guard used the Drill Hall as their meeting place and occasionally would show us how to do rifle drill, or other kinds of drill or aircraft recognition. We had mostly Regular Army instructors who were very good and would teach us to shoot on the rifle range at the back of the Drill Hall. We went on a trip to an Army camp at Perranporth in Cornwall, we stayed in tents and did all kinds of training, route marches and drill, and it was good fun.'

The Drill Hall on Imperial Road

The Girls Training Corps

The G.T.C. Girls Training Corps was set up to introduce 16 year old girls to military training and procedures.

Rene Ide

'We were taught by the Home Guard how to shoot, and were drilled by an N.C.O. from Exton Depot. The A.T.C taught us aircraft recognition and the Fire Guard, fire fighting techniques, like how to put out incendiary bombs using a stirrup pump.

We were taught boat drill by the Sea Cadets and the officers in charge took the girls on camps in the summer. Members of the G.T.C. were guaranteed entry in to the A.T.S. when they reached the age of 17 and a half.'

Rene Ide in her Girls Training Corps uniform, 1945

Plastic Army Cadet Force badge

Cardboard milk top.

Chapter 11
Wartime Christmas

Decorations

Wartime Christmas decorations were made from pipe cleaners, cotton reels scrap paper, cardboard and painted fir cones. Small candles and home-made sweets were hung on the tree along with wool decorations, such as pom-poms. Christmas paper and hanging decorations were used, ironed and put away for the following year.

Brown paper was used for wrapping presents, when you could get it and children drew on it, or stuck pictures cut out from newspapers on to it. Hours were spent making paper chains, out of any coloured scrap paper, glue was difficult to get and you couldn't use flour and water, as flour was scarce. Christmas cards were remade from last year's cards, by cutting out the images and gluing them to a plain piece of card with a fresh message.

Presents

Christmas stockings would be put up on chimney breasts or at the end of beds and, if you were really lucky, an orange which came through the Mediterranean would be in your stocking.

Geoff Perriam
'I wasn't very interested in sweets, but I missed citrus fruit, oranges in particular.'

Fred Butler
'Early in the war my favourite toys for Christmas were metal "Minic" cars, they had a spring motor that you wound up with a key then let them go. I also had a fantastic large wind up Rolls Royce car which when the bumpers hit anything, the car would change direction, I loved it!'

Early war toys usually reflected adult role models for children and this remained the same during the war. As the war progressed, most games were of a cheap and easy to produce nature, because of the lack of raw materials. Flicker books with moving matchstick men, dancing or walking, cardboard squeaking trumpets and clicker frogs were popular items.

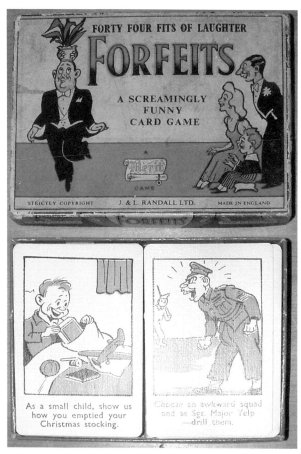

Forfeits - an early wartime game

Winifred Gliddon
'After the Cross had been bombed, one of the buildings which had been flattened had a lot of small mosaic tiles on the floor, I used to pick these tiles out of the damaged floor with one of my Dad's tools and played five stones (Jacks) with the pieces for hours – just sat there on the floor.'

Joy Penwarden
'I stayed in the home most of the time during the war and served in the shop even though I was still very young. I was an only child and to be honest I missed company. When I did play games with my friends, sometimes in The Strand Gardens we played games like, "What's the time Mr. Wolf?" I played with Tina

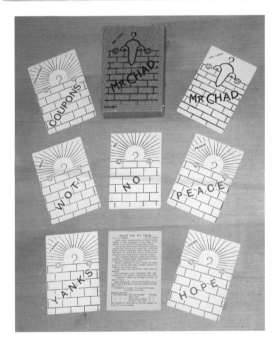

Above from left to right: *Metal Dinky Police Patrolman; Metal Dinky toy Fairey Fulmar; Metal Dinky toy Hawker Hurricane*

Left: *Early war lead toys and Mazac alloy toys*

Below: *Monopoly game still sold today*

Above: *Mr. Chad graffiti cartoon utility card game*

Right: *The "Victory" table tennis set*

Pre-war boy's book   The Splendid Book for Girls

Ewings, Marion Parker and Cynthia Rowe; sometimes we played skipping, hopscotch, jacks and charades – great fun.'

Christmas Sweets

Every child had an extra ration of sweets at Christmas and it was small things like this that made all the difference to the morale of the nation.

Fred Butler
'My favourite sweets were called "cream bars". They were made in milk and plain chocolate. My favourite was milk, but as the war went on you could only get plain chocolate. The Christmas before rationing, my Dad bought a whole boxful for our family.'

Joy Penwarden
'Even though I worked in the sweet shop, I couldn't just help myself. As a customer, you couldn't just have what you wanted either. We prepared mixed bags of loose sweets, so people had an equal chance of having a bit of everything. You then had to exchange the correct amount of coupons for the sweets.'

Joan Middleton
'Sweets I loved them! Pear drops were a favourite and brazil nut chocolates before the war. When rationing

came in and the coupons appeared, sweets were available in the shops but only in small quantities.'

Mary Ashleigh
'My Father was in the Merchant Navy and rarely visited home. We were never allowed to tell our school chums what daddy had brought us home from America, Hershey Bars, Star Bars, Mars Bars with nuts and black chewing gum etc. It was unfair as they couldn't have such luxuries.'

It didn't matter how much money you had you still needed the coupons to get sweets sometimes as little as 2ozs a week. Some bright sparks with a sweet tooth, found out "Where there is a will there is a way"

Joy Penwarden
'Food and clothing were rationed, and the sweets that we had for sale in our shop were bagged up and you had to have what you were given according to how many coupons that you had.'

Ivor Pike
'I had a friend called Jack Neale, his Mother Mrs. Neale used to ask me to run errands for her for pennies. I ran errands for her to get money and errands for someone else to get coupons. I liked mostly boiled sweets and liquorice. The sweets were

kept in glass jars with labels on and very colourful. My favourite sweet shop was in Exeter Road opposite the Park Hotel, it was called Sprittles. I had bright-yellow ice cream at the end of the war. It was made from custard powder I think?'

Mike Slater

'The Americans had vitamin C impregnated sweets called sourballs, they were green, they used to give them to us, and I loved them.'

The Ministry of Food regularly published cost-effective ways of creating nutritious and cheap meals. This is a recipe for wartime Christmas pudding.

Wartime Christmas Pudding

Ingredients

4 oz Breadcrumbs
4 oz flour
3oz Suet
2 oz Sugar
A pinch of salt
1 Tablespoon of treacle

4 oz Raisins
4oz Sultanas
2 oz prunes
Half a teaspoonful of bicarbonate of soda.
1 medium grated carrot
1 grated apple
1 teaspoon of nutmeg
1 reconstituted powdered egg.

Joe Radgick

'We lived in Victoria Road opposite the Y.M.C.A., my Mother, Edith Radgick, did a lot of work for the canteen. On Christmas day 1943, dad went out into the street and invited in two American Soldiers for Christmas dinner, even though we barely had enough rations for ourselves to go round. One of the Americans, Nick Scandalis was 2,000miles from home and still a teenager. He survived the war and wrote to my mother every Christmas from New York.'

Chapter 12
Food Rationing

Wartime Currency

Coin Common Name And Its Value	Date
1. "Half-a-Crown" 2 shillings and sixpence (thirty pennies)	1945
2. "Florin" 2 shillings. "Two Bob" (twenty four pennies)	1941
3. "Shilling" (twelve pennies) a "Bob"	1939
4. "Sixpence" (six pennies)	1939
5. "Thre'penny bit" Silver (three pennies) "thruppence"	1939
6. "Thre'penny bit. Brass (three pennies) "thruppence"	1942
7. "Penny"	1942
8. "Ha'penny" a half-penny piece.	1943
9. "Farthing" (one quarter of a penny)	1940

The coins of the realm in wartime Britain

National Savings Certificates cost 15/- 6d and were worth 20/-6d in 10 years time. Everyone was encouraged to save. They could be bought outright or in instalments using the savings stamps scheme in denominations of 6d, 2/-6d or 5/- from the Post Office or the Trustee Savings Bank.

Shopping

Before the days of the electronic till and calculator people used "Ready Reckoner" tables to work out prices and weights and measures for rationing. People shopped daily and only for necessities.

Jean Acton

'Sometimes we took a bowl or a saucepan to the shops when we went shopping, because bags were in short supply or non-existent. If you could get hold of a paper bag, they fell apart if it rained, due to the poor quality; even wicker shopping baskets were scarce.'

Authors Note

During the war the currency was a duo-decimal system (Multiplications and divisions by 12) and there were 240d (pence) in the pound.

You could buy an off-the-peg man's suit for 30s (£1.50) and a made-to-measure suit for £2. A new bicycle would cost £3 19s 6d (£3.97) and a new eight-horsepower Ford car about £100.

National Savings

The Government was extremely short of money during the war and as well as the re-cycling, and "Waste Not Want Not" campaigns, people were encouraged invest in war bonds.

Rationing

Food Rationing was first introduced in January1940. Every person in Britain had to have a ration book. It ensured that food was distributed fairly and evenly between the people. Swapping went on for certain items. Ration books had to be kept in a safe place to prevent them from being stolen and the used on the black market. They had to be kept clean and in good order, often in a case and never folded. Any ration books which looked too rough or "dodgy" were refused and reported by shopkeepers.

Examples of Wartime Rationing Amounts

This basic list was compiled with information from Lipton's on The Parade, Exmouth. It was compiled by Mrs P. Hocking, who was 15 at the time. The list is now held in Exmouth Museum. Additional information was added by interviewees. Rationing amounts changed during the war continually as circumstances changed.

Weekly ration per person (adult) 1941-1943 highest and lowest examples in Exmouth

Butter 2-8 ounces (grams).
Cheese 2-4 ounces
Bacon 4-8 ounces
Milk very scarce as and when it became available.
Fresh Eggs 1 per week, later 1 per month.
Lard 2 oz
Margarine 4oz
Tea 4oz
Sugar 8oz-2oz

Eggs

Eggs became extremely scarce. Your egg ration could be used to buy chicken feed in place of eggs. This encouraged people to keep chickens instead, which would then lay eggs for them. Cracked eggs with thin shells became available occasionally from the shops and these were not rationed.

Geoff Perriam

'At times fresh eggs were rationed to as little as one a month, a person could forego their egg allowance and claim an allowance of bird feed instead. Thus using the chickens to lay fresh eggs, then later using the birds for the pot as they grew too old to lay.'

Roy Hole's post-war ration book dated 1953-54, 9 years after the end of WWII!

Coupons still inside Roy's ration book

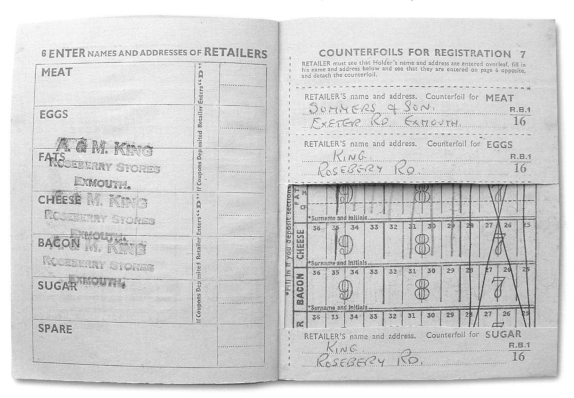

Joy Thorn

'I liked powdered-egg omelettes made with the top of the milk when it was available, lovely!"

Ken Parker

'Powdered eggs were nice! You just had to add water. We had scrambled eggs, omelettes, or mixed them with flour to make pancakes or cakes.'

Milk

One pint of milk a day was made available. Free of charge to all children, expectant mothers and invalids. 30,000 people were needed just to keep the milk flowing. Five million pints of milk were needed every day to satisfy the demand for children's milk. The Women's Land Army played a huge part in ensuring that the local dairy herds were looked after and milked regularly.

Jack Humphries

'My Sister was married to Harry Palmer. He had a dairy business selling milk, butter and cream in Fore Street. At the beginning of the war he was called up, so there was no one to deliver the milk. My sisters then had to look after the shop and organise the milk rounds. Dorothy and Gwen were recruited to deliver the milk around Exmouth on small hand carts, which were made with old pram wheels. They pushed the large churns around the town and had three special measuring ladles for a gill (quarter pint), half pint and pint which they used to measure into people's jugs at the door.'

Ministry of Food "National Dried Milk gas-proof tin

Dried milk from America and Canada was used as a substitute for fresh milk and most people said that it was bearable.

Bread

Mary Ashleigh

'We used to have round milk loaves from the Exeter Road Bakeries. The Viennese loaves had crispy points, so mum had to cut off a slice then divide it in two so we all had a crispy piece.'

Cheese

Ray Challis

'Our cheese ration was 2oz a week! You'd eat that in one mouthful these days!'

Sausages

Mary Ashleigh

'Sausages were on sale at the Co-Op Butchers' I think this was in Exeter Road too! Mum sent David Pocock and me to buy some. I ate them raw on the way home. I can still remember the blue bags of sugar and the hessian sacks of dog biscuits in the Co-Op – I nicked one once!'

Barry Clarke

'The queues for Porky Downs' sausages just after the war, when the rationing changed, were very long. Sometimes stretching right up to the Gas Works.'

Cakes

Ken Parker

'We caught rabbits in the country at harvest time. We would follow the binder round at harvest time, catching the rabbits as they hid in the decreasing circle of wheat. We then skinned and dressed the rabbits and made rabbit pie, or just baked them like a chicken. They tasted quite good.'

Joan Dyke

'We had no electric fridge, just a larder. A small room with shelves in it. There was a marble slab, on which we kept any meat, cheese, butter and margarine and it did the job very well.'

'I was never aware of anyone getting food poisoning, from the food etc. because it wasn't kept in a fridge. When milk bottles were available we kept them in a bucket of cold water to keep the milk cool.'

* * *

Fish

Fish was not rationed and fish and chips became the "National Dish" during WWII. Being an island, Britain was surrounded by water, and fish could be caught and landed relatively easily.

Some of the established local fisherman, Will Newcombe, Will Horn and Frank Rowsell, managed to keep their boats and managed to have an understanding with the authorities which allowed them to continue fishing. These fisherman ran the risk of being sunk by attacks by German fighters, so it was risky business being a fisherman during the war. Because of this fishing was only supposed to be permitted in the mouth of the river and estuary.

Potatoes

Exmouth experienced several raids where the Germans attempted to burn crops with incendiary raids on cereal fields. The Ministry of Food decided to grow more potatoes as a high carbohydrate food supplement for wheat. The potato harvest could be virtually guaranteed in Britain's temperate climate which had a greater chance of survival in bad weather conditions.

Roy Pemberthy
'I used to go round to Dommett's on a Friday to buy fish and chips and a bottle of cider. Mr Dommett used to serve them with lots of salt and vinegar, in a grease-proof bag with the fish on the top. They were then placed on a piece of white paper, which was then wrapped in newspaper to keep them warm. Delicious!

Mary Ashleigh
'Smiths crisps were sold in a red and white bag, but they used no blue ink on them during the war, as it would save a lot of ink. They were 2d a packet with dark blue paper screws or twists of salt.'

Roy Pemberthy
'Mum made bread pudding, but the fruit was always hard because it was dried.'

The National Federation of Women's Institutes

Rose hips provided a natural source of Vitamin C which was crucial to the health of growing children. The W.I. organised local children into groups to pick rose hips from the hedgerows which were then made into rose hip syrup. Gooseberry jam became popular due to the shortage of other soft fruits such as strawberries and raspberries. Blackberries were picked from the hedgerows in August and September. Apples and pears were also grown in gardens and carefully looked after.

The Women's Institute gave talks on jam-making at Littleham W.I. Miss Gunnels' talks on marmalade-making, using the pulp from rowanberries, proved very popular.

People re-used jam jars with screw-top lids for storing home-made jams and chutneys. People would also store food like salted meat and fish, pickled eggs, potted meats, and made fish paste from scraps.

Joy Penwarden
'All our vegetables and fruit were grown in our gardens or allotments. We planted and picked them and some were preserved and put into Kilner jars. Fruit was boiled, then strained through muslin and made into jam or jelly.'

Cakes and Puddings

During March 1941, jam and syrup rations were reduced to 1/2 lb per person per month, people used barley sugar sweets, melted down to sweeten puddings.

Mary Ashleigh
'Mum used to boil up old bones to get the fat out as it was scarce and use this to make macaroons with almond essence.'

The following recipe was taken from the cookery book below. It tastes similar the famous Cadbury's "Crunchie" bar.

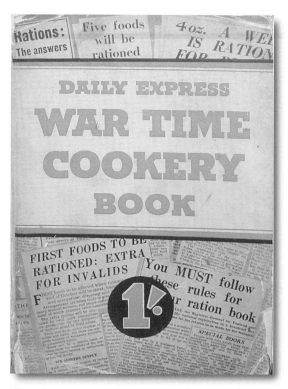

The Daily Express *Wartime Cookery Book*

Cinder Toffee (Honey Comb) Recipe

INGREDIENTS:

10 ½ oz. Castor sugar
7 oz Lyle's golden syrup
2 Tablespoon of white wine vinegar
2 Tablespoon bicarbonate of soda
5 fl oz cold water

Put sugar, cold water, syrup and vinegar in a large saucepan.
Heat until sugar has dissolved. Bring to the boil. Remove from heat. Stir bicarbonate of soda into 1 desert spoon of cold water.
Add to pan. Swirl the pan and let the mixture bubble up. Pour into greased tin and leave to set. When set, turn out of tin and break up.

For added taste cover the broken pieces in melted chocolate.

The British Restaurant

There was a British Restaurant in Exmouth. They were part of a national chain where you could eat value-for-money meals made from staples. Meals for children were 4d, and 8d for and adult. The British Restaurant had a series of plastic tokens they used in place of money, these had varying values corresponding to the currency of the day. The Exmouth restaurant ran at a bad loss and, was a source of constant consternation to the operators, the council and the users who said the food was, quite frankly, terrible. Tea was 2d a cup, jam and cream buns 2d (when you could get them) and plain buns 1d.

It was a criminal offence to waste food in the war, even at a restaurant. This is where the "doggie bag" idea came from. You would have to take your uneaten food home with you. Only the smallest of scraps would go into the restaurant's pig bin.

Feeding Animals

Robert Knowling

'When The Strand was bombed in 1943 Betty's Milk Bar was destroyed along with most of its food stocks. Mr Williamson, the owner, had a lot of pre-war ice cream wafers which he had sealed in glass air-tight jars, knowing that because they were a dried food they would keep for a very long time. Ice creams were in very short supply during the war due to milk shortages.'

'During the salvage operations at the shop, after the bomb, these ice cream wafers were found everywhere in the debris. Some still in the remains of the broken

glass jar. The wafers would have course been inedible, because of the risk of internal haemorrhaging, but it was decided that rather than waste the food it could be fed to chickens who would then safely supply eggs for home consumption, which would not be affected by the broken glass. It meant that the chickens could then not be eaten, again because of the risk to people, but at least the spoilt food could be turned into another usable food source.'

'The broken wafer pieces were retrieved by hand, one by one from the wreckage and were then sieved. The tainted chicken feed was then used for some time to come.'

Vitamins

As the U-boat noose tightened around Britain it became virtually impossible to get any kind of fresh fruit from overseas.

The Government knew that diseases such as scurvy and rickets would soon take their grip on the children of the nation, as this had already been experienced in the food shortages in WWI.

Concentrated orange juice and oranges themselves occasionally made it through the blockade. Much of these products came through the Mediterranean as the Allies still had control of the seas in this part of the world.

Swedes and parsnips could be grown easily and were a good source of vitamin C. Children were encouraged to eat them, although they were not a popular choice for most children.

Jim Dyer

'Mum used to make mock bananas using parsnips and banana essence. They were alright.'

Vitamin A was available from carrots and this was a crop which could easily be grown in Britain and was guaranteed to come up every year. "Cat's Eyes" Cunningham, a famous night fighter ace, was used as an example to the nation's children. The tales of his successes in the newspapers were used to try and get everyone eating carrots as they would "Help You to See in the Blackout". The real reason was to get people eating carrots as they were a guaranteed food source. Recipes such as carrot cake then became popular during the war. Nobody knew that "Cat's Eyes" Cunningham had a new radar system installed in his aircraft.

As the war progressed margarine was manufactured, which was impregnated with vitamins. Consequently most young children had a better supply of vitamins than they ever had before in any point in history.

Chapter 13
Dig for Victory

Smallholdings and Allotments

Most Exmothians had smallholdings or allotments. Some families had their own allotments and some shared communal allotments. Every available space in the town was turned over to growing seasonal vegetables.

Ivor Pike

'Dad had an allotment behind the All Saints Church; we used to grow all sorts of seasonal veg there.'

Ray Challis

'We had a garden and an allotment at Mudbank Lane and another behind the Devoncourt Hotel, these allotments were built on what used to be the last nine holes of the Maer golf course; we used to grow all sorts of seasonal vegetables and fruits there.'

Roy Hole

'As part of our "Dig for Victory" campaign, our school had its own allotments at Mudbank at the end of Carter Avenue, near the old brickworks, in which we used to grow seasonal vegetables. We also had allotments in Phear Park, in the dip where the giant oak tree lays fallen down, and also at our School.'

'With all this "Dig for Victory" activity going on, there was never any vandalism or damage done to the allotments. Firstly it was too important to everyone to be able to eat, and secondly we wouldn't dare too!'

Mushrooms were a good source of protein as meat was scarce. People who knew where to find them locally would pick field and horse mushrooms from the fields and penny-bun (porcini) mushrooms from oak roots in the woodland in late September-October time. A lot of people were worried about being made ill by eating mushrooms and toadstools, thinking the risk of poisoning was too high and so kept well away.

The Women's Land Army (Land Girls)

The Women's Land Army eventually recruited 71,000 women and many of them were based in Devon as it was one of the largest and most important farming

The Ministry Of Agriculture *"Dig for Victory"* Leaflet No. 1

counties in Britain. Six million acres of land was turned over to growing food. The good jobs were the lambing seasons and looking after the cows, most of the Land Girls had real affections for the cows.

Land Girls were responsible for haymaking, potato picking and milking amongst other chores. The only job that was really hated was sprout picking where the sprouts had to be cut from stalks. Squatting in the pouring rain or freezing cold, with extremely sharp knives, their hands got so cold that they quite often cut themselves without realising. There is no doubt that Britain owes a great debt to these young women.

Joining the Women's Land Army

Polly Perkins

'I joined in the Women's land Army in 1942 at the labour exchange Lesse Street in Liverpool. I was nearly 18 years old when I enrolled and was looking forward to the change. We had already been evacuated twice from our home in Liverpool as it was very badly bombed.'

'I travelled to Exeter in my uniform, with my gas mask. It was the train that left Lime Street Station Liverpool, via Sefton Park, which is where I boarded the train. The L.M.S. (London Midland Scottish) train took me all the way to Salisbury where I changed to a Southern Region service which took me to Exeter Central.'

Dorothy Jerrett

'When war broke out I was living in Bournemouth. I volunteered for the Women's Land Army in 1941 and was sent straight to a Devon. I was based at Houstern Farm in the centre of Otterton, which was owned by a Mr Dowell and his family, his wife, son Bob and daughter Kathy. They were all very nice people, but he treated them very badly, especially his wife who he would only ever refer to her as "Woman" in a gruff voice. He never called her by her name. Needless to say after about 5 months of working on the farm for him, I fell out with him and left, refusing to work for him because of his manner.'

'My jobs included, getting up at 6 to milk the cows, then cleaned out their stalls, There was always 25-30 cows which needed milking Bob and I would quite often do this together. After we'd finished I would load up the milk crates on to a bike and deliver the milk to the houses in Otterton. I rode a man's bike with a big box on the front in which were put the milk bottles, when it was full it was very heavy.'

W.L.A. shoulder titles and armband

'I also helped with the harvest. Everyone in the village did. The farms had to grow a certain amount of wheat to feed the nation and the Government insisted that a certain amount of available land was turned over to this use. The farms also had to grow sugar beet which was then refined to make sugar as this was also in very short supply. I had to load the trucks with the hessian sacks filled with the sugar beet and they were very heavy. It was really hard work. The rest of the farm was grass fields for the cows to graze on.'

Polly Perkins

'I would get up at 5 o'clock and get washed and dressed and then have some breakfast. After breakfast I would call the cows in for milking. I would have ten to twelve cows and took them into the milking parlour, I started by washing the udders down with warm soapy water, which was changed regularly by one of the ladies that worked there. I had a three legged milking stool and an aluminium bucket, very light. It was my own and we carried these two items round the parlour with us from stall to stall.'

'The cows were lovely when I got use to them. I was a little frightened of the cows initially, but I had to get used to them. They were very strong and they would kick you when they were uncomfortable or if you hurt them, you had to be very gentle with them but very also very firm.'

'It would then be time for the other jobs that I had to do on the farm. I used to feed the cows, turn out the dirty hay and clean and wash out the cowshed, then replace the straw and hay before getting ready to milk the cows again in the afternoon.'

'Between the hours of 3.30–5.30 we repeated the same procedure as we had carried out in the morning, but got slightly less milk.'

Women's Land Army Uniform.

Polly Perkins

'I was issued immediately with two pairs of corduroy breeches. They were lovely and warm. They were thorn proof and very comfortable. Ideally suited to the hard work. We used one pair for work which we constantly mended and patched and kept one pair for smarter occasions such as parades and church or any other official functions that we attended.'

'We were also issued with two pairs of cotton dungarees, with a bib for the summer, they were very thin though and the thorns and pine needles would poke through them. "We had to constantly repair the buttons on the braces as they were always pulling off when we bent down or got up.'

Women's Land Army hat

Women's Land Army badge

'The hat was like a large felt trilby it was a khaki colour with a badge on the front and everyone's hat looked slightly different. We tended to "style" them in the way we liked them to look. My own hat I turned up at the side and it looked more like an Australian hat.'

'We had two green woollen jerseys, a half-belt khaki serge over-coat which kept us very warm in the cold weather, but we tended to keep this for best or for travelling to an from the workplace. A pair of good quality, lace up shoes of brown leather, with Blakey's iron protectors in them was issued to us and we really had to look after them. We also had plimsolls for light summer work and issued with strong boots when we transferred to the "Women's Timber Corps" and worked in the forests; they went up under the knee and were very tough.'

'We were issued with knitted woollen stockings (socks), 3 pairs were issued to us – these were khaki in colour, 3 pale khaki shirts in "Aertex" which we rotated.'

The Women's Timber Corps

The Women's Timber Corps had a very tough time and although they were working in Woodbury during WWII, Polly was sent to the Savenake Forest, but the work was the same.

Polly Perkins

'I was sent to work for the newly formed Forestry Corps as it was first called, this later became the Women's Timber Corps. Britain was desperate for timber for pit props for the coal mines and for quick growing timber to help build certain parts of vessels for the D-Day invasion fleet, so in 1943 I went to the Savenake forest for a while to work, planting trees.'

'Most of the girls were injured by septic wounds caused by cuts at some point in their life in the Timber Corps and occasionally the wounds became so infected that you would need some time off to recover as the work was arduous and you needed to be fit to be able to do it. We had a large bottle of disinfectant that we carried with us to put on the scratches we sustained from the thorns and pine needles. We got hundreds of these. Apart from these annoyances, we lived a very healthy outdoor life and were well fed. Mostly we were in really good health, which I must say I really enjoyed. Being a city girl, it made such a change to be in the countryside.'

'Most of our time was spent hand planting new saplings on our hands and knees using a trowel. Although the earth was tilled, turned and drilled prior to our arrival, we worked from 8 in the morning till 4 at night and it was back-breaking work.'

Dorothy Jerrett

'There were Women's Timber Corps Girls working on Woodbury Common, but we didn't get to see much of them, except occasionally at the country dances organised by a Mrs Grant. I really enjoyed these dances but they were always over too soon, I had to get up early in the morning, as did most people and so the dances would finish at 8.30 so everyone could get to bed.'

Chapter 14
Clothes and Fashion

New Clothing

Clothes rationing was introduced on June 1 1941.

Rene Ide

'I was 14 when I started work in the shop, I had to wear a black dress when I worked in Louvil's, all the time. We weren't earning very much, coats were expensive to buy and at least 18 coupons. Nice stockings were nearly impossible to get hold of once the shops quota for them had gone. Decent knitwear was also impossible to get. We used to stock Braemarle and Pringle before the war, but the supplies dried up, we would put people's names on the waiting list, really knowing that there was no chance of getting anything.'

'We had a lot a titled people living in Exmouth at the time. They had moved away from the city areas for safety. Two Countesses' used to shop with us, one was a foreign lady and the other had a strange name!'

This table shows how many clothes coupons were required from your clothing ration book to buy specific items. The coupons could be used on any items of clothing that you preferred, or were in desperate need of. Once they were used up for the specific period of time, no more were made available until the following year.

Theoretically you could spend all your coupons in one day on 66 suspenders belts or ties, but that would mean you would have spent your clothing allowance for the whole year.

Try and work out what you would spend your money and coupons on in one year.

Remember: The total adult yearly allowance was only 66 Coupons

Men	Coupons
Suit	26
Shoes	7
Shirt	5
Shirt Collar	1
Socks (pair)	3
Tie	1
Pants	4
Vest	4
Pyjamas	8
Dressing Gown	8

Women	Coupons
Suit	18
Shoes	5 later 7
Outdoor Coat Lined	18
Cotton or Rayon Unlined	7
Wool Unlined	11
Blouse or Jumper	5
Stockings	2
Vest	3
Knickers	3
Bra	1
Suspender Belts	1

The original clothing coupons were used from the old food ration book, which had 26 unused margarine coupons left in it after the full margarine quota had been used up by the individual for that year.

Later on, 40 additional clothes coupons were introduced printed on special green cards which became the first clothes ration book proper.

By April 1941 clothes prices had risen by 72% of their highest 1939 prices.

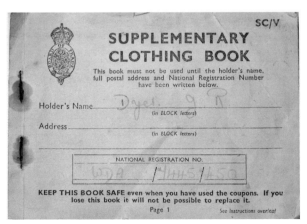

Jim Dyer's Supplementary Clothing ration book

Children's Clothing

A child under the age of three's clothing was not rationed, whilst for a child over this age clothing was rationed from August 1941. At this point, half the amount of adult coupons were used to buy the equivalent garment in a child's size.

Children carried leather satchels to school and wore caps and blazers. Boys wore short trousers until the age of 14 due to material shortages and school uniforms were constantly being repaired. They were in short supply you had to look after your clothing. The first children's ration books were introduced in 1943.

Peggy Gibbins

'I had the same gymslip all through my senior school. Mum just moved the buttons as I grew and repaired it, money was so tight.'

Furs and animal skins were not rationed, furs were popular but expensive. If you had the money, they were a great source of warmth outside as well as in the home, as fuel was rationed and life in the winter was cold.

When the 1943-44 clothing ration books were introduced further cuts in the coupons were made, to the lowest level during the war of 40 coupons for the whole year!

At this point, dress hire and hired evening dress for men came in, as purchasing suits became too expensive and the material was unavailable.

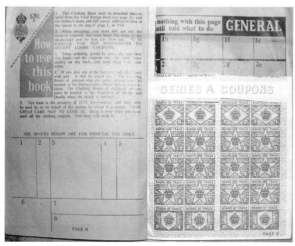

Late war period clothing ration book still with some coupons inside

Austerity Rationing

This was introduced to counter the problems of supply caused by the shortage of raw materials. New laws were introduced governing the making of clothes and limitations of cloth usage.

These new laws dictated how much clothing a manufacturer could produce, or prohibited the use of certain materials. It also forbade the use of embroidery, limited the depth of hems and restricted the width of lapels. On men's clothing, double-breasted jackets were banned, as were turned up trousers. The amount of stitching was limited on each garment and the amount of buttons used on a single garment was also reduced.

Utility Rationing

Because manufacturers and suppliers tended to make and stock higher-priced goods to earn a living. Cheaper items of clothing were becoming virtually unobtainable by early in 1941. Utility rationing used ingenious methods to make every thing stretch further. Smaller patterns on cloth were introduced, to make repeating patterns easier to match up and less visible if they couldn't be matched exactly, thus saving cloth.

The Utility Mark

The CC41, Civilian Clothing 1941 mark was a guarantee of quality whilst using as few materials as possible, to produce a stylish garment. Nicknamed "The Two Cheeses" it was introduced in September 1941.

Items carrying this mark were exempt from purchase tax and conformed to a standardisation and simplification of design.

The utility programme was brought in for many objects not just clothes. Bed and household linen, shoes and handbags, all started to carry the mark which eventually spread to other items including furniture.

Government Appointed Utility Designers

The Government employed the services of top designers, Norman Hartnell, Digby Morten, Worth; Hardy Amies, Bianca Mosca, Peter Ryssell, Victor Stiebel, and Creed all introduced a spring collection in the shops by 1942. Utility wardrobe would consist of coat, suit, afternoon dress, cotton overall dress. In all 32 different outfits could be created using utility designs.

Second Hand Clothes

Second hand clothes were exempt from rationing and a thriving trade in swapping and bartering existed in Exmouth. As children out-grew their clothes they were handed down to their younger brothers and sisters, or more distant relatives. Friends and neighbours would swap and exchange any item of clothing which could be traded; especially women who always needed a new look for that special date!

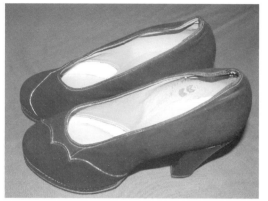

Above: *Utility designed Women's shoes*

Top Left: *Hazel Bradford sitting on a bench in Withycombe wearing women's clothing typical of 1944*

Bottom Left: *Hazel's sister Connie photographed on the same day in 1944*

Below left: *Utility Mark in long johns*

Below right: *Utility mark in Lisle and rayon stockings*

Bottom: *Utility rayon stockings*

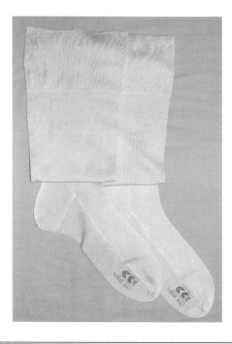

Pearl Cawse
'I had a second hand adults black coat which a seamstress cut and turned by taking it all apart by hand. It fitted very well. Second hand coats were scarce.'

"Make Do and Mend"

Joy Penwarden
'There was always sewing going on in households. Sheets were turned sides to middle. Cuffs and collars turned. Socks darned with the aid of a wooden mushroom, for support. Old jumpers were unpicked, put into hanks, washed, put into balls and knitted up again.'

Stockings

Stockings were scarce. Rayon and nylon were new products and a lot had come from America at the beginning of the war. The U-boats made it impossible for anything other than crucial equipment and foodstuffs for the war to be brought across the Atlantic. Women were constantly mending stockings and when they wore out and became unusable they developed very clever ways of looking their best. Women found that by boiling nylon stockings all together in a saucepan, that this would go a long way to equalising the colour of them. Then once a stocking from a pair had been mended so many times to render it useless, the other one could then be used as the colours would match and not look odd.

Emergency Measures

In times when stockings became completely unavailable, some women would use a mixture of gravy browning and other dyes, including boot polish to stain their legs a light brown colour. This was similar to the artificial tanning creams that women use today. After the legs had dried a seam line was drawn up the back of the leg to imitate the look of real stockings. I have seen this done and it looks incredibly effective. Especially in a dark dance hall.

Jack Humphries
'My sisters were always swapping clothing and getting ready to go to the local dances at the Pavilion. They used to colour their legs as they could not get any stockings during the war. They mostly used Camp Coffee. A liquid coffee substitute in a bottle. It was made from chicory. They would smooth it on to their legs. They made me use an eyebrow pencil to draw seams down the back their legs before they went off to the dances, which required a steady hand!'

Rene Ide
'Quality underwear was extremely hard to find. Silk was at a premium. Peggy, a girl in our work, got hold of an American Army parachute and made knickers from it for us. They weren't bad. You really felt more glamorous because of the feel the silk but nobody got to see them!'

'We were so desperate to create new fashions and got so bored with the same old clothes we would do anything to make something new. We would swap clothes, or combine two dresses of similar patterns, or different colours to create new styles and colour schemes.'

Mrs Sew and Sew

Mrs Sew and Sew was a character designed for the "Make Do and Mend" Government Information films and poster campaigns throughout the war. She always had tips and helpful hints to help people make new clothes from their old ones or how to repair and spruce up old clothing, to make it more desirable and fashionable. Exmouth's Women's Voluntary Service ran local knitting circles and Make Do and Mend groups where, resources, skills and materials could be pooled to alter and repair clothing.

Jim Dyer
'You had to have coupons for new clothing, so patches were put on everything. If you tore anything, it was mended. Leather was on worn elbows. The cuffs would wear out and have leather patches sewn round them. People still took pride in their appearance though. Most people had uniforms as they were in the services and you could only wear uniform. Never civvies.'

Moths

One of the greatest dangers to people's clothing was moths during the war. Most clothing was manufactured from "edible" natural materials, such as cotton and wool and people had to be extremely careful with how they stored their clothing, using mothballs, camphor impregnated balls of wood. Moths disliked the smell and the balls therefore acted as a deterrent.

Chapter 15
Fuel and Water Supplies

Petrol Rationing

Petrol was strictly rationed in the war. It was such a precious commodity that even petrol for cigarette lighters was rationed.

Roy Hole
'Dad had a small petrol allowance for his Austin 10 to allow him to go to Bristol to pick up HT batteries for radios'

Gas

The Government suggested heating one room in the house only. Usually the kitchen or dining room. The upstairs of the house was never heated. The door from the heated room downstairs was opened last thing at night, to allow the heat to rise and heat the upstairs. Some people would take up a few embers to put in the grate up stairs or put them in a bed pan to heat the bed. Most used a hot water bottle in the winter.

The oven was used as little as possible. When it was lit as much stuff as possible was put in. People were encouraged to bake once a week and wash clothes once a week.

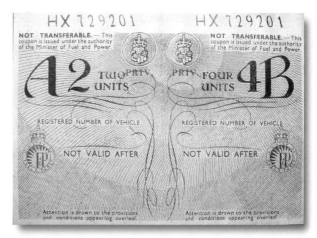

Petrol ration coupon and train ticket with gas economy slogan on the reverse

Coal

Coal was essential for munitions production and alternative energy production, such as, electricity and gas, for heating and lighting.

Coal merchants in Exmouth delivered coal by horse and cart. One such merchant was E.V. Perry of Bicton Street. Three shovelsful of coal a day was the maximum consumption allowed per household. The occupants of the house had to leave a running total of the amount of coal used on a card in the front window, so the coal merchant could check the amounts used.

Water Rationing

The reservoirs needed to be kept as full as possible to make sure the fire services had enough water in the event of large scale incendiary raids. One cup of water only, was to be used in each saucepan for boiling vegetables.

This seemed ironic to some of the locals as Exmouth was at the mouth of an enormous river and right by the sea. Static rainwater tanks were erected at sites all over the town and a 150mm pipe ran from the docks along Victoria Road to the corner of The Strand, assuring a supply of sea water for use in the event of a bad raid.

Washing and Bathing

Most working class homes had no bathrooms. Just a large zinc bath. This could be used in front of the fire in the winter or more usually, in front of the range in the kitchen to make it easy to fill with pans of hot water from the stove. Only a maximum of 10cms of water was allowed in the bath. People frequently marked this line on the bath with paint.

Roy Hole

'I remember having a bath every Saturday night; it was a tin bath we kept out in the yard and was brought in. Mum had to boil enough water to bath 5 children and 2 adults. It must have been very hard work.'

Barry Clarke

'The family used to bath in the kitchen in a zinc bath filling the bath up from saucepans from the stove'

Toilet paper on string

Toilets

The great percentage of working-class homes had outside toilets only and it wasn't unusual to see old newspapers, cut into squares and threaded on a piece of string, which was then hung on the back of the toilet door.

Barry Clarke

'In my American Red Cross parcel box that the G.I.s gave me was soft toilet tissue absolute luxury!

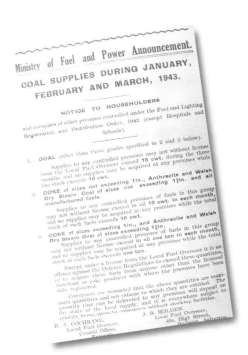

Chapter 16
Recycling and Salvage

Britain was becoming desperate for raw materials by the end of 1941. The national and Local press allocated space in their publications to draw the public's attention to the problem. Loudspeaker vans, touring the streets making public announcements, were also used.

Rubber

Old tyres and inner tubes, hot water bottles pencil rubbers old soles of shoes were recycled and rubber was essential for making tyres, lifebelts, lifejackets, gas masks and dinghies.

Paper

Waste paper drives were in operation throughout the war. Even the smallest scraps of paper were deemed useful and it was an offence not to save waste paper.

Left: Joy Penwarden shows the pans to the camera collected for Lord Beaverbrook's appeal

Below left: Shoe polish in a lightweight war economy tin

Below: Envelope sent to John Fletcher made from reused blue Tate & Lyle sugar bag and the inside of the recycled envelope

Train ticket with paper salvage slogan printed on the rear

Things like small train tickets have become scarce items as most were surrendered during the war to help the recycling drives.

Waste paper was collected by Girl Guides, Rangers and Boy Scouts on Saturday's pushing hand carts round the streets. The paper was then sent back to the papermill's for processing and turned into new paper products. Nearly seven tons were collected in September 1941, which for a town the size of Exmouth was an excellent result.

Jack Humphries

'We used to have to collect cardboard and paper for the war effort. A hand-operated compressing machine was used to squash the cardboard to save space; everything was recycled where it could be.'

Bones

Once bones had all the edible meat removed from them and had been boiled to remove the marrow, which was used for sauces soups and gravies, only then would the bones be sent to the bone bins for recycling.

The recycling of bones was essential to the war effort. Nitrates could be extracted from heated and crushed bones and thus they provided a valuable supply essential to both the armaments and fertilizer industries.

Disappointed bird, looking for scraps in the bone bin

They WERE Kettles

Behind the W.V.S. depot at the Strand, up to Wednesday, lay an amazing collection of cast-off domestic utensils in the shape of aluminium pots and pans which have served their purpose in a peaceful manner and are being salvaged to be turned into instruments of war to defend the country from the threats of a ruthless enemy. The pots and pans, some in a very good state, were sent from hundreds of Exmouth households following the broadcast appeal for aluminium to help in the further construction of aeroplanes.

The collection filled the room almost from floor to ceiling and it was removed on Wednesday by rail to go to a factory in another part of the country.

The ladies who undertook the collection were Mrs. H. P. Hodgson and Mrs. Gray (in charge of the depot), assisted by Miss B. Miller, Mesdames Sugg, A. B. Hosken, J. Moore, E. L. W and Valpy French.

Wanted !

Odd Scraps of Wool are urgently needed by the Exmouth and District Anglo-Russian Council. Any Colours. Garments suitable for unravelling would do.

Clothes and Woollens, suitable to send to Russia also needed. Hand to Mrs. Ware, 7, Rosebery Road.

The Exmouth and District Anglo Russian Council.

Chapter 17
The Dock and Estuary

Joy Thorn

'I used to cycle to the seafront and to the docks. There was always a lot of ships coming and going from the docks. Exmouth was a busy port. Sometimes you could see a dozen or more ships out to sea on the horizon.'

The estuary was used by German raiders as a navigational aid to find Exeter as it was easily recognizable from the air due to its distinctive shape and size. On 10th of June 1940 a letter from The Admiralty, Secretary to the Commander-in-Chief, Western Approaches at Mount Wise Devonport, ordered the removal of the buoys at the mouth of the Exe estuary, as they provided a good reference point for German aircraft, or invading forces intending to raid Exeter up the river.

The Exmouth Lifeboat

In December 1943 a south coaster ran aground on pole sands and the lifeboat under the supervision of the new coxswain Reginald Searle, rescued 13 men from the stricken ship.

December 1944 a Dutch coaster was in trouble a destroyer and Exmouth lifeboat rescued 11 men from the stricken vessel. A tug boat towed the ship to safety.

H.M.S. Tennyson

The Royal Navy requisitioned the Imperial Hotel to be used as a shore establishment and was named H.M.S. *Tennyson*. Later in the war as the Americans declared war on Germany and Japan, American naval officers were billeted here

Peter Mattholie

'We stayed in the Imperial Hotel on Exmouth seafront for a while, which was called H.M.S. Tennyson. It was a Royal Naval shore establishment and contained all the officers and Combined Operations staff. Me and my friend Jock were "volunteered" for duty, waiting on tables for a while, in the officer's mess.'

R.A.F. Marine Branch A.S.R.U. No.38 Exmouth

Based at Exmouth docks and initially equipped with two pinnace launches. These were general purpose launches whose design was initially intended to service and re-supply sea planes. They were ideal for this purpose. However they proved far to slow to be of any use to Air Sea Rescue units.

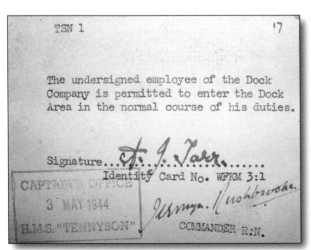

H.M.S. Tennyson Admiralty issued dock pass

An Air Sea Rescue unit launch

Later on these were replaced by Thornycroft High Speed Launches serial numbers 191 and 193. These had a top speed of approx 30 Knots and were incredibly noisy. They were equipped with Thornycroft's own engines and were responsible for waking up the local population on many occasions, when they were started.

There job was to rescue airman of all nationalities, including the enemy, they also recovered bodies of downed airmen. Duty crews slept in "Waterside" a small green hut, converted to an office opposite the steps to the Starcross ferry.

Jim Shapter

'100's of landing craft, barges and other small ships were in the dock and estuary most of them kept between Shelly Beach and Starcross. The dock was absolutely full of them prior to D-Day.'

Thames lighters, large slow moving barges used for carrying freight, coal and bricks down the River Thames. Four hundred of these large boats were converted by the Admiralty and put to use during the D-Day landings as supply vessels.

Peter Mattholie

'The Thames river barges or lighters, were approx 60' long and 20' wide. They were painted a Blackish

DKX 178364 stoker 1st Class Peter Mattholie aged 18

colour. They had a small wheel house at the rear of the boat and completely flat for the rest of the length of the boat for storing cargo and equipment. They cut off the stern of the standard barges and fitted and bulkhead across the back and two Huge Chrysler petrol engines port and starboard. The front was cut off and a wooden drop-down ramp was then fitted to it so it could run on to the beach. Our barge was numbered in white letters LBV 41(Landing Barge Vehicle). There must have been 40-50 barges in the estuary and Shelly Gut area amongst the other boats, but I'm not sure what they were.'

'Some of our barges were highly specialised, one we called a "Cook", it was a floating cook house and bakery it had a huge built up top heavy look with "H" shaped chimneys sticking out of it. These were designed to be anchored off-shore at Omaha and Utah beach. They would then be supplied with the raw material to cook fresh food and bake bread which was then transferred to the shore by the other barges and landing craft.'

'There was also a barge with an American truck permanently mounted on board. It had power take-offs and heavy tools for making pattern parts and repairing items in need of heavy engineering.'

As D-Day approached the Landing Craft and a whole host of other vessels including an Exmouth based, privately owned motor yacht, which had been commandeered by the Admiralty and pressed into service as H.M.S. *Alvista* left for Portsmouth and Poole harbour. The *Alvista* was used as the command ship of convoy TM 4 by Lieutenant Commander L.J. McMillan R.N.V.R. during the disastrous Exercise Tiger D-Day rehearsals, where American landing ships were attacked by E-Boats out in Lyme Bay on the 28th April 1944.

Once at the harbours they were they were loaded with ammunition, bridging equipment, vehicles and supplies. They were then split into their specialist convoys, which sailed to Omaha Beach and Utah Beach in the early hours of June 6th 1944.

P.L.U.T.O. Pipe Line Under The Ocean

One wartime project was the construction of P.L.U.T.O. (Pipe Line Under The Ocean) which was to be towed across the Channel on D-Day to supply petrol to the invasion fleet and vehicles.

Jim Shapter

'They stored and tested some of the Pluto equipment by Mudbank. Other sections were also moored off Powderham. Pieces of the pipe were stored all over England. It was towed across on the landings and eventually ran along the bottom of the channel and

kept our invasion forces vehicles filled up with petrol during their advance through France and Germany.'

Joe Radgick

'Later in the war they off-loaded sleepers from the railway which were going to be used for making a platform out in the estuary to be towed across on D-Day to support part of the Pluto petrol delivery system, but it wasn't used in the end. Hiram Thomas worked on this project during the war and it was Top Secret.'

The Royal Naval Patrol Service (R.N.P.S.)

This unit was formed just before the Dunkirk evacuations. They mounted boat patrols just offshore, in the estuary and up and down the River Exe. They also operated a Lewis gun mounted on a pillar by the swing bridge.

Ray Towill

'The Docks garage was owned by Harold Rowland, it was commandeered by the Royal Navy at the beginning of the war. The Royal Naval Patrol Service was set up, a bit like the Home Guard in boats! The volunteers that staffed the launches became known as "Rowland's Navy" they patrolled the river and estuary and also operated the steel turret for a while.'

John Pascoe-Watson

'My Father Bill was in the Royal Naval Patrol Service. They had small motor launches and rowing boats and were based down at the Dock. Amongst their responsibilities was running a hawser from the boom out across to the Warren to prevent an enemy attack via the river. The Headquarters for the R.N.P.S. was in Rowland's Garage near the swing bridge.'

Joe Radgick

'We used to take our canoes across the river at night when we were 16 and drank cider in the Anchor Inn at Cockwood. We didn't really think about it at the time, but we could easily have been shot as enemy spies if found in the estuary, in the dark, they may have thought we were retrieving soil samples for an invasion or making sketches.'

The Sea Cadets

Joe Radgick

'We went on Parades through the town centre I was keen on the Royal Navy and wanted to join, but at the time my father wanted me to learn a craft, so I could join the navy later as an artificer, which had better pay and career prospects. My father was insistent that I learned the trade as they were sinking ships faster than they were being built.'

Sea Cadets and Sea Rangers march past the Pavilion in the Salute the Soldier parade 10th June 1944

Chapter 18
The Observer Corps

Initially, during the Battle of Britain the Observer Corps was made up mainly from ex police officers, or special constabulary members. It was set up to monitor enemy aircraft movements over the coast and all over the British Isles as the first line of the national air defences. Exmouth's Observation Post (Fox Four), was at the top of Foxholes Hill, near the Coast Guard Cottages.

Mr. P. Oswin was the Chief Observer. The post was staffed 24 hours a day by a full time staff and a part time staff. A four-man, full-time observer staff team worked in shifts, 48 hours per week and a contingent of 16 part time staff shared these watches working sixteen to 24 hours per week.

Originally it was just a circular concrete pit in the grass but as the war progressed, a look-out tower and huts were built on the site. These were surrounded by layers of protective sand bags. It was staffed every day of the year, in all weathers and was attacked by German raiders on several occasions.

The Post Instrument
(Micklethwaite Predictor)

Direction was calculated by points of the compass written on a compass rose on the post instrument pit. Height was calculated by the Micklethwaite Predictor and this coupled with the estimations of numbers and speeds proved a reasonably accurate system for calculating the speed, direction and weight of the attack.

The Observer Corps often had a busy time recording the numbers of aircraft flying in and out of Exmouth airspace. Virtually every night aircraft were spotted between June 1940 and late 1941 usually sometime just after dusk. It was possible to hear the sound of bombs detonating and anti-aircraft barrages going up all the time during the night.

The men of the Observer Corps recorded that aircraft could often be seen in the early morning light returning from night raids. Heinkel He 111s, Junkers Ju88s, Dornier 17s and 217s, were all seen over the town. A lot of reports suggested that these bombers were flying very low on return journeys to stay below radar detection systems and below the depression of anti-aircraft guns.

Mike Heard

'Incoming and outgoing aircraft were overhead continuously during night and day. The noise of engines was nearly constant at some points, but you got used to it. The German planes sounded different to our own and you gradually got used to the sounds of them, knowing when there could be trouble and when it was safe.'

Later in the war as German air attacks became fewer the Observer Corps role shifted to counting allied aircraft in and out as they made bombing raids on Europe and travelled to France in the massed glider and paratroop assaults for the Normandy landings.

Incendiary bomb

Chapter 19
Air Raid Precautions

The Need for A.R.P.

Between the start of the Second World War in September 1939 and the end of 1941, civilian casualties on the British mainland far out-numbered those of servicemen fighting at the front.

Government maps made by those planning defence strategies for the Great Britain show that although high civilian casualties were anticipated, it was thought these were most likely to occur in and around London and the industrial areas further north.

The National A.R.P.

Planning for an Air Raid precautions service had started back in 1935. The Government knew well that the Germans had bombed London using Zeppelins in WWI and now had newer, more efficient way of delivering bombs and poisonous gas to the British Isles.

After the lessons learned in 1937 from the bombing of Guernica, during the Spanish Civil War, it was crucial to have trained individuals ready to respond to Luftwaffe aerial attacks against a defenceless population. It was quickly recognized that an efficient search and rescue and first aid service would have to be set up in countries at risk from air raids.

The government passed the Air Raid Precautions Act in Autumn 1937, requesting 800,000 volunteers to undergo training in this new service. On the 1st of January 1938 the amended Air Raid Precautions Act came in to force outlining that:

'The Armed Forces would remain the front line of defence against an attack from an aggressor and the unarmed A.R.P. would deal with training, sheltering, reporting and logistic to deal with raids, using a mixture of preventative measures and well organised first-response reactions to air attacks to minimise casualties and destruction of property.'

In July of 1938 the Civil Defence Acts definition of itself stated that:

'Civil Defence encompasses all the organisations that contribute to the limitation of death, damage and disruption from enemy bombing, but would rely primarily on the Air Raid Precautions organization.'

Staffing the A.R.P. with volunteers was a continuing struggle throughout the war, as more and more Men and Women were called up into the armed services. People were constantly leaving and joining, which meant that a continuing programme of instruction, lectures and training had to be kept in place throughout the war.

The Exmouth A.R.P.

The Exmouth A.R.P. started organising the towns Civil Defence structure from early March 1938. Local papers carried adverts asking for volunteers to help set up the system and to work as Wardens, Rescue Workers, Fire Guards, First Aid personnel and Gas Detection Squads. These people were also required to help the locals with the fitting and maintaining of gas masks and safe sheltering. By August 1939 the A.R.P. Services had already instructed most of the local populace in gas mask fitting and air raid drills.

Training A.R.P. Volunteers

As printed material was not yet available, the A.R.P. volunteers had to take notes, when attending lectures. The topics covered were; organization, reporting, first aid, the blackout, rescue services, and assembling Anderson shelters.

Thankfully gas was never used in WWII and as the decontamination exercises during the war showed, it was virtually impossible to protect the population against gas attacks. It was intended to be sprayed from aircraft and covered anything it touched with a long release burning vapour which smelled of garlic. This could then be transferred from the road to your shoes without you even knowing. Then, when you took your shoes off at night they would fill the room with vapour that would burn the sensitive linings to your lungs, rendering them useless.

A.R.P. Printed Literature

Pamphlets were prepared and printed outlining preparations for precautionary measures such as clearing lofts of inflammable material and to improve access for Fire Guards. Vast numbers of pamphlets were issued to households covering the topics of public air raid shelters, Anderson shelters, Morrison shelters, gas attacks and gas masks, first aid, the blackout and how to survive in the event of an invasion.

Regular talks and instructional courses were presented for A.R.P. Volunteers and the general public at the Control Centre on Exeter Road during the course of the war. Topics for these courses included, Gas detection and decontamination, Incendiary Bombs, High Explosive Bombs. Mr. B.R. Stevenson gave a large percentage of these lectures. Full scale mock air raid exercises were also staged.

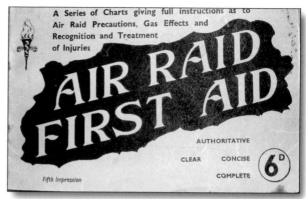

Air Raid Precautions first-aid book

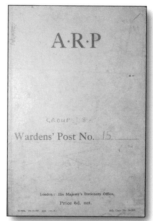

Right: *Harry Stocker's A.R.P. Warden's notebook*
Far right: *Home Office A.R.P. pamphlet*

A.R.P., Civil Defence, Police and Fire Guard Equipment

Wills cigarettes cards A.R.P. training book

The Structure of the Exmouth A.R.P.

The Control Centre

During the early months at the Centre, it was used as a training establishment and lecture hall, where volunteers could learn the new skills and responsibilities required by the A.R.P. service.

Into this building was installed a small exchange system and additional telephone extensions to deal with incoming reports. Incoming and outgoing messages regarding incidents could be received, coordinated and acted upon at the centre. The Centre was activated in 1939 and was initially staffed 24 hours a day by volunteers, working eight hour shifts. A total of 120 staff could be mustered from the centre in the event of a large scale emergency. The Centre was staffed every day of the year until the 10th June1945.

Duty's At The Control Centre
(The Library Exeter Road)

Rotating shifts of eight people were on duty from 8.00 a.m. – 8.00 p.m. on three nights a week. There

Now Exmouth library, once the site of the A.R.P. Control Centre

were wooden framed, canvas military beds in the section which is now the main library room, where the duty personnel could sleep, whilst two duty officers took it in turns to operate the phones.

Part of the building had a glass roof and it was never protected during the course of WWII, despite the many complaints of A.R.P. Staff who slept under it whilst on duty during the raids. It was obvious that a direct hit would destroy any building but their real worry was being hit by small 1kg incendiary bombs, debris and shrapnel from bomb explosions nearby. Later in the war, "Butterfly" bombs, lethal area deprivation bombs, filled with high explosive and ball bearings, became an even bigger source of worry. Fortunately these were not used on Exmouth but were used in Exeter to devastating effect, killing and seriously wounding several people.

Jean Acton

'My older sister Mary, was to go into military service in 1940, but was stopped by her dad to help run the business as mother was ill. The case went to a tribunal in the end and she didn't have to join up and so remained in Exmouth where she joined the Air Raid Precautions Service. She applied for a job as a telephonist and worked at a house called Maervale. It was the A.R.P. Communications Post."

The A.R.P. Telephone Centre Cyprus Road

Mary Acton

'I joined the A.R.P. in 1942 aged 18 years I was not called up, as I was taking the place of my Father's male assistant at W.H. Smith Bookstall on Exmouth Station. I had to go before a Tribunal and was told I would have to join the Civil Defence, as I was happy to do.'

'I was first stationed at the old infant school in Exeter Road. We had a very smart uniform. Navy double breasted greatcoat, navy beret, navy trousers and a navy long sleeved overall with ties at the back. By common consent we all wore our own white blouses.' 'We had a very nice Controller a Mr. Clinchy. He was a frail looking man, who suffered from asthma, but he was very kind and helpful and soon got us into our routine.'

'We had to use our telephones wearing our special respirators which had a protrusion on one side for the telephone receiver I remember there was laughter as we tried it all out. The respirators made rude noises with the air outlet!'

The Civilian Duty Respirator (Gas Mask)

Civilian Duty Respirators were used by people who would need to perform vital functions in the event of a gas attack. A.R.P. workers, switchboard telephonists, gas workers, First Aid Party members

Early Civilian Duty Respirator

A.R.P. Warden's Mk II steel helmet

and drivers for the A.F.S. were all issued with this type of mask as it was much tougher than the civilian model.

People who had volunteered for work with the A.R.P. were expected to work in any conditions, including gas attacks.

These gas masks were supplied in a hessian or linen sack, to people who would have to work, or remain at their station throughout an attack.

Mary Acton

'We soon moved to a large detached house in Cyprus Road, the drawing room had been re-enforced with heavy wooden beams and sandbags and our phones sat in state, in the middle. We were on duty, I think three nights a week and sometimes were called during the day. I seem to remember that when the air raid warning sounded it was mostly to R.A.F. Exeter that I spoke. They had a Polish Squadron stationed there and I knew they were a great asset during the Battle of Britain. We all slept in tiered bunks, with heavy black screens at the windows.'

'Exmouth suffered quite heavy bombing and casualties. I used to leave A.R.P. Headquarters at 6.00

a.m. and cycle to the railway station in my uniform, respirator and tin hat (steel helmet). The paper train arrived about 6.15 a.m. and the different paper rounds had to be marked up.'

'At the end of hostilities we were "stood down". We were allowed to keep our greatcoats (very cosy!) and our tin hats and everything else was returned.'

'I was given a solid silver A.R.P. badge in a red case, of which I am very proud!'

Alerts

The Control Centre could be alerted at extremely short notice and put into action, because of the staffing commitment. In a matter of minutes the staff were woken up and manning their post in the event of a warning, or raid. In an alert, telephone reports were dealt with from sector posts and also from the A.R.P. headquarters in Exeter. They were then relayed to the relevant sector posts and the Police.

There were many tense and boring hours of wondering whether the enemy would come, and if so where and when would they attack. Some nights, alerts lasted several hours. Some nights there were several short alerts and some nights nothing. It is a wonder that anyone ever got any sleep at all. During an air raid the centre became a hive of activity, organising the other emergency services such as, Rescue Squads, Ambulances and the Fire Brigade, to arrive at an incident in a co-ordinated, cohesive force, able to deal with any eventuality.

Late war Woman's A.R.P. uniform jacket

Exmouth Urban District Council.

Council Offices,
Exmouth.
October, 1938.

AIR RAID PRECAUTIONS

Dear Sir or Madam,

The Air Raid Wardens who have been appointed by the Town Council to the Sector in which you reside will be visiting you shortly to fit respirators and register the sizes required by you and members of your household in the event of an emergency, and it will be appreciated if you will afford them the necessary assistance.

Wardens can be recognised by the silver A.R.P. Badge or Brooch which they wear. They are also in possession of a card of appointment issued on the Council's behalf.

Yours truly,

A. L. E. BERLYN,

Chairman, Air Raid Precautions Committee.

"Journal" Exmouth.

October 1938 A.R.P. leaflet arranging appointments to fit gas masks

The Civil Defence and Air Raid Precautions service motto was "Go to it!" and the Exmouth A.R.P. certain lived up to this motto dealing with around 1,300 alerts and bombings during six years of war.

The Messenger Boys

In the event of the new central electronic telephone exchange at Rolle Street being hit, or put out of action because of power failure during an air raid, a Messenger Boy system was set up to take notes from The Report Centre to the Sector Warden's Post's and other important establishments. The local Boy Scouts based on Marpool hill in the WWI army huts, supplied quite a few of these young lads, as did the A.T.C., Army Cadets and Sea Scouts during the course of the war.

During raids and alerts the telephones would become extremely busy and so the messenger service was also used then. The young boys would either run, or cycle through the most hazardous conditions, even during raids, sometimes in the blackout, or over debris, damaged and unsafe terrain to get the message through.

Jack Humphries
'At the age of 14 and above you could be taken on as an A.R.P. Messenger. I was a Messenger boy for a time. I had to have my own bicycle. At the time' (1944) the air raids never came as it was too late in the war.'

'I was based at an A.R.P. Post in the Avenues. We were always waiting, playing Ludo or Dominoes and we used to chat endlessly about the war and what it would be like after the war.'

'I was issued with an armband, I think it was pale blue and it had A.R.P. written on it in white writing, we had to take our gas masks with us and were issued with a helmet that used to hang on pegs at the A.R.P. post.'

'In the event of an air raid and the telephone system being destroyed or damaged, we were sent to the important services, the Fire Brigade, The Police, Hospital or other services.'

Jim Dyer did travel to Exmouth during the war to relax and enjoy what he could of the beach and entertainments, but at the time lived and worked in Exeter. In the evenings Jim was an A.R.P. Messenger and was delivering messages during the nights of May 3rd and 4th 1942, when Exeter was blitzed.

'I Joined the Messengers in 1942, when I was 15 years old; I joined up with a friend. At the time we were all encouraged to join something like the A.T.C., Sea Scouts or some other service but I decided to be a Civil Defence messenger. The Messengers were used when the phones became too busy or damaged in a raid. We took vital messages from the control centres to the sectors and brought back, the reports from the sectors.'

Jim Dyer
'We were then issued with one uniform, a dark blue battledress and trousers and a "Tammy" hat (beret). You could only be issued with one uniform due to war time restrictions.'

Top: *Jim Dyer's Civil Defence "Roof over Britain" Armband*

Above: *Jim Dyer's Civil Defence Messenger side cap*

'We had yellow lanyards issued which we wore over the left shoulder, but didn't carry a whistle like the wardens did, we had metal A.R.P. badges with pins on the back to fix them to our hats.'

'I bought my own, side cap (field service cap) I wore it whilst on duty but was not allowed to wear them on parade, when the issue beret had to be worn.'

Jim Dyer

'You were called out when the siren went if it was your turn on duty. If there was no actual raid, you just stayed at the A.R.P. Post, mostly playing darts until the all-clear. Luckily they didn't bomb the town every time there was an alert.'

The Messenger boys did a fantastic job and it is a shame that they received very little recognition for the part they played nationally during the war, especially in the heavily bombed larger cities. Jim's time spent working for the A.R.P. was counted towards the award for the Defence Medal, which is at least something.

The Wardens

The Exmouth district had been divided into Sectors, to which a Wardens post was allotted. Telephone reporting posts had been erected where a Wardens post building could not be set up. By 1940, 160 wardens had been appointed in Exmouth, with some vacancies for Wardens still available. The Warden's

Above left: *Group 8 Sector 15 Warden Harry Stocker.* Above right: *Exmouth Corps of Air Raid Wardens Sector 16-18 1944.*
Below: *Sector 15 Air Raid Wardens at All Saints Church 1942. See Appendix V p.156-7 for key to names in these photographs*

gave advice to pedestrians and householders in preparation for and during raids to prevent panic and general instruction in all aspects of civil defence. Initially the Wardens were issued only with armbands, steel helmets, whistles and gas masks. Once the war had started serge uniforms were supplied.

Michael Slater

'One night we forgot to blackout a room. The street A.R.P. Warden knocked on our front door and told my mum to put the light out, or cover the windows up.'

The Rescue Squads

Rescue Squads were organised, mainly from council staff. They were called out after raids to rescue people trapped in the debris and were called out several times during the war. It was extremely hazardous work in the wrecked buildings sometimes amongst U.X.B.s

They were also sent to other cities several times. Mainly to Exeter, Plymouth, and Bristol during the heavy incendiary raids.

Mr. Harold Bond Receives the B.E.M.

Harold Bond was the Superintendent in Charge of the Rescue Parties and for services to the community he received the B.E.M.

Civil Defence Worker Honoured.

Exmothian Receives B.E.M. From the King

Few wartime honours will be more enthusiastically acclaimed in Exmouth than that accorded Mr. Harold Bond, Superintendant of Exmouth's Civil Defence Rescue Services who received the British Empire Medal at the hands of H.M. the King this week. Mr. Bond, member of a well known local family and for many years a prominent builder in the district, has accomplished magnificent work throughout nearly four years of war in the local area. He resides in Bradham Lane.

Ideal in every respect to fill a post of this nature, Mr. Bond has shown ingenuity, enterprise and plenty of physical courage in the dangerous tasks he has been called upon to perform since 1939. Colleagues and townspeople, who had worked under his direction, were delighted to learn that the King had officially recognised his services.

The Gas Decontamination Squad

The Decontamination Squad was formed where possible, from people who had a background in chemistry or experience in using steam cleaning

Exmouth Council's C.D. Rescue Squad and Truck

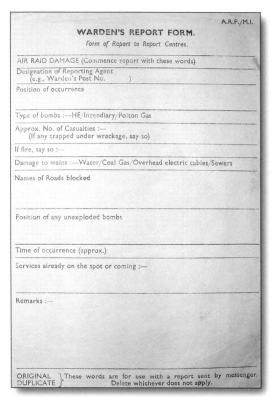
Warden's incident report form

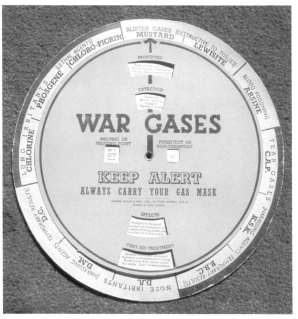
Gas Decontamination Squad's gas detection dial

equipment. They were trained in gas detection using specially prepared chemical kits as well.

Gas decontamination would have proved a real problem if gasses had been used. These gasses, in particular mustard gas would have been sprayed in a liquid form from low flying aircraft over, on the up wind side of the town. The oily liquid which smelled of garlic, then stuck to every thing that it touched and was then transferred by everything else it touched (soles of boots, clothing vehicles etc) to other parts of the town. Mustard was a persistent gas, which meant that it continued working for some time after the attack, gradually being released in a vapour over long periods of time.

If someone had a small amount of mustard gas liquid on their shoes which they had not noticed and then went to bed at night, with their shoes in the same room, the chances are that they would be dead in the morning by the time the gas had fully vaporised. The linings of their lungs would have become badly blistered by the irritant gas and unable to transfer oxygen to the blood.

Mustard gas was a "Vesicant" gas which meant that if it came in contact with the skin it would burn badly if not washed of and treated with bleaching agents, which neutralised the active ingredients in the liquid. Because of this burning and blistering nature of this gas, lungs were very susceptible to injury from the vapour, which is why gas masks had been issued.

It was because of the threat of mustard gas, that Exmouth Urban District council placed adverts in the local newspapers asking that people who had baths with running water available (which was only a small percentage of the population at the time), to put notices on their gates that a bath and stirrup pump were available here. These items could then be used by the local decontamination squads.

The thought of people stripping naked in the streets outside one of these houses, to be initially hosed down by a stirrup pump and then transferred to the bath room caused some difficult decisions at the council offices. In the Minutes of a Council meeting published in the *Exmouth Journal* Saturday 8th November 1941, It was decided that.

'As immediate treatment was imperative, all that was required was that people who had been contaminated would go to the house, take off their outer clothing, boots and hat outside the door and then go in their underclothes straight to the bathroom. Anti-gas ointments would be wanted and also a means of washing the eyes. As Exmouth was not the Garden of Eden, something must be done after the bath to clothe the person, either by lending him a suit of clothes,

dressing gown or pyjamas, or sending to his home for clothing.'

The contaminated clothes would then need to be aired in a safe place for 48 hours, prior to a 2 hour boil wash and treated with bleaching agents, to ensure they were safe, to be worn again. The prospect of dealing with hundreds of potential gas casualties in a small town would have resulted in a nightmare for the gas decontamination squads and medical services, with the possibility of hundreds of dead and severely wounded and very little chance of treating them effectively.

Although this unit trained, but never saw action in its primary role, due to the Germans decision not to use gas, they still had to report to the A.R.P. centre on Exeter Road, each time the air raid siren sounded. One Sunday they had a full scale practice drill at the docks utilising the whole of Exmouth's Civil Defence Services. The control centre overlooked that the squad were still stood to when the practise alert had finished. They remained at their posts for several hours and missed their Sunday dinners.

Dennis Pratt witnessed a gas decontamination exercise in the town.

Dennis Pratt
'One Such "action" I witnessed came when a suspected area was tested for gas and ringed with bleach-powder.'

'Using a substitute for the powder, the squad went to work, moving into the suspected area, dressed in oilskins, gas masks and steel helmets.'

'They spread the substitute for the powder over the ground. Under active conditions the powder would have (reacted with the gas) causing the gas to burn, gradually minimising the poison, eventually to wipe out all traces.'

Gas squads gas detection kit case

ANTI-GAS

Contaminated persons
may wash here.

"You may wash here", these signs were hung in the windows with bath room facilities

Civilian respirator (gas mask) issued to all children over the age of three and all adults

'A surface shelter which was also suspected of being contaminated" with liquid gas, was washed down with bleach paste, a mixture of bleach powder and water.'

'All traces of gas in the area were removed. Then the men decontaminated their implements, smeared their hands with anti-gas ointment and boarded a lorry ready to rush to another area.'

Civilian gas masks and protective cases

Gas masks

Civilian Respirator (Gas mask)

Most adults and children above the age of three were issued with the Civilian Respirator. It was manufactured in three sizes, Small, Medium and Large. Mr. J. Horn was a sail-maker at the old sail loft in Camperdown Terrace who would make and repair cases for Civilian Respirators. It was very quickly realised that the poor quality cardboard boxes would not stand up to the rigours of everyday life especially where children and wet weather were concerned.

Jack Humphries
'I remember gas masks being issued, fear of gas from parents who knew of its use from in the First World War was rife, and my parents were relieved that they were issued.'

'We had to carry it everywhere. It was the law. The gas mask was in a beige cardboard box. We had gas mask training at school and had to sit with them on for half an hour whilst we continued our work.'

'There was also a real fear of bombing, as people knew what had happened to other countries which had been attacked by the Germans. Every child was asked to make a matchbox which contained a small partition in it half way down. One half was filled with cotton wool the other half was filled with Vaseline. These had to be brought to school everyday and kept in your gas mask box. The idea was to make earplugs

PACKING OF RESPIRATOR
The Respirator should be placed in box with heavy end (container) standing on bottom of box. The Transparent Eyepiece should lie evenly on the top of container and at full length without any deformation.

When Respirator is required for use.
1. Hold Respirator by the straps.
2. Put on by first putting chin into the Facepiece and then draw the straps over the head. Adjust straps to obtain close but comfortable fit.
3. Take off by pulling the straps over the head from the back.
DO NOT TAKE RESPIRATOR OFF BY PULLING THE CONTAINER UPWARDS OVER THE FACE

Instructions for the gas mask on the box lid

to protect our ears from the air pressure in a bomb blast.'

'On the lid of the matchbox was stuck a piece of paper, on which we had to write this rhyme and learn it off by heart.'
'I'm a guard against bangs and shocks,
Keep me in your gas mask box.
'til you need me, keep wool dry
grease rots rubber, reason why.'

Roy Hole

'*You had to always carry your gas mask in the early war years and were in serious trouble if you forgot it. There were regular checks by teachers to make sure we had them. There were gas mask drills where we had to put them on and check that they fitted and would work. They would steam up badly, especially on cold days making it virtually impossible to see out of. You weren't allowed to play with your gas mask either, as if it became damaged, it wouldn't work, but I'm sure some children did.*'

Jean Acton

'*We did have gas mask drills in school; you got a detention if you didn't have it. We practiced en-masse and after we had put them on. We stayed like that still working, for half an hour and sometimes more. They had a horrible rubber smell and we found that we could make "farty" noises if we breathed out real hard. Some boys did it on purpose to annoy the teacher. They steamed up badly so it was suggested to rub soap on the eyepiece to stop it steaming up, but never did this.*'

The mobile gas mask testing vans

These were driven around the town in the early stages of the war, stopping at the A.R.P. Posts. Although it was compulsory to have your gas mask fitted and checked by the local warden, it was not compulsory, only advised, to check it for leaks in one of these gas vans. The vans were sealed and had a system for releasing tear-gas into them from a pressurised cylinder. People would enter them, one at a time to see if their gas mask was functioning correctly. After a short while you were asked to take off the gas mask and take a small sniff which would then make your eyes water and make you cough, but was non harmful in such a short time, other than being a nasty irritant for around 30 minutes. Dennis Pratt had his gas mask tested in one of these vans.

Dennis Pratt

'*Volunteers went through a gas van to test their masks and get some experience of obnoxious fumes. After a while the instructions were, to loosen the mask and sniff the gas. I took a good whiff and regretted it, tear-gas stung my eyes and nose and the weeping continued for a long time afterwards!*'

The Mickey Mouse gas mask

This respirator had to be made from a special type of extremely soft rubber, which would fit round the contours of a child's face in order to make an air tight seal. It was decided to make this in red rubber and attach a blue filter to the end, to make it a more attractive item to a child as black was considered to be too "scary". It was suggested to parents that they told their children to "Put it on and you'll look like Mickey Mouse."

Joy Penwarden

'*We all had to carry gas masks. Mine was a Mickey Mouse one. It was claustrophobic and smelled of rubber. We carried it in a square brown box around our necks. Luckily we never had to use it.*'

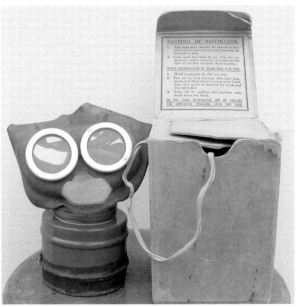

Child's (under 3) "Mickey Mouse" Respirator

THIS SPECIAL RESPIRATOR FOR A SMALL CHILD IS GOVERNMENT PROPERTY. ANY PERSON WHO HAS IT IN HIS POSSESSION IS RESPONSIBLE IN LAW FOR USING CARE TO KEEP IT IN GOOD CONDITION. IT IS TO BE RETURNED TO THE LOCAL AUTHORITY IN WHOSE AREA THE POSSESSOR MAY BE AT ANY TIME, EITHER ON REQUEST OR WHEN NO LONGER REQUIRED.

PACKING OF RESPIRATOR.

1. The respirator should be placed in box with heavy end (container) standing on bottom of box.
2. Care must be taken to see that the expiratory outlet valve lies flat against the side of the box without deformation.

WHEN RESPIRATOR IS REQUIRED FOR USE.

1. Hold respirator by the harness.
2. Put on by first putting chin into face-piece and then draw harness over head. Join free parts of harness by hook and eye provided.
3. Take off by pulling the harness over head from the back.

DO NOT TAKE RESPIRATOR OFF BY PULLING THE CONTAINER UPWARDS OVER THE FACE.

Chapter 20
The Red Cross and St John Ambulance Brigade

The First Aid Post (F.A.P.)

The F.A.P. and Ambulances were stationed at the Cranford Club. These could be sent to the scene of an emergency, with V.A.D. and F.A.P. personnel. Both Men and Women drove the ambulances and took teams of first aid trained volunteers to the scenes of attacks. Six ambulances in total were available, three equipped to take walking wounded and seated injured and another three equipped to take seriously injured and stretcher cases.

Bastin Hall was at Elm Grove, the Home of the St John Ambulance Brigade. It was also designated as a secondary First Aid Post to be used in the event of large scale raids, or if the First Aid Post at the Cranford Club was hit and put out of action.

Bystock House was a hospital for rehabilitating soldiers and airmen during the war. The patients were mainly Polish and a large number of them were wounded at the battle of Monte Casino in Italy. The Immobile V.A.D. (permanent staff) carried out the general nursing duties at the hospital.

The Doctor

If you had to call a doctor in an emergency, as no National Health Service was available until 1948, you had to pay. Most families kept 2/- 6d available to pay the Doctors call out charge. It could be a real life saver when a serious situation or illness was discovered.

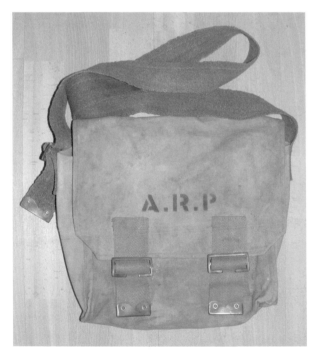

Above left: *St John Ambulance Brigade woven breast badge*

Above right: *St John Ambulance Brigade silver lapel badge*

Left, above: *A.R.P. first aid haversack dated 1939*

Left, below: *A.R.P. shell dressing (bandage) dated 1939*

Below: *Ambulance driver's Mk II steel helmet*

Top left: *The V.A.D. and St John Ambulance members outside Bastin Hall*

Top right: *The Bastin Hall today*

Left: *Bystock House "Immobile" V.A.D. staff in the early war years*

Above left: *Red Cross nursing proficiency medal 1943*

Above right: *Red Cross Air raid Precautions training medal 1943*

Above left: *The St John Ambulance Brigade junior Girls and G.T.C. march through The Strand on Salute the Soldier Week*

Above right: *The "Mobile" V.A.D. march through The Strand in the Salute the Soldier parade*

Left: *The staff of Bystock House Hospital with patients, 1944*

Below: *Red Cross V.A.D. "Plasfort" early plastic helmet*

Chapter 21
Air Raid Sirens and Shelters

Air raid Warnings

Exmouth's first air raid warning device was to be the steam whistle mounted on the gasworks building. The raiders approaching warning was given by a series of sharp intermittent blasts where A.R.P. staff would have to cease working all over the town and report for duty. The all clear would be marked by a long slow blast on the whistle. The same signal would be repeated by Police on duty and early volunteers for the A.R.P. services who would make the same sounds on their whistles.

To explain the significance of these whistle warnings Mike Slater takes up the story.

Mike Slater
'I was outdoors at the top end of Chapel Street walking with my Mother. From somewhere I had managed to get hold of a Police whistle as I was only young it was probably a present from someone. It was some time after the Cross area had been bombed, so people already knew what to expect in an air raid. I was blowing the whistle repeatedly; completely unaware of the significance of the sound it made, just for fun. A Policeman came over and asked my Mother to stop me immediately. He then confiscated the whistle because it may have caused panic.'

Large remote control air raid sirens were placed on high buildings to maximise their range. One was mounted on the spire of All Saints Church on Exeter Road. Withycombe Church Tower and Littleham Church both had sirens mounted in the towers at a later date and the controls for these, were staffed 24 hours a day. The sound was referred to in the *Exmouth Journal* as a "warbling sound" for raiders approaching and a continuous note for the raiders past signal. Exmouth's Police cars were also fitted with sirens at the time and the same applied to the sounds they made. The sound of the siren was soon was christened with the nationally used affectionate nickname "Moaning Minnie" by the locals.

Exmouth's First Air Raid Warning.

Exmouth's first warning of a possible air raid was on the Wednesday 7th August 1940. The siren signalled Raiders Approaching (R.A.) at 11.30 p.m. and All Clear (A.C.) at 1.45 a.m.

Prior to this date the sirens had only been sounded in tests which had always been advertised in the local Press so as not to cause alarm.

Exmouth's Last Air Raid Siren.

The Last All Clear (A.C.) Siren was sounded at 4.30 a.m. on the morning of April 30, 1944.

Shelters at Schools

Ivor Pike
'At the beginning of the war, we were at Exeter Road School, when "Moaning Minnie" sounded we had to go to nearby houses where they had sheltering facilities already in place. The house I had to go to was in Egremont Road. We had to run straight to these houses with our gas masks as they did not want us to be hit by a bomb in school when we were in a large group.'

John Pascoe-Watson remembers the earliest attempts to provide air raid protection at the grammar school. Just imagine hundreds of children climbing in and out of mud filled trenches on rainy days!

John Pascoe-Watson
'Trenches were dug at the Grammar School as the earliest form of sheltering from air raid. They were situated between the playing fields and hockey pitch and the Art Department.'

Roy Hole
'Outside the windows of the school, there were brick screens erected to protect the windows which stood off the wall by about 200 mm, they were to stop the windows blowing in if a bomb exploded nearby.'

Although quite effective against blast, debris and shrapnel these brick blast screens severely limited the amount of natural light entering the classrooms which made them very dark places.

Public Air Raid Shelters

The building of public air raid shelters commenced in July 1940 and initially 22 were erected all over the town, enough to shelter 1,070 people in total. Some of the population already had purpose built or privately purchased, small domestic shelters such as Anderson shelters.

Mary Ashleigh
'On shopping trips to Exeter we'd rush to the air raid shelters or in The Strand when we were in Exmouth.'

Three of The Strand air raid shelters and the Hart's bus, just visible parked outside Lockhart's shop 1942

Air Raid Shelters In Rolle Street.

Anonymous Eyewitness
'As soon as the siren went off, we rushed out and ran to the air raid-shelter at the bottom of Holy Trinity Church Path. It was positioned where the path meets Rolle Street. "Trinity shelter", as we called it would hold approx 20 people standing. After the Bombing of Chapel Street and Church Street, during the nights we would sleep in our Morrison shelter at home. We slept in it every night, whether the siren went or not.'

Exmouth's First Air Raid Shelter.

Exmouth's first private air raid shelter was built at Halsdown House Nursing Home on Exeter Road. Mrs. Hunt the owner had contacted Hooper Brothers Builders, in the run up to WWII.

On the week the A.R.P. issued pamphlets telling people that the safest place would be in a Public

Shelter, in the event of a raid. The *Exmouth Journal* Newspaper was invited to inspect the new shelter, and reported on the construction of this private shelter, as no public shelters had been built yet.

'The chamber, which is 19ft, by 12ft and 6ft 6inches in height, is approached from the ground level by an easy flight of steps, so that stretcher-cases can be taken into the refuge without the slightest difficulty. The concrete roof is supported by steel girders and metal rods, with expanded road-metal reinforcement and the roof itself is covered with tons of earth, which will be used as a garden or a shrubbery, thus giving additional protection, while completely hiding the refuge from the air, or, indeed from casual inspection from the garden itself.'

This design would of course have offered excellent protection, but would still not protect the occupants from a direct hit as was found out later on during the London blitz.

Realizing that the shelter would be an ideal instructional facility for Air Raid Precautions, Mrs. Hunt arranged that the residents of Exmouth could view the shelter by appointment, in a public spirited gesture to help put people's minds at rest.

Advert for air raid shelter advice in the Exmouth Journal *1943 and the entrance to an underground privately-built air raid shelter in Exmouth*

A Group of Exmothians standing on the mound of their Anderson Shelter

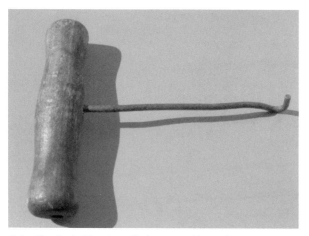

John Fletcher's Morrison Shelter assembly tool

Anderson Shelters

Anderson shelters were made from curved corrugated iron sections and were designed to be placed in a hole, dug in the garden then covered with earth and stones. They proved very successful and undoubtedly saved many lives during the war.

Morrison shelters

Jack Humphries

'We always sheltered under the stairs in the early war years and didn't get our air raid shelter until 1943. It was a Morrison shelter which was erected in the front room. Some of our neighbours had Anderson shelters in their gardens. In our Morrison shelter we had a mattress and blankets in the bottom. I did sleep in it, but not often; we kept a torch and fresh water in there with us.'

Roy Hole

'We had a steel cage Morrison shelter, it was about 6ft long and all 5 children slept in here. One night in the Big Blitz of 1942, all the adults were outside, watching the fires at Exeter burning, you could see it easily from Exmouth. We asked if we could go out but they said it would be too dangerous for us, so we said "why isn't it too dangerous for you then?"'

Ivor Pike

'When I was about 9 years old I had rheumatic fever. My mum made me up a bed downstairs by putting a mattress on top of the Morrison shelter. In the event of an air raid I could then just, "swing under" and get out of the way of falling debris.'

'I can remember sitting on the Morrison shelter and looking at the bright lights in the sky over Exeter when it was blitzed and my Mum saying poor devils, but not really thinking much about it myself other than it looked like a glorified firework night. My wife Alice was caught in this raid at the time and she always said there were a lot of incendiaries'

The Exeter Blitz

Sunday May 3 1942 and Monday May 4 1942

This raid was a direct reprisal for the raid on Lubeck by the R.A.F. The Luftwaffe command used Baedecker tourist guides to choose the cities which would be bombed. Exeter was chosen partly because of the amount of early wooden structured Tudor buildings in its town centre.

The first severe raid on Exeter was on Sunday May 3rd 1942 and during this raid, huge areas of the city were destroyed with heavy casualties. Exmouth's emergency services were sent to help in the aftermath.

Exeter was blitzed for a second night on Monday May 4th 1942 once again causing severe damage and elements of the regular Army's Queens Royal Regiment, The Royal Marines based in Exmouth and Dalditch Camp, Exmouth's Home Guard, Police, Fire Brigade, A.F.S. and Heavy Rescue Services were once again sent to help the emergency services in the city. They were given prioritised instructions to:

1. Search for survivors.
2. Recover human remains.
3. Salvage belongings.
4. Clear away rubble and debris.

Tony Smith

'Whilst stationed with Royal Marine 9th Training Battalion at Dalditch Camp on Woodbury Common, we were called to help clear up after the devastating incendiary air raids in Exeter on May 3 and 4 1942.'

'The raid on Exeter was a very big one I remember, we helped on the outskirts of town for just one night, I cannot remember the date but a few days later some of us went to the Rougemont Hotel and drank in the bar with some of the pilots from Exeter who were strangely silent due to stress from flying on the previous nights.'

John Pascoe-Watson

'I slept on Shelley beach on some nights, when the weather was mild. I remember when Exeter was badly bombed. You could see the flames in the sky up river and burning paper and fine fragments came floating down from the sky following the path of the river. The sound of the aircraft was in the air for what seemed like hours, I was lying on my back I can remember the silhouettes of at least 4 Heinkel HE 111s against the night sky.'

Jack Humphries

'The Exeter Blitz affected us; we could see flashes in the sky and stood watching it from the garden. We could hear the bombs falling and even feel the detonations of the larger bombs.'

Air raid shelter parrafin lamp

Inspection of respirators notice

Harry Stockers first aid equipment advert in the Exmouth Journal

Specialist glasses made to fit under masks

Chapter 22
The Fire Brigade

Exmouth Fire Brigade

Exmouth Fire Station was at 1-3 Church Road, opposite All Saints Church. The Brigade was financed via Exmouth U.D.C. who possessed two fire engines by the outbreak of war. The second larger fire engine was purchased in 1939 on the realisation that war was imminent. These engines were a Merryweather 30 H.P. and the newly purchased Merryweather 65 H.P.

Each had a pumping capability of 400 gallons per minute. Two miles of hoses were available in 1940 with all the relevant couplings, branches and spray nozzles. Other equipment included, escape ladders

and axes, lifelines etc. breathing apparatus and uniforms. Exmouth's Fire Brigade was a highly trained and professional unit before the war and was called out on many occasions to extinguish fires and assist in rescues.

Tragedy

A fire and rescue demonstration was given in Phear Park. After the bombing of the Parade on Saturday March 1 1941 it was decided that a demonstration of civilian fire-fighting and rescue techniques would be given jointly by members of the Exmouth Fire Brigade and the A.F.S. A demonstration was given of the old manual village fire engine. Displays of fighting fires

Exmouth U.D.C. Merryweather fire engine

Fire Engine stowage, nozzles, hoses, unions, branches and pump

The Fire Brigade at work at the Chapel Street bombing 18th January 1941

were given, rescue procedures and also a march past by the combined services of the local fire service with their equipment.

Whilst performing a fireman's lift in an attempt to demonstrate a rescue from a burning building with A.F.S. telephonist Miss Mary Evans, Fireman Edward Nelson lost his footing in the freezing weather conditions. The couple fell 8 metres and both were seriously injured.

Immediately First Aid Personnel rushed to the scene and Fireman Nelson, who was the most seriously injured, was rushed to Hospital in an ambulance. Miss Evans had multiple injuries and was placed on a stretcher before being sent to hospital in a separate ambulance. Mary Evans eventually recovered from her injuries but Fireman Nelson, a father of 2 later died of his injuries.

The Auxiliary Fire Service

Joy Penwarden

'My Dad, Bill Penwarden, was too old to join up, (the Armed Forces) so he had to join the A.F.S. He was away several times a week and so myself my mother and grandmother, who lived with us, had to leave the centre of Exmouth at night, in case of bombing raids. We were picked up by Ambulance and taken to Littlefield House on the Salterton Road where we stayed and were then delivered back to the shop in the morning.'

Joy Penwarden

The A.F.S. Headquarters was behind the shop on the corner of Danby Terrace and Exeter Road. It was a big building, the first house on the right going up. When he was on duty they were called out occasionally to deal with small fires and sometimes

The A.F.S. Sector 6 Firemen

A.F.S. Sector 6 engine crew at All Saints Church September 1943. Bill Penwarden is stood on the rear mudguard

Exmouth A.F.S. members photographed in the bandstand in Manor Gardens 1941. See Appendix VII p.159 for key to names in this photograph

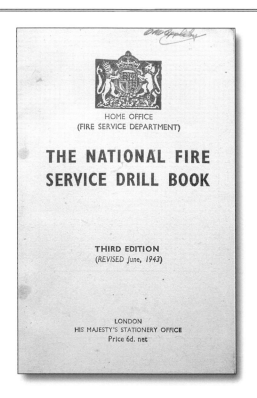

HOME OFFICE
(FIRE SERVICE DEPARTMENT)

THE NATIONAL FIRE SERVICE DRILL BOOK

THIRD EDITION
(REVISED June, 1943)

LONDON
HIS MAJESTY'S STATIONERY OFFICE
Price 6d. net

Above: *N.F.S. Training Manual*

Above left: *A.F.S. Fireman's woollen jacket, Mk II steel helmet, fire axe and webbing belt*

Left: *The old Exmouth Fire Station on Church Road*

Below: *The N.F.S. Firemen and Women march past the Pavilion in the Salute the Soldier Parade*

bombings, they called it a "shout". Dad and other A.F.S. men were called up to the Exeter Blitz, to help with putting out the fires on the nights of 3rd and 4th May 1942. One Exmouth man was killed on Bobby's building in Exeter which was badly on fire and then collapsed.'

The Plymouth Blitz could be seen easily from Exmouth and on the night, Exmouth Fire Brigade and the A.F.S. went to the aid of the Plymouth Fire Brigade.

The N.F.S.

In August 1941 the National Fire Service (N.F.S.) was created. It amalgamated the Local Fire Brigades structure with the volunteer based A.F.S. The A.F.S. members then became full time, rather than part time firemen and women. The N.F.S. was controlled centrally from the Home Office which then standardised procedures and equipment on a regional and national level for brigades all over Britain.

These regional brigades would then have the autonomy to react and work with other brigades in the area, knowing well that training procedures would be the same and that basic equipment would "marry up" and be used collectively to fight large scale fires. The N.F.S. was finally disbanded in 1948 to make way for the system we have now.

Pearl Cawse
'My Uncle, George Willatts was the Park Keeper and lived at Phear Park Up lodge up until approx 1942. We joined the N.F.S. during the war and was based at the Church Road Fire Station.'

From left to right: *Women's Auxiliary Fire Service tunic badge; N.F.S. Officer's cap badge; N.F.S. metal button; N.F.S. Fireman's cap badge; N.F.S. late war plastic button.*

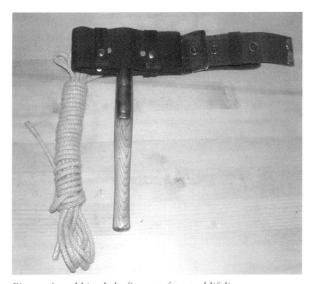

Fireman's webbing belt, fire axe, frog and lifeline.

Exmouth fire station recess and enquiries bell

Chapter 23
The Fire Guard

The Formation of the Fire Guard

The Fire Guard were formed to bolster the facilities of the fire Brigade and A.R.P. services and were a purely voluntary organisation, until 1943 when changes were made to the structure and it became compulsory. The Fire Guard's sole function was looking for 1 kg incendiary bombs and small fires and extinguishing them. They had to spend a lot of time on roofs, or in the confined spaces of lofts so needed simple, portable equipment.

By training the Fire Guard to deal with this specific threat, it allowed the Fire Brigade and A.F.S. to deal with the bigger fires using larger, more complicated equipment systems, only needing to attend the most serious incidents, or to remain on "Alert" in case a larger raid came later.

Without a doubt the Fire Guard saved millions of pounds worth of industrial property and homes during WWII. They were also responsible for saving many lives and rescuing injured people from burning buildings in some cases, before the professional services arrived. They did a remarkable job considering the training and equipment that they were given.

Above: *Sector 109 91 1944*
Below: *Sector 104/c Fire Guards at All Saints Church 1941*
See Appendix VI p.158 for key to individual's names in these photographs

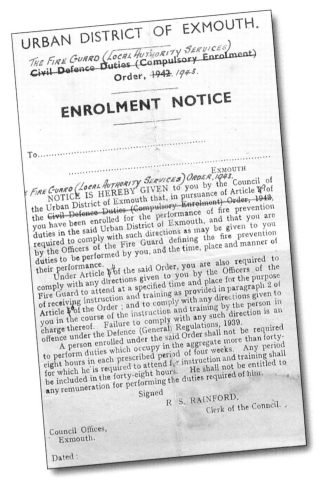

Above: *Fire Guard's arm band*

Left: *Compulsory Fire Guard enrolment form 1943*

Below: *Fire Guard Solly Zuckerman's steel helmet*

Uniforms

The Fire Guard were formed into small three person fire parties. They had to go through a course of instruction before they were permitted to wear the arm band on their left arm. From 1941 they were issued with the distinctive Solly Zuckerman helmet and used the standard civilian respirator for gas protection.

The pressed mild-steel construction of the helmet, made it cheap to produce and the high crown would allow it to absorb impact from falling shrapnel and masonry etc., bending inwards on impact without harming the wearers head.

Incendiary Bombs

The 1 kg Incendiary bombs were used mainly on corn field raids in and around Exmouth and used stirrup pumps, sand bags and fire buckets, some filled with wet sand and others filled with water to deal with these bombs quickly and efficiently.

The stirrup pump was produced as a cheap and efficient way to extinguish incendiary bombs and was designed by the incendiary bomb committee. The pump sprayed water on the up and down stroke at a rate of 3 litres of water a minute, with a spray radius

of approx 4 metres. This simple device saved an incalculable amount of property which would have otherwise burned down or been severely damaged during the war.

This item is held in great affection by people who used it. Simple design, portability and efficiency made its name famous throughout Britain. It was mentioned in songs, became the butt of cartoonist's jokes. When it was finally taken out of service from the Civil Defence stores after the cold war, gardeners used it allotments and gardens for watering up. Some are still in use today.

Training as a Fire Guard

From the age of 15 boys could join the Fire Guard or Fire Watch at local businesses and sixth form schools, for up to 12 hours a week. The Fire Guards were trained to lie on their stomachs using brick walls and metal structures as cover to protect themselves from the sparking and exploding incendiary bombs.

They were trained to operate a stirrup pump, to keep the room wet, if they could not actually direct the stirrup pump spray at the bomb. Apart from the blitzes of major cities, cigarettes left still burning were still the biggest cause of fires during this period of history.

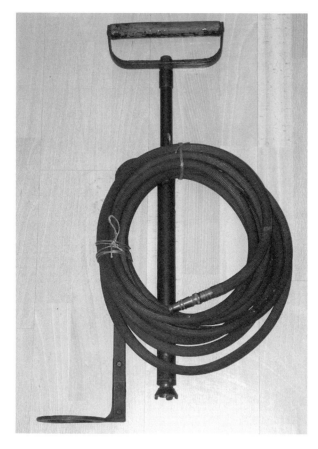

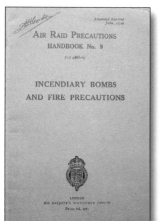

Above: *Fire Guard Elaine Madge's stirrup pump*

Left: *Fire Guard incendiary bomb training manual*

Fire Guard Duties

Jim Dyer

'We used the stirrup pump to put out the incendiary bombs which were on fire in the house next door, I had to run and get the water in a bucket. Some incendiary bombs had a small amount of explosive, which would detonate to keep you away from dealing with them.'

Roy Penberthy

'I was a Fire Watcher at the Savoy Cinema, I had a stirrup pump and bucket, I used to put my foot on the base of the pump and then pumped like mad to get the water out. I was on my own on my fire watching duties, but I used to meet up with other members of The Strand and Parade Fire Watchers who used to go for a cup of tea in Forte's Café on the Parade during their shifts. Although I practised putting out fires I never once had to deal with an incendiary bomb.'

John Pascoe-Watson

'The Grammar School had to set up its own fire watching scheme. It was set up by Harry Bamfylde and some of the other Masters. It was only Prefects that could be a Fire Watcher.'

'We carried out our watches one night a week, on a rota basis. We slept on canvas camp beds in the Masters staff room and the Masters slept in the Women's staff room. We were only woken up when an alert sounded and we then had to stand by for duty. The rest of the time was spent chatting, playing board games or sleeping.'

'We received no training whatsoever and were expected to climb up on the roof of the school to throw off burning incendiary bombs or douse them with water or wet sand using a very long-handled scoop (Redhill Scoop) or a stirrup pump. This was made harder by the fact that they had not supplied us with any ladders to reach the roofs. We had no safety helmets, uniforms or armbands. Only utility blankets to use on our beds.'

Elizabeth Maycock

'When I was 17, I enlisted as a Fire Watcher I would have to keep a look out for fires in the Littleham area. One night Exeter was bombed in May 1942. I was under the care and instruction of the Manager of Lloyds Bank. We were stationed in an empty field in Littleham. It was part of the dairy farm by the railway station just beyond Littleham Cross.'

'The sky was all red and pink and a huge glow filled the sky. It was in the blackout and really was quite something. You could see the movement of the flames in it. I did not see, or hear any aircraft flying overhead but was aware that a lot of small pink burning and smoking objects were floating down all around me." All of a sudden The Bank manager decide he would go and try and find out what was happening and left me on my own in the field until I finally decided to go home on my own at around 2.00 a.m. in the morning. Nothing had happened in Exmouth that night, but when I got home I told Mother that something dreadful must have happened in Exeter.'

The floating, burning objects were cinders from the fires at Exeter they can travel for miles on the wind and this is what Elizabeth experienced.

Chapter 24
The Air Attacks

Tuesday 3 September 1940
Incendiary Raid On Cornfields

The Raid

Exmouth siren sounded. R.A. (Raid Alert) 09.11.p.m. – A.C. (All Clear) 11.33 p.m.

This was the first recorded air raid on Exmouth. Prior to this date the Exmouth A.R.P. and Fire Services had only had to deal with rehearsals and false alarms. Because phase two of the Battle of Britain was at its peak around this time. There was a lot of aerial activity all over Devon. Sidmouth was also bombed on this night.

The A.R.P's Response to the Raid

The alarm was raised by a Home Guard patrol on their way to Budleigh Salterton from Exmouth, who saw and heard the plane swoop low over the town, then let out showers of bombs. The bombs, which, according to eyewitnesses fell in a wide arc and detonated in the field and the surrounding area, were all incendiaries. The bombs burned a few bare patches into the cornfields and set light to some small stacks of corn standing in the fields. The A.F.S. the Home Guard with the help of local volunteers quickly got the fires under control. The workers received a commendation for their prompt and effective action.

Saturday 14 September 1940
Orcombe Point Incendiary Raid

The Battle of Britain

The date August 30th 1940 was the peak of the Battle of Britain, but after this date although they were suffering massive casualties amongst bomber crews, German pilots continued to press home their attacks in day time raids. By now phase 2 of the Battle of Britain was in full swing with the Germans having switched their strategy from bombing R.A.F. airfields to bombing London and other cities, in mainly day-time raids.

Exmouth

Exmouth sirens sounded R.A. 3.20 p.m. – A.C. 3.55 p.m.

A lone German bomber, dropped incendiaries in cornfields and at Orcombe Point. There were no casualties recorded in this raid. During the raid the Royal Ordnance Corps Observation Post (Fox Four), at Orcombe Point was machine gunned and hit by incendiaries. Some of the incendiaries fell offshore.

Mike Heard

'On the top of Foxholes Hill, was the R.O.C. Observation Post. It was manned 24 hours a day. It was near the Coast Guard cottages and was a wooden hut covered with sand bags. All around it and on to Sandy Bay was cornfields, one night it was attacked by a plane with incendiary bombs.'

'Mr. Oswin, the Observer Corps Chief, had a boat down at Lavis's boat yard and I used to talk to him some times when he came down to work on his boat. He knew everyone wanted to collect shrapnel so he and his men on duty extinguished the bombs which had detonated in the raid and took some de-activated ones to the Exmouth Journal offices in the morning.

They thought they could be sold as "souvenirs" to raise money for war charities but government censorship wouldn't allow it, as it would confirm the raid had been successful. He ended up just selling them to friends and people that collected shrapnel.'

Thursday 19 September 1940
Bonds Lane Area

Situated near Foxholes Hill running between Gore Lane and Orcombe Point, this area was used for growing cereal crops during WWII. It was also very close to the route of the Home Guard's cliff patrol to Budleigh Salterton. There is very little information about the raid except for a mention in Harry Stockers Wardens note book and Bill Sleeman's diary and notebook.

Bill Sleeman's Diary Entry 19 September 1940

7 bombs dropped on the district

Bill Sleeman's Notebook

'Went out on patrol 8-6.30 a.m., at Bond's Lane. 7 bombs dropped.'

Saturday 4 January 1941
Orcombe Point Incendiaries

Exmouth Siren. R.A. 6.58 p.m - A.C. 1.32 a.m.

The Raid

It is thought that the bombs were jettisoned by enemy aircraft returning from a raid on Bristol's Avonmouth Docks. Incendiaries were also dropped en masse offshore at Orcombe Point.

Harry Stocker's A.R.P. Report Book Section 15

Siren Sounded 18.58

All on duty until 21.00 then team 3 took over. Mrs Sheppard, Mr. Sheppard, Mr. Fairchild and Mr. Rusling.

Numerous incendiaries dropped in easterly direction. Heavy anti-aircraft fire heard immediately afterwards.

All Clear 01.32

H.W. Stocker.

Post Warden.

(600-1,000 incendiaries reported found between Peak Hill and Dotton Water Works)

Friday 10 First Damage January 1941
Exmouth Lime Kiln Lane / Watery Lane

A solitary aircraft, thought to be returning from a raid elsewhere in Britain jettisoned its high explosive bomb-load before returning across the channel to its base in France. Two of the bombs exploded on impact. No siren was sounded before the raid.

Exmouth siren sounded R.A. 6.45 p.m. - A.C. 8.25 p.m.

Lime Kiln Lane

Bomb 1

The site where the bombs landed was open ground at next to Lime Kiln Lane approx half way down on the left hand side. The first bomb detonated on impact.

Bomb 2

The second bomb again detonated on impact close to the first impact. It landed in the wet mud nearby, an area which was sometimes referred to locally as the "Brickworks" or "Watery Lane".

Bomb 3

This bomb fell into a small area of woodland on the east side of Lime Kiln Lane and failed to explode. It was recorded by Warden Harry Stocker as a delayed action bomb. The bomb eventually detonated on the morning of 13th January at 1.00 a.m.

There were no casualties except for the pride of a local Police Constable.

Lime Kiln Lane Bomb

Ron Lee

'We had been given information that it was on the Douglas Avenue end of the lane and the Bomb Disposal Unit were checking it. Sergeant Buckingham decided we should go and see what was happening and, on arrival, we found that the bomb disposal officer was checking it. He called us over to come and have a look at it and when we were there he started hitting it with a large hammer saying "what do you think of this then?" Asking if it was likely to go up, he informed me that he was still checking it. Upon receiving this information and as it was our first local U.X.B. bomb I decided right away that I didn't want to be the first in Exmouth to be blown up! I quickly put my self at a greater distance from it.'

'A few minutes later we were told that the bomb was ticking and it was a bomb that would explode later. It did go up in the early hours of the next morning when one of our constables, Ozzie Boyd, a Geordie boy, was keeping watch to make sure no members of the public came too close. He told me later that he was eating a sandwich when next thing he new, he was in Maer Road. Fortunately he was not injured but he was, very shaken.'

Elizabeth Maycock

'Early in the war we lived in a house called "Mansfield", it was situated on the corner of Douglas Avenue and Cranford Avenue. The back garden ran down to a bank which was the side of Watery Lane. Watery lane ran from Hospital Corner on the Salterton Road to Douglas Avenue. One night there was a terrific explosion which smashed a lot of the local house's windows and caused some damage to the buildings, mainly to the backs and the sides of the houses.'

'When the bomb exploded, my mother heard glass breaking, and went to check what had happened. My younger sisters bedroom was damaged and windows were broken, but we were unharmed.'

Ray Challis

'*The following day I went with my father to see the damage. There was a crater approximately 15ft wide and about 6ft deep where the bomb had detonated. I can't remember seeing the place where the other bombs had fallen.*'

Friday 17 January 1941
Enemy Raiders over Exmouth
Air Raid Alerts

Friday 17th January

Exmouth Sirens Sounded

1st Alert   R. A.10.30 p.m. - A.C. 11.20 p.m.

2nd Alert   R.A. 11.58 p.m. - A.C. 3.15 a.m.
                        Saturday 18th 3.15 a.m.

Hurricanes from 504 Squadron R.A.F. Exeter were principally engaged on monotonous convoy patrols, but on 17 January 1941, intercepted and damaged a He111 bomber to the south of Start Point. It was believed that this aircraft was returning from the third heavy raid on Swansea.

Saturday 18 January
The Cross/Chapel Street Bombing

The Cross was a very busy part of town in pre-war Exmouth. It was full of small local businesses which thrived on a brisk local trade. It was also home to people renting rooms above shops. The Cross itself also provided a useful landmark as a meeting place for locals and visitors alike.

On Friday 17th January and Saturday 18th January, Swansea was a target for German bombers and was heavily bombed with H.E. bombs. The Luftwaffe often used the mouth of the Exe estuary as a navigational land-mark, to take bearings, as it could be easily seen from the air on a clear night. Wartime Luftwaffe intelligence maps dated 1940, which had been converted from British pre-war Ordnance Survey maps show the estuary clearly, with Exeter highlighted. German planes had been flying regular sorties over the South West between the Dates of 9th – 18th January and the Royal Devon and Exeter Hospital was hit in a raid on Friday 17th Jan.

The Raid

At 1.50 a.m. on the morning on Saturday 18th January, the area of the Cross was hit by three SC 500, 500 kg H.E. bombs. The bombs were thought to have been jettisoned by a raider, most likely a Dornier Do 17z, returning from a mission elsewhere in Britain. The Exmouth bombs followed a line towards the gasworks and it was assumed this was the target. According to eyewitnesses German aircraft had been flying across the coast and over Exmouth in large numbers during the early hours of darkness.

Bomb 1 Frederick Place

Bomb 2 The Cross

Bomb 3 Chapel Street

John Middleton

'*We were living in Halsdon Road at the time of the Chapel Street bombing. I was lying in bed and we heard the bombs go off, great big bangs, it was in the early part of the war.*'

The Bomber which carried out the raid was flying extremely low and was seen quite clearly by several Air Raid Precautions personnel on the night.

Harry Stockers Warden's Notebook

January 18th.

Siren Sounded 00.02

Team one again on duty.

Heavy explosions heard at 1.06 a.m.

Wardens reported no damage in Sector.

Heavy pall of black dust or smoke seen to drift up river. Senior Warden having ascertained where damage was. ——— i.e. Chapel Street area, left Mr. Fudge in charge and went to incident taking wardens Sheppard, Rusling, Franks and Burrows with him, Senior warden arriving first found shock case –(lady of 80) in house adjoining, Dolphin and with the aid of a sailor removed her to London Inn. Afterwards removed her sister from the same house with L. Gage, Rusling and others helped with children from Dommett's. Senior Warden seeing everything was under control sent Franks and Sheppard back to sector with Burrows and Rusling. Helped search damaged houses in vicinity for minor casualties. Child rescued from demolished house next to French's Butchers shop, taken to St John Ambulance Hall. Two found unhurt after being found pinned for two hours, four others in same house killed.

Assisted Doctor Stevenson until all clear 03.30.

Found billets for shock cases (taken to London Inn) earlier in Roseberry Road.

Wardens dismissed at 08.45 a.m. and returned to the scene of incident.
Helped Doctor Stevenson again and also with

removable of rubble in search of casualties at Dommett's.

Fire at Walton's at 5.30 approx. Gutted in 20 mins. Gas offices also alight.

Arrival of Exeter Brigade with turn tower enabling water to be pumped behind flames saved Rolle Street.

Left Scene at 8.45.

H.W. Stocker.

Bombs 2 or 3 in number.
1 between Wilson's store and French's shop.
1 behind Dommett's shop in the Cross.
Third not confirmed but believed to be through back of Andersons in Chapel Street.
12-14 Killed.
3 Injured.
About 20 Shock cases.

Bomb 1 Frederick Place

Roy Hatten
'During the War we lived for the mostly at 50 Victoria Road Exmouth. My Mum was Marjorie May Dommett, the Daughter of Hubert Dommett. On the night of the Cross and Chapel Street bombings there had been sirens during the night, and I woke up when I heard crumps and bangs.'

'Mum had said that Grandmother was sheltering under the stairs after the siren had sounded, as they didn't have an air raid shelter. Grandmother went up stairs to her bedroom to collect her life savings which were hidden under the bed. She was killed instantly in the raid by a direct hit.'

'We went to look at the site the following day, but could not get any closer than Rolle Street as there was a cordon around the damaged area. It was a complete shambles. I was upset at the time; I hated the Germans even more after this.'

Fatalities

EMMA MARY DOMMETT

Ron Lee one of Exmouth's wartime Policemen was at the scene.

Ron Lee
'The area was in a really bad state. It had been smashed right up, The Sergeant told us what to do, I had to clear people out from the old Post Office on Rolle Street to the end of the Parade as it was unknown if there were any more bombs dropped in the area at that time because the damage was so bad.'

We set up a cordon and put red tapes across the entrances to certain roads and buildings to seal off the area.' All of the regular Police were there and the specials would turn out when there was an emergency on. The Home Guard helped set up the cordon and I remember Harry Lavis, Ron's Father was there.'

Fatalities

JOHN ALBERT JEFFERY
PATRICIA JEFFERY

Bomb 2 The Cross

Peggy Gibbins
'Chapel Street and the Cross was the centre of town, it was badly bombed in January 1941. The morning after the bombing I went to see my Grandmother and she took me to see the bomb damage. The Salvation Army were there giving out tea and sandwiches to the workers. My Grandparents lived in Anne Street. What stuck in my mind was the Cobblers shop called Batten's was completely destroyed. Ivy Batten and her husband were both in the Salvation Army and they had helped the evacuees by putting up a family from London called the Masons. Mr. Mason was a Captain in the Salvation Army and Mrs. Batten was also a member. They had a lot of Children and quite a few were killed in this air raid, one of the children was in my class at school but I can't remember his name.'

Fatalities

MADGE WALKDEN-GOODALL
IVY MAY BATTEN

The Mason Family

Winifred Gliddon
'My Dad was a Captain in the Salvation Army and so was my Mother, she was called Highness Maude Gliddon, everyone knew her as Aunty High.' 'Edith Mason was a family friend from the Salvation Army, who had two sons Ronald and Bernard who were trapped under the wreckage of their house when the bombs dropped on their house at the Cross and survived, the Mason family's smaller children and Mrs. Mason were killed. Ivy Batten another Salvation Army member and good friend of my Dad had put the Mason family up as they were evacuees and looked after the boys occasionally.'

Fatalities

EDITH MARY MASON
EDWIN DAVID MASON
BERYL MASON
NORMAN MASON
RAYMOND MASON

Roy Pemberthy

'On the way to work that morning, the streets were full of rubble and glass and the rescue services were still working at the scene. We went into the roof space to check for damage and noticed that a big sandstone block, which was very heavy had been blown in through the roof smashing all the slates and battens and had landed on the water pipes and beams. It took two of us to lift. We had to get it free from the pipes then lifted it down through the ceiling on a rope. The hole in the roof we covered with a tarpaulin and it stayed there for some time to come.'

Bomb 3. Chapel Street

Fatalities

PRIMROSE MAY BROOKS
DOROTHY ETHEL COLES

Peggy Gibbins

'Margaret Street, Princes Street where the Old Barrel is now, down the bottom, across the road to the Volunteer Pub where the Royal Marines drank; were all badly damaged. Dommett's Fish and Chip shop, near the Cross, Battens shoe shop, Densham's wet fish shop, a tobacconists, Oliver's shoe shop, the grocery store, Wilson's provisions store, Griffith's a pasty shop, Mrs. Coomes the Jewellers, Andrew's Dairy near the Cross, Webbers the Butchers, they had an abattoir at the back of the butchers, all were either destroyed or badly damaged. Thorns the carriers, with their horses drawn carts. Porky Downs the Butchers, Weston's the Dairy, a greengrocer's run by two sisters, Mrs Edwards and Mrs Wakely was also damaged.'

22 Chapel Street. H. W. Down Master Butchers

Exmouth's longest established (1900) Butchers, affectionately known as "Porky Down's" have been at the same address for many years. Mr. H.W. Down, who owned the shop in WWII was the leader of Exmouth Urban District Council during the war and was a popular man. Amongst many other things he organised the welcoming of London's first young evacuees with parties at the Savoy Cinema on Rolle Road.

The Butchers shop was damaged in the raid of 70 years ago, but thankfully still survives today as the last remaining Exmouth family business to be still trading from its pre-war premises in Chapel Street.

Miss. Hayman.

'I was woken by a terrific noise, Father had said "quick downstairs," I hurried downstairs with bare feet and in night clothes in the freezing cold.'

'Rene" (Irene Perry) carried her son called Brian down the stairs with one hand and had a chamber stick candle in the other. She shouted "close the door" to her Mother, as she was worried about the blackout, "we've got no bloody door" came the terse reply'

Barry Clarke

'St Saviours Church was in Church Street and badly damaged by a bomb which fell close by at the bottom end of Church Street this part of the street was badly damaged and then later demolished by the council. Chapel Street had buildings completely destroyed by the bombs.'

Peggy Gibbins

'We got as close to the damage as we could, walking down Fore Street from the gasworks to have a look.

Above: *The view down Chapel Street from a similar position today*

Left: *A Policeman and a demolition worker inspect the damage to Chapel Street. In the background a considerable crowd has gathered in Church Street at the edge of the cordon*

There were craters, wrecked buildings and rubbish everywhere, Church Street was badly damaged on both sides by one bomb and others had fallen in the Cross area, destroying a lot of the small shops there.'

Walton and Co. Departmental Store

Walton's was a departmental store which specialised in fashion clothes, millinery, underwear, hosiery, baby linen, knitwear, furnishings and household linen.

The threat of explosions from escaping gas due to a fractured main, further complicated rescue attempts, by risk of further explosions and fire in the pitch black aftermath. Lights could not be turned on and only small torches could be used by the rescuers, for fear of attracting more German bombs.

Mike Heard

'Walton's wasn't too badly damaged in the raid, but their goods were blown out onto the streets, good-willed rescuers and passers by, put all the things back in to the shop premises which later caught fire at around four in the morning. The A.F.S. service at the scene thought it was probably an electrical fire which started in the lift shaft, consequently destroying a lot of rationed items which were badly needed by the community at the time.'

Walton's shop dummies had been blown into the street and were buried in the wreckage; there were many surprises as the Rescue Squads uncovered what they thought initially were bodies, but were in fact the fully clothed, shop window mannequins.

Tributes

Tributes were paid to the civilian volunteer helpers, the Police, the Home Guard, A.R.P. and Fire Brigade.

Tuesday 25 February 1941 The Dock

A German bomber approached Exmouth from the south-east. It was visible from Orcombe Point flying at high level. The raid took place at around 1.00- 1.30 a.m. in the morning. There was no siren sounded at any point in the raid and Exeter Control was not notified.

A mixed load of 4 x SC 250 (250 kg) and 1 x SC 500 (500 kg) bombs were used on this raid and they fell in the following areas.

Bomb 1. 114 St Andrews Road, U.X.B. (SC 500)

Bomb 2. Victoria Road, outside Wilson's Wood Yard. U.X.B.

Bomb 3. The Docks. U.X.B. (Possibly Still There!)

Top: *The A.R.P., Firemen and the rescue services working in the smoking ruins of Walton's departmental store.*

Above: *The scene at the still smouldering Walton's on the18th January 1941. The officers from the fire brigade and A.R.P. are present, visible by their white helmets*

Bomb 4. Shelley Flats. U.X.B.

Bomb 5. The Bull Hill Sandbank.

Joe Radgick

'One bomb dropped on the Cockle Sands on Shelley Beach, which did not go off, One U.X.B. fell outside the corner of the Beachcomber Bar on Victoria Road, near the tunnel that goes through to the docks now, this was later defused, another fell on a house in St Andrews Road but did not explode and another in the docks.'

Harry Stockers Warden's Notebook
Feb. 25

Explosions heard 01.05.
Wardens quickly separated. Sector Searched. "Cordite" smelt strongly but no traces found.

Centre rang at 01.30. Informed H.E. had dropped in St Andrews Road and no need to stand by.
Proceeded with wardens to St Andrews Road leaving Miss Stocker at post.

Helped keep people from coming into the area as unexploded bombs had been found in St Andrews Road. (Bomb passed through No. 114 killing one man.—-a Mr. Hill.)

In Victoria Road —- Mr. Wilson's Timber Yard and in Camperdown Terrace Bomb and/or bombs which did not explode, evidently pitched on cockle beds.

Area evacuated. 250 people moved to senior school amongst other measures. Bombs proved to be "Duds" on examination.

Bomb 1. 114 St Andrews Road

A 500 kg bomb fell through the front side of the roof of the house, which was split in to flats. It passed through the upper floor which was a bedroom in the home of two sisters, Miss Mabel and Miss Edith Pearse. The impact covered them in dust and debris but luckily they were not injured. The bomb failed to explode and continued its journey through the floorboards and ceiling of the room below.

This room was a bedroom occupied by Mr. Arthur John Harding Hill. He was killed instantly by the impact of a 500 kg bomb which landed on top of him whilst he slept.

Fatalities

ARTHUR JOHN HARDING HILL

The A.R.P. services and Police had been called to the scene and arrived "almost at once" according to one report. They started knocking on doors notifying neighbours and people in the immediate area as to what had happened.

Bomb2. Victoria Road

This bomb did not detonate but lodged itself in the pavement Approximately 150 metres from the New Beach Hotel. It was fortunate that this bomb did not detonate at the docks as only a few days earlier, remotely controlled sea mines had been stored in the dock's number three store, ready for installation in the estuary.

Mike Heard
'A Royal Naval minelayer had removed about 20 mines which could be detonated by remote control which was housed in the Harbour View building. These mines were laid from Maer rocks to Orcombe Point, just two days before the raid. If the store had been hit by a live bomb and the mines had been there and exploded, a large part of the docks and Exmouth would have been razed to the ground in this one raid.'

Around 70 houses were evacuated until the Royal Engineer Bomb Disposal Squad could arrive from Exeter to defuse the bombs

People were evacuated by the Y.M.C.A. who provided temporary accommodation for some evacuees in Schools and Churches in the town until later in the day. Others managed to stay with relatives and friends until the danger had passed and the bombs had been defused and removed to a safe place.

Roy Hatten
'In the early hours of the morning, the Police knocked on the door to wake us up and we were evacuated to our Grandfather's second hand furniture shop, above Lipton's on the higher parade until the bomb disposal squad had finished disarming the bomb. In the shop, Grandad had a show room for his second hand furniture we actually stayed here for two days in the show room sleeping on the furniture.'

Bomb 3. The Dock

It was thought that bombs had dropped into dock at the time but no one was sure, as there was no explosion from the area. When morning broke it became clear that something had happened and at least one bomb had fallen into the dock but had not detonated.

Ray Towill
'Turps Dixon and me were working repairing a boat called the "Valhalla" in the dock. It was afloat right over where a bomb had fallen. He said to me, "There is a bomb down there", pointing over the edge of the boat it was dropped about six months before I started work at the boatyard.'

'I said to the Dock Master Bill Peters, one day in 1941, when he was doing the moorings one day, "What had happened to the bomb?", He said, there was a big splat of mud all over the boats which must have been made by the falling bomb, but not enough mud to have come from an exploded bomb. The bomb disposal team felt around in the mud with long poles and although they could feel something hard it was thought best to leave the U.X.B. where it was, as it might prove more difficult and dangerous to remove it.'

Joe Radgick
'One night a German bomber dropped high explosive bombs in the Docks area. One fell into the dock but did not explode. We knew something had fallen in because the side of the boats were all covered with mud in one area. The dock was dredged and the U.X.B. squad tried to find it but it didn't show up. People think it could still be there today!'

Bomb 4. Shelly Beach

This bomb did not explode and has very little information about it, possibly because it had very little significance at the time compared with the more serious damage caused by the other bombs.

John Pascoe-Watson
'*After the Bomb Disposal Squad had defused the bomb on Shelley Beach, the Home Guard were instructed to dispose of the explosive content by setting fire to it on the beach.*

Whilst the Home Guard officer and an Army friend had a cup of tea in a house nearby the plastic explosive burned badly, with masses of thick black smoke which went all over the adjacent houses and marked them.'

Bomb 5 The Bull Hill Sand Bank

This bomb detonated in the Exe estuary and the explosion was heard all over the town and was reported in the newspapers as "waking several residents." Its detonation caused some damage to windows in the Shelly bungalows.

German Radio broadcast on Wednesday 26 February 1941

William Joyce, commonly known as Lord Haw Haw reported.

'*Dock and harbour installations at Exmouth were among the objectives attacked last night.*'

The following day the Royal Engineers U.X.B. squad from Exeter squad defused the St Andrews Road Bomb, The Victoria Road bomb and the Shelley Beach Bomb. But although there was still thought to be a bomb in the docks. Divers and dredging could not locate it.

Saturday 1 March 1941 The Parade

It was a fine evening for the time of the year and this was reflected in the amount of people who were in the town on this evening. The bomb load is thought to have been 4 x SC 250 (250 kg) bombs and 1 x SC 500 (500kg) bomb. They were dropped, at around 7.50 p.m. in the evening.

Only two of the high explosive bombs detonated, one at the Parade and one in Phear Park, causing four fatalities and some minor injuries. The remaining three bombs failed to detonate.

Exmouth Sirens   R.A. 7.59 p.m. – A.C. 8.45 p.m.

Locations of Bombs

Bomb 1. The Strand Gardens U.X.B. (SC 500)

Bomb 2. The Savoy Cinema U.X.B.

Bomb 3. The Upper Parade.

Bomb 4. The Exmouth Inn Exeter Road U.X.B.

Bomb 5. Phear Park Lodge

Bomb 1 The Strand Gardens U.X.B.

Mike Heard
'*The first bomb fell in the soft soil of The Strand Gardens, just along from where the zebra crossing is situated now, causing no casualties. This bomb did not detonate and was later defused by the Royal Engineers U.X.B. squad. The remains were then "dug out" by the Home Guard on cordon duty at the incident who later that day, along with the Savoy Cinema bomb pushed it into the back of an open lorry for removal from the scene.*'

'*The big bomb's casing was intact, with very little damage visible. It was later cleaned up and made into a collecting box for war savings and stood outside a shop in The Strand.*'

Rene Lewis
'*As we emerged from the cinema, someone came screaming and shouting along the road saying that the Parade had been hit. We thought it best to get home as quick as we could had to go through The Strand Gardens in the pitch black because of the blackout. About half way along The Strand Gardens my cousin Florrie stopped us all and said "Hang on! I've dropped my gloves". In the blackout one of the boys said "I've got a match", so he lit the match and shouted, "Bloody hell! Run for it!" we could see an unexploded bomb right in front of where we were standing, the bomb was approximately half way down The Strand Gardens.*'

Bomb 2 The Savoy Cinema U.X.B.

At around 8.00 P.M. a large crowd was in the Savoy Cinema in Rolle Street enjoying the film at the time this bomb dropped. They were watching the Universal film "The Boys from Syracuse". There were no casualties reported at the scene of this bomb.

An SC 250, 250 kg bomb fell in through the Foyer and bounced under the stairs imbedding itself under the balcony next to the annexe building, but fortunately did not detonate. The Savoy was on the same spot as it is today, but it occupies less space.

Mike Heard

'The air raid sirens didn't sound until after the bombs had fallen. When they got a bit more organised, the Savoy Cinema flashed up on the screen to please leave the theatre quickly and quietly. People had already decided to start leaving the building as something was obviously wrong and the lights went up.'

'The manager climbed on to the stage to appeal to people to leave the building quietly and calmly, to reassure people. Some of the people insisted that their money should be refunded at the time, but only a few, most were well aware that the situation could have been a lot worse. People generally left in an orderly fashion more or less, some by the main entrance and some by the Emergency Exit into Crudges lane.'

'The Home Guard members then had to go home, put on our uniforms on and reassemble in The Strand, to cordon off the area to keep the people safe from the U.X.B's'

Ron Lee

'That evening, I arranged with Aimee, my girlfriend at the time, to meet her at the Savoy Cinema entrance at 7 o'clock and we would see a film-show. We were in the circle upstairs and there was a full house of about 400 or more people. It was a very funny film with much laughter, when suddenly at around 8 o'clock there was a terrific explosion. Immediately there was pandemonium with people shouting, squealing and rushing to get out. I told those near to me to stay where they were, because anything that was going to happen had already done so and it wasn't much use being crushed in the rush to leave. After this bomb, we heard another more distant explosion.'

'When we got outside, I saw two or three men lifting up a large wooden bill board against the front entrance wall. I left Aimee at that point; telling her to go home and I went to the Police Station as we had been instructed to do in emergencies, to give help.'

'It was learned eventually that 5 bombs had dropped but only two of them had exploded, but we had found only another two of the U.X.B's, one was still missing. The Bomb Disposal Unit Officer, said that one unexploded bomb had landed on The Strand and one exploded on the Parade. This had killed four people and badly damaged the Parade Methodist Church, Millicans Cooked Meat Shop and Wills Shop, were also destroyed. One U.X.B. had fallen on Exeter Road and one bomb exploded at Phear Park, damaging the Park Keepers house. These were thought to have been 250 Kg bombs. The problem was to find the fifth bomb had been dropped. We thought about the drop order of the bombs and felt that it had been before The Strand or after Phear Park.'

'The next morning, when I was on duty I remembered the two men outside the cinema lifting up the bill board. With two men of the bomb disposal unit, we pulled the board down and there about six feet inside the building, was the missing fifth bomb.'

'You can see the damage that was done on the Parade. I shudder to think of how many would have been killed or maimed if the Savoy bomb had exploded.'

The Home Guard remained on duty over night in The Strand and the Royal Engineers Bomb Disposal Squad from Exeter arrived, they removed the fuses from the bomb in the Cinema and the one stuck in the soil of The Strand Gardens. After they had been made safe, Mike and his mates in the Home Guard had to roll these bombs onto the back of a waiting lorry, by pushing them up two planks.

Mike Heard

'No one had told us!, but the U.X.B. Squad had decided to detonate the fuses of these bombs in a controlled explosion in a Strand air raid shelter, in order to make them safe. As we were pushing one of these big bombs up the planks there was a sharp bang and we jumped out of our skins! Thinking we were going to be killed by the explosion!'

He said it, with an amused look on his face, but added, '...we were absolutely terrified at the time!'

Bomb 3. The Upper Parade

The bomb in the Parade detonated and completely destroyed two shops, Wills Brothers a popular Drapers shop and Millicans a provisions shop. Other buildings damaged on the upper Parade were, The Methodist Church, Woolworths, Walrond's Radio shop, all of these businesses were situated on the upper Parade. On the lower Parade, Smerdon's Electrical shop, Ackland's the Tobacconist, and the Express and Echo offices who shared the same shop premises were damaged along with many other businesses.

The damage caused to the lower Parade shops March 1st 1941

Fatalities

GLADYS GWENDOLINE JACKMAN
LILIAN IRENE TAYLOR
VICTOR JOHN DAVIE
JOHN PATCH

John Fletcher

'My Uncle Leonard Will's Drapers shop was destroyed in one of the bombing raids. Leonard, his wife Nellie, their daughter Jean Wills were all living above the shop at the time along with two family friends who were staying with them, Helen and Julie.'

'At the time of this raid I had just been to the Regal to watch a film with my dad and brother. We had just walked along the Parade and heard an aircraft engine approaching. My Dad who was down from London at the time was a Fire Watcher and he didn't like the sound of it. As the aircraft appeared he pushed us into a shop doorway near Capel's Fish and Chip shop. We heard a big explosion, but didn't go back afterwards to see where had been hit, we carried straight on to Camperdown Terrace, because Dad had said where bombs have fallen there are likely to be others.'

'The Draper's shop was destroyed and it was a big building three storeys and a basement, but Luckily none of my uncle's family were killed or hurt in the raid.'

Bomb 4. The Exmouth Inn Exeter Road U.X.B.

An SC 250, 250 kg bomb fell outside the Exeter Road entrance of the Exmouth Inn, which is now the Exmouth Arms. The Pub is situated on the corner of Exeter Road and Sheppard's Row.

Kathleen Bryant

'I lived in Exeter Road above Edwards the Motorcycle shop at the beginning of the war. It was right next to Sleeman's the Gentleman's Outfitters. Opposite me was Pickett's the chip shop and the Exmouth Inn, as it was then. One night we had an unexploded bomb drop opposite which was stuck in the pavement.'

Bill Sleeman remembers this incident as he was in his fathers shop on Exeter Road at the time which is almost directly opposite the pub. The attack was made by a lone German raider, he thinks it was probably a Heinkel HE 111 from what he had heard at the time.

Bill Sleeman

'I was stood inside my shop doorway in Exeter Road on this Saturday night. I couldn't see anything at first due to the blackout and it was the noise of the Parade bomb detonating which alerted me to this bomb.'

Members of the Home Guard and members of staff clear up Wills' Shop on the upper Parade

Clearing up Millicans and Wills' Shop on the upper Parade

Men from the Home Guard, the "West Surreys" the Rescue Squad and the Police clearing the debris on the upper Parade the morning of 2nd March 1941

'I went outside the shop door to take a closer look. A bomb had fallen in the doorway of the pub. It as around 3-4 feet tall, of which, most of the tail was sticking out of the ground. The 500lb bomb had crashed into the pavement right outside the door of the Exmouth Inn fortunately it did not go off, as there were many people in the pub.'

'The Home Guard, of which I was a member was then summoned to the alert to arrange a cordon around the area from Clarence Road, George Street, Albion Street, the Parade, New Street and Rolle Street (to Creedy's Corner), Exeter Road and The Strand and waited for the Royal Engineers Bomb Disposal Squad from Exeter come and defused the 3 U.X.B.'s. I was on duty until 7 o'clock in the morning and very tired by the time we stood down.'

Muriel Thorn. (Bill Sleeman's Cousin)

'Bill Sleeman brought home an enormous piece of shrapnel from somewhere, it was on the night of the Parade bombing. It was all he could do to carry it! I'll still never know how he got it home! It was from the floor to his chest in size. We were in the kitchen of his house at the time when he struggled in with it.'

Bomb 5. Phear Park Lodge

Another SC 250 fell here and detonated. Several people went to see the damage caused by the bomb the following day. There were no casualties at the scene of this detonation.

Geoff Perriam

'The Bomb fell about 10 metres behind the Park Keepers Lodge in Phear Park, making a crater about 3 metres wide and 2 metres deep. It had fallen in the soft earth; my own house was hit by a splodge of mud.'

Thursday 6 March 1941
German Bomber Scared Off

A lone German bomber was spotted approaching Exmouth and was pursued by Hurricanes based at R.A.F. Exeter.

Exmouth siren sounded. R.A. 6.30 p.m. - A.C. 7.30 p.m.

Newspaper report the *Exmouth Journal* Saturday 8th March 1941

LEFT IN A HURRY

'British fighters gave a decided shock to a Nazi sneak raider which tried to pay a visit to a South-West coastal town at dusk on Thursday.'

'The Nazi in charge decided that the neighbourhood was particularly unhealthy for him and left in a terrific hurry, dropping his bombs into the sea as he went.'

By dropping its bomb-load of approx 2,200 kg, the plane would have more power and speed available to evade the pursuing R.A.F. fighters. There is no evidence that this plane was shot down, or even damaged.

Wednesday 2 April 1941
Heinkel HE 111 Shot Down

Exmouth

Exmouth siren sounded. R.A. 7.00 a.m. – A.C. 7.40 a.m.

The Raider

On Wednesday 2nd April 1941 a Heinkel HE 111 P-27 (call sign G1+IR), Wk Nr 2137 from 7/ KG 55 based at Villacoublay set out for a routine reconnaissance flight over the English Channel.

The aircraft was shot down by Flight Lieutenant P.T. Parsons, in a Hurricane from No. 504 (County of Nottingham) Squadron based at R.A.F. Exeter. It finally crashed into the sea approx 2-3 kilometres from the shore between Exmouth and Budleigh. The 5 crew members were killed.

One Exmouth A.S.R.U. launch was deployed and the crew upon arriving on the scene found that the aircraft had sunk leaving an oil slick on the surface of the water. They spotted two bodies in the water. One body sank and the remaining body taken on board the boat.

Some members of the Exmouth Dock Home Guard were present at the North Jetty when the body was landed by the A.S.R.U. and remember an Iron Cross on the body of what they thought was the pilot.

The Fate of the Raiders

The recovered body was actually, the Observer, Oberleutnant Hans-Ludwig Wolff. He was wearing his Iron Cross 1st class on his flying uniform at the time of the crash. Three days later he was buried at the Higher Cemetery Exeter, with full military honours.

The remaining crew members were all killed by machine gun fire, by the impact of the crash, or by failure to escape the sinking aircraft and thus drowning.

Friday 11 April 1941 Good Friday Raid

Exmouth Machine gunned

A lone raider, thought to have been looking for R.A.F. Exeter flew down Exeter Road and fired burst of machine gun fire at ground targets.

Exmouth

Exmouth siren sounded R.A. 09.36 p.m. - A.C. 02.35 a.m.

Harry Stockers Wardens Notebook
Siren Sounded 21.34.

All on duty except Mrs. Sheppard and Flook until 22.00. Then Stocker, Rusling, Franks, Harris and Copp took over.

No Incidents.

Reported to Centre :————————

2 burst of machine gun fire 01.53 (single gun) Twin-engine bomber came over the viaduct at 500ft approx. Flying due south over Exeter Road. Port and Starboard engines and nose all lit up as though on fire, but no smoke visible.

All Clear 05.05

Saturday 12 April 1941 the seafront

A single enemy raider, reported as a Junkers JU 88 by eyewitnesses, dropped bombs on the centre of the town and the seafront, on a fine and warm Easter weekend.

The Raid
R.A.F. Exeter

Exeter siren sounded R.A. 8.52 p.m. – A.C. 11.20 p.m.

On the nights of 3rd, 5th, 12th, (and subsequently the 13th, 14th, 16th and 17th) of April, air raids caused extensive damage to buildings including hangars, huts, and the Officers' mess at R.A.F. Exeter. During the raids a considerable number of aircraft were destroyed or damaged including Hawker Hurricanes, a Bristol Blenheim and an Armstrong Whitworth Whitley bomber.

Exmouth

Exmouth siren sounded R.A. 08.45 p.m - A.C. 11.15 p.m.

Time of Raid. 10.55 p.m.

Bomb 1. Elm Grove, the Hotel by Bastin Hall

Bomb 2. Temple Steps,

Bomb 3. 30 metres from the Sea Wall.

Bomb 4. Further out to sea.

The enemy raider is thought to have been looking for R.A.F. Exeter and was in danger of running low on fuel, as it had been in the area for some time. It would seem most likely that the Raider jettisoned his bombs on Exmouth prior to returning home.

Bomb 1 The Hotel next to Bastin Hall in Elm Grove

It has not been possible to trace the name of this hotel. Very little information is available from eyewitness accounts of this bomb and the subsequent damage.

Newspaper Article
(paper and date Unknown)

Lieutenant Ronnie Brooks, son of Mr. J.E. Brooks had an almost miraculous escape in the course of a recent blitz on a South-West Coastal Town. He was spending the evening with friends, and they moved to a different room in the house. The party had scarcely moved when the room they had previously occupied was completely demolished. Had they been there they would have been killed.

As it was they were buried in debris, but were able to extricate themselves and escaped by the window. They Came under machine gun fire when they went to the hotel that Lieutenant brooks was staying in. when they got there the hotel was destroyed and all of his belongings.

The bomb damage to the Hotel in Elm Grove April 12th 1941

Bomb 2 Temple Steps the Seafront

This bomb fell very close to a Home Guard patrol and Supplementary Fire Party on duty on the esplanade. The blast caused minor damage to the large hotels and houses in Morton Crescent and Morton Road. The Jubilee clock tower's roof and seaward facing clock face were damaged by flying debris, as was the nearby seafront public shelter which had its glass broken.

Eyewitness Bill Gorfin

Article in the *Exmouth Journal* 1 February 1975
'I spotted the raider diving and we went flat, right at the top of the steps and nothing happened. I decided it would not be particularly healthy to be so close to the stonework of the sea wall if a bomb exploded and we made a dash for a flower bed in front of Morton crescent. Still nothing happened, and we made for the entrance to Morton crescent to find the raider coming back from the direction of the Maer with machine guns blazing.'

'We went to earth again and after the raider vanished. The "all clear" sounded and people began to pour down Temple Road eagerly enquiring where the bomb had dropped. We assured them there was an unexploded bomb somewhere and managed to keep them back from the seafront.'

Bomb 3 The Beach

This bomb exploded under the water, approx 30 metres from the sea wall, throwing up a lot of sand and water but inflicting no real damage. The crater left wasn't noticed until the tide had receded.

Bomb 4. Off Shore

Mike Heard
'I was on patrol one night when I saw a Ju88 machine gun the beach. It had also dropped a "dud" bomb which landed in the sea opposite the old Lifeboat Station. I did not actually see the bomb go in, but I was told of it by my Home Guard friends.'

Sunday 11 May 1941
flares dropped on the town and river

Exeter

R.A.F. Exeter bombed.

Exmouth

Exmouth sirens sounded.
R.A. 07.20 p.m.   A.C. 09.50 p.m.
R.A. 11.40 p.m.   A.C. 05.10 a.m.

A flare path was laid up the river towards Exeter. Reported as being a very bad night for enemy activity overhead, but no damage sustained to Exmouth.

Harry Stockers Warden's Notebook
11 May 1941

Eleven fighters constantly patrolling area at great height.

Lots of flares dropped at 8.30

Ack-ack firing.

Bill Sleeman's Diary
May 11th and 12th 1941.

The night of the 11th May and the morning of the 12th, Exmouth had 3 alerts. The town was machine gunned and many flares were dropped over the town.

Monday 12 May 1941
flares dropped and town strafed

R.A.F. Exeter was bombed on this night. The aircraft that attacked Exmouth were thought to have been returning from this raid. The types of aircraft are unknown.

At 02.05 a.m. A lone bomber fired bursts of tracer down a searchlight beam and then flew back over the town from the Exeter direction firing from front and rear machine guns. This happened another 4 times with four different planes during the course of the night and early hours of the morning.

Exmouth

First Alert
Exmouth siren sounded R.A. 05.20 a.m. - A.C. 05.50 a.m.

Second Alert
Exmouth siren sounded R.A. 11.40 p.m. - A.C. 05.07 a.m.

Harry Stockers Wardens Notebook
May 12 1941

Siren. 23.40

Stocker, Mrs. Sheppard, Fairchild, Flook and Mitchell on duty.

23.40 ———— 00.10 ———— 'Flaming Onions' ——- Airport Direction.

02.00 ———— Same as Above.
02.05 ———— Plane fired burst of tracers down the beam of a searchlight and then flew back over the town from the Exeter direction with front and rear machine guns blazing. All other Wardens reported on duty except for Wotton.

The above performance was repeated at:

02.55, 02.58, 03.30, 04.10.

No reports of casualties but planes were low on

bullets, seemed to hit the ground within 50 yards of the post.

Answering tracer fire seen from the dock area and seafront. Some bursts appearing very near flames.

All Clear 05.07. (Heavy gunfire and bombs in distance just before all clear).

(Second Alert)

Siren 05.17. Same team on duty. Very distant gunfire and bombs heard 05.23.

All Clear. 05.55.

Tuesday 13 May 1941 Crazy Bombs

The Raid

Exmouth siren sounded. R.A. 03.40 a.m. – A.C. 4.00 a.m.

At 03.40 a.m. lone raider thought to have been looking for R.A.F. Exeter, dropped a stick of five bombs which behaved in a strange way. A Home Guard patrol walking near the Bath House on the seafront saw the bombs drop.

They reported seeing "small bombs on fire and jumping about". These were the new type of German incendiaries intended to spread fire and prevent people from extinguishing them. A secondary timed explosive charge was stored in the casing of the bombs. It was because of the strange antics of these bombs, the raid was christened "Crazy Bombs" by the locals.

Harry Stocker's Warden's Notebook
May 13 1941

Siren. 03.40.

Bomber passed up river over Egremont Road. Low

03.43   Bomber Roared back in over viaduct, very low behind houses on left hand side coming in. Bomb traps seen to open before plane passed out of view five bumps heard. Four explosions seen.

03.45   Glow seen over where bombs pitched lasting about 1 minute.

On Duty:-
Stocker, Burrows, Fudge, Miss Stocker, Harris, Franks, Herbert, Wotton.
All Clear.   03.56

Five bombs dropped.

4 x 500 lb and 1x 1,100 lb.

 Incendiaries attached to the fins of 500 lb bombs. (Accounting for glow recorded above)

Bomb 1. Exploded at foot of Rock Garden near Madeira Walk

Bomb 2. Unexploded on footpath Carlton Hill against swimming pool wall.

Bomb 3. Unexploded. Shelter of Rose Garden opposite Swimming Pool. – bomb badly dented.

Bomb 4. (1,100lb) Found in front of Harbour View. Burst and scattered unexploded T.N.T. across road.

Bomb 5. Exploded on Sea-Wall on left hand side of lifeboat slipway.

H. Stocker.

The incendiaries were attached to numbers 1, 2, 3 and 5 it would have been unusual to attach incendiary bombs to the fins of an SC 500 and so it was presumably left unaltered.

Unexploded incendiaries were found in close proximity to the lifeboat station. When the main bomb detonated these would have been spread over a wide area.

Bomb 1

An SC 250 with 4 x 1kg incendiary bombs attached to the tail fins, dropped behind the Pavilion, where it skidded and left a crater, approx 5 metres long in the soft earth and ended up exploding against the wall of Carlton Hill in the rockeries and flower beds of the Pavilion Gardens.

Mike Heard
'I was on patrol with the Home Guard on the night, but didn't see the bombs fall. When I returned later and reached the spot where they had landed there were a lot of people, my friends in the Home Guard thought that the bombs had been dropped by a JU 88. There were large bombs, with several small incendiary bombs and some did not detonate. Some of the small incendiaries did go off. Members of 477 R.A. Home Guard saw them jumping around on the road surface and the Pavilion Gardens.'

The Home Guard and the Fire Guard put the fires out and made the area safe.

Ray Challis
'The bombing on the seafront was quite odd really; most of them didn't go off. We were told that one

dropped behind the Pavilion and another bomb dropped in the corner of the gardens and skidded near to where the new bowling alley development is now. One crater was still there for years afterwards where a bomb had exploded in the ground.'

Bomb 2 U.X.B.

This bomb, an SC 250 with 4 incendiary bombs attached, landed on the grass of the Pavilion Gardens, it then slid across the ground, knocked down the railings and part of the dividing wall between the Pavilion Gardens and Carlton Hill and then continued its journey, embedding itself in the wall of the open air swimming pool causing a sizeable hole. This bomb did not detonate.

Mike Slater

'I was walking along Plantation walk with my Mother towards the swimming pool shortly after the raid; I could see that the wall was damaged. We stopped and looked at the wall where the bomb went through. It seemed like an enormous hole at the time and could I see the water in the pool.'

Bomb 3 U.X.B.

The third Bomb, another SC 250 with incendiary bombs attached dropped at the bottom of Carlton Hill. It hit the road between the swimming pool and the beach gardens opposite.

This bomb failed to detonate, after skidding along the ground demolishing a park bench in the beach gardens shelter.

Bomb 4 U.X.B.

This was an SC 500 HE, 500 Kg bomb, which hit the road where, Marine Drive joins Carlton Hill. The bomb casing burst open on impact and scattered its explosive content across the road and surrounding area.

What was left of the bomb casing continued its journey through the beach garden, over the hedge and into the garden of Harbour View bungalow.

The Police and Home Guard knew that the plastic explosives that had been shed by the bomb could only explode with the help of an internal detonation and therefore it was quite safe to handle, which is why nobody seemed to worry too much about it being handled by children later. Similarly, it could have been taken away from the scene where it may have exploded elsewhere.

Mike Heard

'I suppose the bomb must have released about a hundred weight or so of the explosive, it looked a bit

like candy, the Home Guard gathered it all up and took it down by the docks, for burning'

Geoff is one of Exmouth's finest historian's, possessing a wealth of knowledge about the history and people of Exmouth. He is a volunteer at Exmouth Museum and a member of the Exmouth Local History Society.

Geoff collected shrapnel during WWII as did most children and some adults! Someone gave him a souvenir of this particular raid, in the shape of some of high explosive taken from one of the bombs, which split open on the seafront.

In our interview at Exmouth Museum, he referred to this explosive material as "Manna from Heaven" When I asked him about what he did with the plastic explosive, he laughed and said:

Geoff Perriam

'All of the local children tried to get hold of some as a "Souvenir". It was quite safe really. It could only explode with the help of an internal detonation. It was, (he showed me a similar colour) *a light mustard yellow colour and had a smooth surface a bit like candle wax. We used to set it alight but it didn't burn very well, When it burned, it burned very slowly with a thick brown smoke, I threw mine away when I got bored with it.'*

Ray Challis

'One bomb fell and it broke open, leaving lots of the plastic explosive from the inside all over the place. It was a browny-yellow colour, solid like greasy wax and smelt slightly of marzipan. We managed to get hold of some and used to try and set it on fire, but surprisingly! It didn't burn easily.'

Bomb 5

This bomb, another SC 250 did explode. It fell in the garden (facing the sea), of the Harbour View bungalow which was situated opposite the original lifeboat station. The bomb detonated close to the sea wall and right beside the lifeboat slipway. The explosion caused some damage to the bungalows windows and roof structure and woke up the Naval Officer and staff who were resident there.

The lifeboat station received minor structural damage and one of the doors was blown from its hinges. Six small incendiaries were also found here.

Wednesday 28 May 1941
Woodville Road and Carter Avenue

Weather Conditions

A clear night, no rain or cloud.

The Raiders

Were thought to have been from 1/KG 54 "Totenkopf" Deaths-Head squadron Based at Evreux in France. The Squadrons JU 88's, who were very busy bombing all areas of Britain at the time, were thought to have been trying to find Exeter.

Exeter

Exeter sirens sounded.   R.A. 01.15 a.m. - A.C. 03.35 a.m.

Exmouth
The First Raid. Bomber 1

Exmouth siren sounded. R.A. 00.15 a.m. - A.C. 03.35 a.m.

This raid was made by a raider at around 1.50 a.m. The bomber had flown over Exmouth from the south-east, very low looking for a target. It dropped five H.E. SC 250 bombs which detonated in fields at West Down Farm near Sandy Bay, near to where the World of Country Life exhibition is now. There were no casualties or serious damage sustained in this raid.

Report from Harry Stocker's Warden's Notebook
Siren: 00.15

Sheppard, Fairchild, Mitchell, Flook, Stocker on duty.

01.55   Bombs heard in easterly direction, after heavy bomber had flown low across town. (-5 H.E. dropped at West Down Farm no damage or casualties.

The Second Raid. Bomber 2

The raider released an incandescent flare and then a stick of 6 bombs during the early hours of the morning at around 3.30 a.m. Killing 9 people and badly injuring 8 more who were taken to Exmouth Hospital. This aircraft having already over-flown the town form the south-east, made its bombing run, flying from the Exeter direction.

Parachute Flare

The flare was released at a point above Halsdon Lane.

Bomb 1

This bomb fell and detonated behind Tower House at the top of Belle Vue Road. The explosion caused no casualties or damage.

Bomb 2 U.X.B.

Fell in Belle Vue Road between a Dr. Halls House and

Cliff End, near the disused brickworks. No casualties or damage were sustained here.

Ray Challis

'I was sat by the fire at around 1.30 in the morning, it was quite usual for children to still be up at this time during alerts. I was still up, sat there dozing off. I heard the sound of the bomb whistling, aeroplane engines and then an explosion. This Bomb had fallen behind Belle Vue Road, between there and Halsdon Avenue now.'

Bomb 3

Fell behind No. 7 Carter Avenue. The bomb detonated on impact in Mudbank Lane causing damaged to the roofs and windows of several houses in the area.

Fatalities

CHARLES HENRY MORTIMER

The Gardens at the back of Carter Avenue as they are today

Bomb 4

Fell on Southern Road and detonated on the roadway near the Motordrome Garage. Minor damage was caused to several buildings. Two soldiers injured.

Bomb 5

The bomb was a direct hit on the railway track. No casualties were sustained here.

Ray Challis

'The bomb went off, right on the railway line and blew it to pieces. We went up to see the damage, you could see there was a large crater and the railway tracks were all twisted.'

Bomb 6

This bomb destroyed and damaged five, houses at Woodville Road. Numbers 18, 20 and 22 were completely destroyed and numbers 16 and 24 were seriously damaged. Minor damage to several other houses was sustained.

Ray Challis

'The Noise of the explosion was tremendous; I was living at No. 6 Woodville Road, a few doors up from where the bomb fell.'

'We could hear the noise of the aircraft flying over throughout the night and it kept us awake. I was sat by the fire and just dozing off. The first I knew was a loud rushing sound, then boom! We went outside to look. Bricks, glass and heaps of rubble was strewn all over the road. The road was sealed off by A.R.P. and Police some small fires had started.'

'Slates were blown off the roof of our house and some windows were broken. The builders came and repaired the house within a few days.'

Report from Harry Stocker's Warden's notebook
Siren: 00.15

Sheppard, Fairchild, Mitchell, Hook, Stocker on duty.

02.51   Bomber came in fairly low over Exeter Road from the sea and flew inland. Suddenly heard to turn and appear to dive back. (02.52).

Wardens ordered to take cover by Stocker and immediately sky lit up by flare and earth began to rock. Actual explosions drowned by noise of bomb crashing down. - Not a whistle but sounded like express train.

Dirt and stones rained down on the Wardens lying on ground outside the post. Glass roof of dispensary (Chemists) of post broken in two places.

The sound of hundreds of large stones and bits of debris penetrating the surrounding roofs together with the light of the flare gave impression that hundreds of incendiaries were being dropped.

Wardens jumped to their feet and ran to the corner of Woodville Road. Glare could be seen from Carter Road as if fire had been caused. Stirrup pump and buckets of water seized from post in case fire broke out near where gable end of house was seen to be silhouetted against glare from Carter Avenue. In Woodville Road gable, having been tipped right over. Wardens raced to the spot and found H.E. had made direct hit on backs of numbers 18, 20, 22 Woodville Road. Casualties buried under debris.

Coal Gas leaking. This report phoned through at 02.56.

All Wardens reported by this time and rescue work was carried on with help of volunteers until arrival of official rescue squad. (03.20) approx.

Doctors phoned for from post twice and from Police Incident Post which had been established by this time.

Considerable delay occurred before Doctor arrived.

After arrival of Police establishment of Incident Post No further reports were put through from the post to the centre.

Stocker working with P.C. Morgan- Incident Officer, putting all reports through him.

Wardens searched all adjoining houses for slight casualties and by questioning neighbours helped Police materially in ascertaining No. of people in affected houses and No. of casualties.

All Clear 03.55

05.35 Crater discovered on railway. Track affected. Rescue work continued until last casualties were removed at 07.35 approx.

Wardens dismissed at 08.00 on permission of the Police.

Doubt about the identity of Female corpse. Not cleared up until 14.30. Stocker remaining with P.C. Morgan until identity established.

Position of Bombs

1. Behind Tower House. – Exploded – no casualties or damage.

2. Unexploded in Belle Vue Road. Roadway between Dr. Halls and Cliff End.

3. Mud Bank Lane – middle of lane. No casualties. Exploded. Damage to roof of houses in Carter Avenue.

4. Southern Road. Exploded. 1 killed in house 2 Soldiers injured by Motordrome. Several houses had roofs and windows damaged.

5. Direct hit on Railway. Rails shifted several feet (12-20) But track not broken. Stones hurled through garages adjoining. No casualties.

6. Woodville Road. No.'s 18, 20, 22 demolished, 16 and 24 badly damaged. 8 Killed, 3 badly injured, 8 or 9 slightly injured.

18 Woodville Road

This was the home of the Pannell family.

Fatalities

DORIS MAY PANNELL

20 Woodville Road

This was the home of the Bradford family. Percy and his family were popular in the town and he was known to the local evacuees as "Uncle" Percy.

Fatalities

PERCY BRADFORD
EVELYN WINIFRED GRIFFITHS
MAUREEN ANNE GRIFFITHS

22 Woodville Road

Fatalities

JANIE BRYANT
ANNE PEMBERTHY
JOYCE HEATH

Kathleen Mary Bryant

'There was a bad bombing at Woodville Road, during the war my Mother in law's house (22) was completely destroyed and the houses next door were destroyed or damaged. There was nothing left of the house except rubble. They had rented the house and everything in it was gone, including the outside toilet and the shed at the bottom of the garden.'

'My Mother in Law, Sydney's Mother was called Janie Bryant. She was injured by the blast and falling bricks. She was rescued from the wreckage along with his Aunt and they had been taken to Exmouth Hospital with head wounds, but only lasted two days. Bill sat by her bed for the full two days. The Aunt died first and then his mother.'

The re-built houses in Woodville Road as they are today

24 Woodville Road

This was the home of Railway Worker Mr. A. Bulling and his wife. They had billeted evacuees Ronald Feagan and his Brother William with them when they arrived from London in 1939.

Fatalities

RONALD R. FEAGAN

26 Woodville Road

This was the home of Mr. G.W. Tilke and Mrs. F.R. Tilke. The house was badly damaged.

Wednesday 11 June 1941 Westland Lysander Shot Down

Roy Hole
'A Westland Lysander was attacked one day as it approached Exmouth. It was shot down by German Planes and ended up perched on top of a house in Cranford Avenue somewhere. Both the R.A.F. Crew were killed.'

The Raiders

The raiders on this occasion were 4 x Messerschmitt 109s from III/JG 2 and 7 /JG2 based at Rocquancort in France. They were flying a combination of Bf 109 E3s and F2s.

Exmouth

1st Alert
11th Wednesday R.A. 05.16 p.m. A.C. 05.30 p.m.
No Incidents.

2nd Alert
11th Wednesday R.A. 06.51 p.m. A.C. 07.40 p.m.
The Time of the attack was 19.06 p.m.

The Attack

A Westland Lysander IIIA, number V9510 , from No. 16 Squadron based at Weston Zoyland was flying at around 1,000 ft towards Exmouth from the Paignton direction was attacked over the Maer and Queens Drive.

Two Messerschmitt BF 109s from a total of 4 German Raiders, which were returning from a raid on Teignmouth, flew over Exmouth and attacked the Lysander. It was hit by two bursts of cannon and machine gun fire from one of the enemy aircraft, as it approached the town. The young German Pilot confirmed as shooting down the plane was Feldwebbel Wolfgang Falkinger, Flying an Me 109 E3 "Emil". Wk Nr. 37029.

The Lysander crashed, out of control in smoke and flames on the roof of the house "Deveron", No.8 Cranford Avenue. The house had its roof and top floor badly damaged by the crash and the resulting fire. The inhabitants of the house escaped but the two R.A.F. crew members were killed.

R.A.F. Fatalities

DONALD WALKER
FRANK PERRY

The Pilot, Squadron Leader Donald Walker and Observer / Air Gunner, Flight Sergeant Frank Perry were killed in the attack.

John Middleton
'I was in the estuary picking cockles with friends when a Lysander was attacked by Messerschmitts we heard the aircraft engines first, the German planes approached from over Starcross way, we could see the Lysander trying to get away and then we heard the machine guns, it didn't stand a chance really I think Lysanders were armed with two Lewis guns but they weren't very fast. The aircraft was shot down and went on to crash somewhere in Cranford Avenue.'

Ray Challis
'Initially we thought the Lysander was an enemy plane, so we were cheering and thinking great! It's being shot down. We could see the two planes fly up behind it, but we thought they were our planes, Spitfires or Hurricanes or something. We saw the plane crash in flames, we didn't know where, because we were quite a way off. It was somewhere up near Elvis Road. When we found out it was one of ours we felt terrible and disappointed, the pilot was killed and the spotter too.'

Roy Penberthy
'The plane was soon removed, but the engine ended up in the driveway and was stood there for a quite a while before it was collected for salvage. I thought it was British planes chasing a German to start with.'

Witnesses at "Deveron"
8 Cranford Avenue.

Rene Lewis
'I was walking down Cranford Avenue with a boy, headed towards the seafront. We had arrived just where Cranford Avenue turns a corner to the left. The plane crashed around there somewhere. First we heard shooting and the engines of aircraft, then we saw it, it drifted across to the side of us on our left and crash-landed just out of sight. We went to see if we could see what had happened, but people would not let us get past and we had to move away.'

Michael Slater
'One Morning my Brother took me to 8 Cranford Avenue, where a Lysander had been shot down and had crashed into the roof of the house. The fire had been put out and the plane wreckage had been removed.'

Bill Sleeman was in Cranford Avenue at the time of the attack, waiting for his girlfriend and took a photo of this event.

Bill Sleeman's Diary
'Four Messerschmitt 109s were spotted headed for Teignmouth and dropped some bombs, then came around coast to Exmouth where they spotted a Lysander flying about 1,000 ft. They gave it one burst of machine-gun fire (or perhaps cannon), the Lysander was hit in two places, fell to the earth on its side crashing on a house in Cranford Avenue. The occupant's of the plane being killed. The Me 109s then made out over the sea again. The house was destroyed; the plane caught fire on hitting the house. Only two of the Me 109s attacked the Lysander.'

Tuesday June 17 1941
Incendiary Raid in Hulham Road area

The Attack on Exeter

Exeter was attacked on this night, at 1.20 a.m. Ten minutes before the sirens were sounded in the City. The planes were carrying high explosive and 1 kg incendiary bombs. Damage to 72 houses and other buildings was caused in Exeter, Topsham and along the path of the Exeter to Exmouth Road.

The Raid

Two raiders from an unknown unit dropped incendiaries on fields and farmland from Lympstone to Orcombe Point.

Exmouth Siren Sounded R.A. 1.55 a.m. – A.C. 2.50 a.m.

Sector 15's Warden Harry Stocker made a not of the raid in his diary.

Harry Stockers Wardens Notebook
June 17 1941

Stocker, Harris, Franks, Copp, Rusling on duty.

No incidents. Bombs heard 1.30 and incendiaries in N.E. Direction.

All Clear 02.52

Incendiaries pitched from Pitt Farm Lympstone in a crescent through Courtland's to Hulham Road.———No damage or casualties.

Saturday 5 July 1941
Attack on Budleigh Salterton and Exmouth

Two Jabo Raiders which were probably from 6 / JG2 flew in from the North-East to attack Budleigh. The aircraft were the brand-new Messerschmitt BF 109 F-2, armed with cannon and two 50 kg (SC 50) bombs slung underneath the fuselage.

The Attack on Budleigh Salterton

The raiders first attacked Budleigh Salterton dropping 4 bombs and then turned there attention on Exmouth, where they strafed the seafront.

The Attack on Exmouth

Exmouth siren sounded. R.A. 2.45 p.m. – A.C. 4.45 p.m.

Fred Butler

'One hot day in summer we went to Dawlish Warren beach on the steam train from Exeter with most of our gang. We played for a while and got up to all sorts of mischief. We then sat on the beach for a while looking out towards the sea across to Exmouth and could hear aeroplane engines. Quick as a flash two Messerschmitt 109s came into view they were travelling very low over the water at a very fast speed. We could see their approach and they flew from right to left along the beach opposite, headed towards Exmouth, they flew over the beach and town strafing as they went. We were scared stiff as we thought we were next so we ran all the way back to the station and caught the first train back.'

The Queens Drive Machine-Gunned

On this Hot Summer Day, Ivor and his friend Ted Gorham were sat on the dwarf wall outside the back of the pavilion waiting for the roller skating to start at 2.30 p.m.

Ivor Pike

'I remember the sound of ricochets and saw bullets hitting the ground; I found it all very exciting. A stranger tried to push us under a wooden bench for safety. I couldn't see the planes; I only heard them, it happened too quickly to see what the aircraft were. It's funny really'

Thursday Feb 12 1942
The Beacon and the *Scharnhorst*

The Channel Dash

The enemy warships *Scharnhorst*, *Gniesenau* and *Prinz Eugen* sheltering at Brest harbour posed such a serious threat to convoys crossing the Atlantic carrying essential food and raw materials. The War Office decided to mount two large scale daylight bomber raids.

The Kriegsmarine realised it was only a matter of time before the R.A.F.'s luck would change and on the 12th of February 1942 the R.A.F. were taken by surprise when the ships escaped via the channel making good use of bad weather.

The Ships had already reached a point of around 30 miles off Exmouth heading into Lyme Bay at approx 4.30 a.m. but still were still due to be in range of aircraft from R.A.F. Exeter for another 5 hours.

The ships eventually reached their home waters, where *Scharnhorst* and *Gniesenau*, previously lightly damaged in the attacks, hit mines and received serious damage.

The Express and Echo City Final Friday 13th February 1942

The Raiders Mission

Three Dornier 217 E-2s, from 7/ KG 2 based at Soesterberg, Holland had been dispatched across the channel to harass the ground defences, bomb the runways and keep the fighters engaged at R.A.F. Exeter.

Exmouth

The Observer Corps post, Fox Four at Orcombe Point spotted the three raiders at around 7.45 a.m. as they came across the coast to follow the line of the river towards Exeter. The bombers flew on to R.A.F. Exeter unhindered and surprised the ground anti-aircraft defences.

The Attack on R.A.F Exeter and Rockbeare

Exeter sirens sounded R.A. 8.00 p.m. - A.C. 8.40 a.m.

The aircraft arrived at Exeter airport and some bombs were dropped and the area strafed. The aircraft were driven off by the anti-aircraft fire and diverted away from R.A.F. Exeter attacking smaller targets.

One of these targets was Rockbeare Nurseries, where one of the Aircraft strafed the area killing two people, Wanda Elizabeth Coombes and James Sydney Pugh, before being shot down by anti-aircraft fire and crashing in a nearby field destroying some greenhouses, beside the A.30, East of Rockbeare Village near Exeter.

Jim Dyer
'Me and my friend Ron Sandford were cycling to school one winter morning and from Clyst Honiton. A German bomber flew over us following the road; they were machine gunning as they came along. We ran and sheltered under the railway bridge whilst the planes shot up the road and surrounding buildings. It was very exciting really. We "mitched" off school for the rest of the day and rode our bikes.'

The bodies of the German Aircrew were later recovered from the wreckage and transported to Exeter, where they were buried in the Exeter Higher Cemetery a few days later. Unfortunately, I cannot ascertain the ranks of the crew members

The aircrew in the crashed Dornier were;

Hermann Drame.
Gerhard Sommer.
Rudolf Baron.
Rolf Guldenpfennig.

The remaining two aircraft withdrew and made a run for the channel using the Exe estuary as a guide to take them back out to sea.

The Exmouth Raid

Exmouth sirens sounded R.A. 8.00 a.m. - A.C. 8.40 a.m.

Time of Raid: Just after 8.00 a.m.

The anti-aircraft guns in the estuary retaliated along with other batteries at various locations in the town. As the bombers were flying so low, the anti-aircraft guns visibility was restricted by buildings and the

chance of hitting friendly targets on the far side of the river and over the town was a high and so they were only allowed a limited time for the response. No hits were recorded on any of the aircraft.

Exmouth Journal Report of Saturday February 14 1941

'The enemy planes were met with a fierce anti-aircraft barrage and it was reported that two had been brought down.'

Mike Heard
'I was about to start work at Lavis's boatyard at around 8 o'clock in the morning. I was playing football in the yard with my workmates. We could hear a lot of flak going up at Exeter which went on for around 10 minutes.'

'After a short while, we heard and then saw two German bombers one quite a way behind the other, following the line of the river towards Exmouth. As they approached Exmouth they peeled away from the line of the river, as we thought they were aiming for the station from the path they were taking. They were flying Dornier 217's I think, at around 20 to 30 metres off the ground at this point and were flying so low we could see the men at the controls as they passed us. They headed over the town gaining height over the Beacon. They were out of sight by now so I couldn't see any more. We were told later that one had dropped a stick of 4 or 5 bombs and that they had exploded at Bicton Place, on the end houses and some women were killed there.'

The First Bomber

Bomb 1 The Stone Masons Workshop Beacon Place

Bomb 2 1, 2, and 3 Bicton Place

Bomb 3 17 Beacon Place

Bomb 4 Louisa Cottages

The Second Bomber

Bomb 5 Louisa Terrace U.X.B.

Bomb 6 The Gun Field Gardens U.X.B.

Bomb 7 The Madeira Walk U.X.B.

Bomb 8 The Harbour View U.X.B.

First Bomber Bomb 1

Elizabeth Maycock
'The Church School's Headmaster, Mr.Marcombe,

Top left: *The Church School now known as the Beacon School.*

Top centre: *The corner of the Beacon Congregational Chapel where the first bomb entered.*

Top right: *The back of the Beacon Congregational chapel as it is now*

Right: *The Rescue Squad, A.R.P. Wardens, Civilians the Home Guard and Men of the West Surreys clearing the debris behind the Congregational Chapel and the junction with Bicton Place and Beacon Place*

lived in a house which was attached to the playground of the school. He told us he was shaving at the time of the raid and was aware of a great crash and a lot of noise. Out of the corner of his eye saw something move out in the playground. He went out to investigate and saw that there was a huge crater in the playground where a bomb had landed bounced and hit the school roof then went up the road a little way and exploded. These houses in Bicton Place, (where we sitting at the time of the interview), were all destroyed and later rebuilt, The bomb also broke all the windows on this side of the Church.'

After leaving the School, the bomb went through the Beacon Congregational Chapel, in Little Bicton Place at ground level. It then continued through the Chapel and detonated against the inside wall of the Stone Masons workshop of Messrs. Easton and Clement, which adjoined the back of the Chapel. It was completely destroyed.

Mr. Battams was a soldier in the 70th Battalion the Queens Royal Regiment and an eyewitness to this stage of the raid.

Mr. G.F. Battams

'Having returned from breakfast, we were busily carrying out the usual chores and preparing for the first parade when the warning wail of the sirens sounded. With a colleague, Corporal Nick Byrne, we ran out of the hall (The Wesleyan Chapel) and up Tower Street towards Bicton Place (The Beacon), a vantage point so we thought, to see what was going on. All to soon we found out'

'On reaching the large open area Chapel Hill with Manor Gardens on our right; we heard the loud noise of an aircraft engine, indicating it was very close. Suddenly, there it was passing overhead and low enough to see the swastika markings. We stood transfixed I suppose, following its flight over the town. Simultaneously we heard a terrific bang and our attention was drawn back towards the Churches. I saw smoke, dust and debris rise from them and the little houses a little distance away. A large piece of masonry bowled along the roadway very close to us. As the air cleared we came across the remains of a fatal casualty in the road near the Congregational Church.'

Bomb 2 Numbers 1, 2 and 3 Bicton Place

The Hamilton Twins

Katherine Anne Hamilton and her twin sister Ellen Margaret Hamilton were both very popular in the Town. The twins lived together, were inseparable throughout their life and went everywhere together. They were thought to have both been in their home at 1 Bicton Place when the bomb detonated, along with Florence Gulliver, who lived at the same address. Katherine Hamilton's body was found on the roof of the church school.

Number 1 Bicton Place

Fatalities

EDITH LOUISA NICKOLS
ELLEN MARGARET HAMILTON
KATHERINE ANNE HAMILTON
ELIZABETH ANN DENMEAD
FLORENCE ELIZABETH GULLIVER

Elizabeth Maycock

'Next door (No.1) the Hamiltons kept a house for elderly people. Out of curiosity just after the raid I came along to see the wreckage of the houses. The chestnut tree opposite the house in the grounds of Holy Trinity Churchyard was full of sheets and bed linen. I also heard later that body parts were found in this tree and the Firemen had a dreadful job recovering these from the tree and the surrounding area.'

The rebuilt houses at 1-3 Bicton Place today

No. 2 Bicton Place

This was the home of Miss. Elizabeth Wickett Aged 70 and Miss Blanche Vallings. They were both badly injured and taken by Ambulance to Exmouth Hospital for treatment and later recovered from their injuries.

No. 3 Bicton Place

This was the home of two sisters. Miss Marjorie Seaton Huie. Aged 58 and Miss Melville Georgina Huie. Aged 61. They were both injured and taken by Ambulance to the First Aid Post at The Cranford Club. They were both treated there and recovered from their injuries.

Holy Trinity Church

Holy Trinity Church as it is now

The early morning congregation had attended the 7.00 a.m. Matins service. Just after the last member of the congregation had left the church grounds the first bomb fell.

The blast from the Bicton Place Bomb caused some damage to the clock on the West face of the tower and minor damage to the stone work. The stained glass windows however took the brunt of the explosion and several of these were irreplaceably damaged. Although the glass was kept only four figures could be reassembled.

Top: *The Rescue Squad and Decontamination Squad clear the wreckage of the numbers 1-3 Bicton Place February 12th 1942*

Above: *The view of the backs of the Beacon Hotels as they are today*

Bomb 3 Beacon Place

This bomb bounced from the Holy Trinity Church gates, damaging them, but failed to explode. It continued its journey in an arc, hitting the Church clock tower, then continuing it's journey hitting the chimney of "Hartley Cottage", finally detonating on the end house of Bicton Place.

An A.R.P. Warden inspects a crushed car at Beacon Place.

Bomb number 3 finally hit No. 17 Beacon Place completely destroying it. The house was re-built at a much later date. A car that was stood nearby was crushed under the rubble.

Bomb 4 Louisa Cottages

This Bomb was a direct hit on a row of 4 small cottages situated on the end of Louisa Place directly behind the grounds of the Dolgorfan Hotel.

Numbers 1 and 2 Louisa Cottages were completely destroyed and numbers 3 and 4 were badly damaged and shortly afterwards demolished This area became the Bombsite where Barry Clarke and his friends played during the war and just after the war when he was about 4-5 years old.

Barry Clarke
'Behind The Dolforgan Hotel in Louisa Terrace, two small houses were hit early one morning by bombs. These houses were completely destroyed and people hurt I think. Other houses nearby were badly damaged. The Council demolished the buildings and it stood derelict for many years after the War. We used to play on it as Kids, calling it the Bombsite.'

The new houses to the right and the original repaired cottages to the left at Louisa Cottages now

Cottage Number 1

This was the home of Mrs. Edith Maud Pulford a well known Nurse in the Volunteer Aid Detachment. Edith was also a member of the Women's Voluntary Service and helped with the billeting of evacuees. This house was completely destroyed in the explosion and was later taken back to ground level.

Elizabeth Maycock
'Louisa Cottage was a lovely little Victorian Cottage on the end of Louisa Place. My Mother always admired it and always said she would love to live there. It was completely destroyed and the occupant, a lady, was killed in there. There were two cottages destroyed there and some other damage done, but I'm not quite sure what. There is a semi-detached house there now just past the turning on the right at the end of Beacon Place.'

Fatalities

EDITH MAUD PULFORD

Other Casualties

Miss O. Pulford. (Aged 26) was the Daughter of Edith Pulford. She was badly injured and taken to Exmouth Hospital where she later recovered from her injuries.

Cottage Number 2

This was the home of Edith's older sister (Aged 69), Mrs. H.F. Pulford. She was badly injured and taken to Exmouth Hospital with her sister and niece and all recovered from their injuries.

Cottage Number 3

Home of Mrs. and Miss Sherriff. It is not known whether the Sherriff's were injured or not. The house was badly damaged but, was later re-built and was habitable again.

Jean Acton
'My friend Miss Sherriff, who lived at Louisa Cottages was bombed out, the bomb exploded and badly damaged the house.'

Cottage Number 4

The home of Mr. and Mrs. C. T. R. Martin: The house was damaged but, was later re-built and was habitable again.

Second Bomber Bomb 5 U.X.B.

This bomb went through two houses which had been converted into a Hotel on Louisa Terrace. The bomb struck the building from the rear corner and passed diagonally through the hotel, causing severe damage. It eventually ended up in the gutter on the opposite side of Louisa Terrace.

Ray Towill

'We were at work and heard the Germans dropped some bombs on the Beacon. It was early in the morning around 8.00, I think. We were just about to start work so it could have been earlier. We could see some smoke and 3 of us went on our bikes straight up to where we thought the bombs had fallen and saw a house that was demolished. We then went up over the Beacon to try and find the other places that had been hit. We had reached the road between the Beacon Hotel and the huge lime stone wall of The Dolforgan Hotel, when I saw a German aircraft come over from the direction of Beacon Place incredibly low'.

'We ducked down behind the wall as quick as we could. I saw two bombs come out, and waited for the explosions. There was a lot of noise, but not a bomb went off! Nothing had happened! We got our bikes and went round to the front of Louisa Terrace and a little way down the road there was a bomb and rubble lying on the road. It was across the road lying in the gutter. Further down the road near Trefusis Terrace, another bomb had bounced and ended up on the seafront.'

Dennis Pratt

'One bomb passed clean through two of the large houses on Louisa Terrace, narrowly missing a shocked and scandalised resident, as he was emerging from his bathroom. It came to rest near the garden on the opposite side of the road.'

Bomb 6 Carlton Hill/Trefusis Terrace U.X.B.

The bomb passed just over the top of Pencarwick House on the corner of Louisa Terrace and Carlton Hill. The bomb left a deep trench in the grass and embedded itself in the mud of the Gun- Field gardens opposite Lion House, on the corner of Trefusis Terrace and Carlton Hill.

Dennis Pratt

'The bomb passed over the low house near the end of Louisa Terrace (Pencarwick House), describing an arc over the sloping field in front of Lion House. The bomb went on to land in the gardens opposite.'

Bomb 7 Madeira Walk U.X.B.

Bill Sleeman (not an Eyewitness)

'The plane which swooped over the town at roof-top height, also dropped a bomb on Madeira walk which fell through the swimming bath wall, jumped the baths, went up some concrete steps and through another wall outside Fortes café.'

The Dolforgan Hotel as it is today

Pencarwick House as it is today

Lion House on the Corner of Trefusis Terrace the sixth bomb landed in the gardens opposite here

Bomb 8 The Harbour View U.X.B.

Bill Sleeman (Not an Eyewitness)

'Another bomb fell outside Harbour view and went under the house.'

The U.X.B's were later defused by the Royal Engineers Bomb Disposal Squad from Exeter. In the mean time the Police and Home Guard had set a cordon in place and the A.R.P. had warned the residents they would need to be evacuated from the houses temporarily. The Y.M.C.A. housed and fed these people.

The Second Alert

Exmouth sirens sounded R.A. 01.40 p.m. - A.C. 02.05 p.m.

A lone bomber of type unknown, returning from a raid on Torquay Harbour, flew over the town at approx 1.50.p.m. It did not attack.

The Raiders After The Raid

Although Exmouth had good ground anti-aircraft defences by this time in the war, these remaining two aircraft made it back to their base in Holland.

Saturday March 7 1942 Hit and Run Raid

Street Cricket Definition

"Hit-and-Run" rule. (also known as "Tip-and-Run").

When the batsman hits or nicks the ball, they are forced to run otherwise they are out; this will speed up the game if there are many players.

The Raiders 13/JG 2

These aircraft came from 13/JG 2 based at Beaumont-le-Roger as they carried out most of the raids on the South Devon coast in March 1942. During this first month of Jabo operations 13/JG 2 carried out 49 "Hit and Run" attacks in their operational area was from Hampshire westwards.

It is thought that this was a reconnaissance raid and rehearsal for subsequent raids in the area. This unit became particularly efficient hit and run attacks. They named themselves "Rotte Fuche", the Red Foxes because of their use of cunning and guile in their tactics. Convoys, Coastal shipping and harbours were their speciality and it was decided that the Squadron badge should be a red fox with a blue broken ship in its mouth.

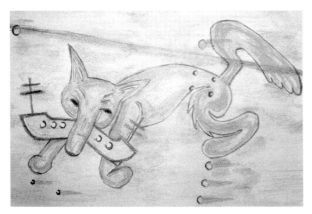

The "Rotte Fuche", Red Foxes squadron badge

The Raid

Exmouth

Exmouth Siren sounded. R.A. 9.35.a.m. – A.C. 10.05 p.m.

The Raiders first attacked Exmouth at 9.25 a.m.; strafing the town they then flew on to Teignmouth, where they attacked the pier and town centre, with machine gun fire. The raiders then returned to Exmouth again at approx 10.00 a.m., to carry out a further machine gun attack on houses in the town, finally heading back out to sea and returning home.

Roy Hatten

'One day Victoria Road was attacked, we were playing cricket in the service road at the back of Victoria Road, right outside of our garage. We saw bullets striking the buildings and heard the noise of planes and the machine guns, but didn't see the aircraft. If you look opposite the back of house No. 50 you can still see bullet holes.'

The R.A.F. Response

R.A.F. 317 (Polish) Squadron's White Section Operations Record Book, Sector Control scrambled 2 spitfires from Bolt Head.

Pilot Sgt. Kazimierz Sztramko in a Spitfire Mk VIB AB215 (call sign JHJ) found himself under attack from the enemy very shortly after take off. He was "jumped" by two Me 109s which dived on him.

Kazimierz Sztramko

'My aircraft was hit, whilst trying to complete a circuit and was forced to make a pancake (wheels up) landing on the 'drome.'

The raiders then made off, the other Spitfire was unable to give chase, as the extremely low altitude made it impossible to receive any commands by radio from Sector Control, as to the direction and height, of the raiders retreat.

Thursday 16 April 1942.
"Hit and Run" raid the estuary

Exmouth Sirens Sounded R.A. 08.12 p.m. – A.C. 08.37 p.m.

This raid was in the early evening and was the first of two consecutive raids on Exmouth, when 3 fighter aircraft, described by witnesses as Me 109s bombed and strafed the town and the estuary area. A railway fireman at Starcross was wounded, no other casualties are reported.

Ron Lavis

'An old wooden boat was moored just off where the sailing club is now. At high tide it looked like the boat was floating and was serviceable but it wasn't. It had plugs put in the bottom which could be removed to sink it and it was intended that it would be used as a block ship, for when the Germans invaded and came up the ferry steps! One evening German planes attacked the estuary area and decided to attack this old boat.'

Derek Rowsell

'One early evening on a spring tide, when high-water was at about 7 o'clock, we were over by the allotments near the dump. There were several of us over there playing. We could see the old barge from where we were. It looked like it was floating because normally, it was just sat there on the bank. It must have looked to the Jerry pilot like it was floating. The Jerry plane that attacked the barge, flew up the river, turned and flew down the river again. We could see him, about 50ft above the level of the water. He fired his cannon and machine guns at the barge in an attempt to sink it. He then flew on out over the water.'

John Fletcher

' On day in the early evening my brother and I were returning to shore in our small boat we had been out during the day and probably over to the warren. We had just tied up on the shore and our friend Roy Knight was just coming ashore in his boat. At this point 3 fighter aircraft flew up the estuary, I had just assumed that they were from one of the Squadrons at Exeter, but when I looked up they were machine gunning and I saw that they had black crosses painted on them. They were Me 109s, we knew exactly what they were as everyone had trained in plane spotting.'

'It was in this raid that two of the old boats which were beached opposite Rowsell's Boatyard, near where we lived, were strafed by the planes. One belonged to the Sea Scouts but that was not hit, but the other one, which was about 45 feet long, was hit by cannon and machine gun fire.'

'The next day there was another attack on the town in the same area and some of our gang were in the boat that had been shot at. Luckily they attacked elsewhere on this day and no-one was hurt.'

Jenny Thompson, resident of St Andrews Cottages, worked as a cockle-picker in the estuary. On this day she witnessed the machine gunning of the train on the line at Starcross by the raiders.

This area was a favourite target of 13/JG 2's Red Foxes a high probability exists that this was the unit that carried out the attack, it cannot be proven as the German records available do not contain enough information at present.

The *Exmouth Chronicle*
Saturday April 18 1942

ENEMY PLANES IN SOUTH WEST

Enemy aircraft were over a coastal district of the South-West on Thursday evening. Enemy planes used machine guns, but they were driven off by anti-aircraft fire.

There was machine-gunning in parts of another South-West town, but no damage or casualties were reported.

A passenger train was attacked by machine-gun fire. The fireman on the train received injuries, but there were no other casualties.

Friday 17 April 1942

Budleigh Salterton and Exmouth "Hit and Run" raid

Exmouth Sirens

Raiders Approaching 1.30 p.m. All Clear 2.15 p.m.

The Raiders

It is my opinion that this attack, was again most likely to have been carried out by 13/JG 2 The "Rotte Fuche" (Red Foxes) under the supervision of Frank Liesendahl, as they were visiting the South-West of England almost daily at this point in the war.
From the path that the raiders took over the towns on this raid, it would seem that they were aiming specifically at Churches on this occasion.

The Raid

On this Friday, 3 Messerschmitt BF 109 F4/B's took of from their base at Beaumont Le Roger in France, carrying two SC 50 High Explosive bombs on each aircraft, mounted on a rack under the fuselage. They Crossed the Channel and after taking approx. 45 minutes to make the journey they first attacked Budleigh Salterton.

Budleigh Salterton

Bomb 1. St Peters Church

St. Peters Church was hit on the North Aisle by an SC 50 bomb. It destroyed most of the wall and the flying buttresses on this side of the Church, seriously damaged the roof and broke all of the windows.

The windows were so badly damaged during the raid

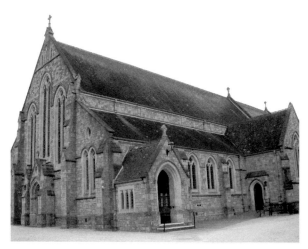

St. Peter's Church Budleigh Salterton as it is today

that nothing was left in a usable condition. The War Damage Commission did pay some money to have the Church and stained glass windows repaired but the majority of the funding had to be raised by members of the Congregation and the local parish.

Bomb 2. East Terrace

On the same raid two houses in East Terrace, Myrtle Cottage and Sunnydale were struck by bombs.

Bomb 3. Chapel Street

"Lyndale" in Chapel Street was also hit and badly damaged.

Other Damage

Damage to roofs and buildings in the town was sustained and in Granary Lane a chimney was knocked off a house and destroyed by machine gun fire. On the bottom end of Cliff Road houses were damaged by machine-gun and cannon fire.

Marker's war time shop damaged by cannon fire and still visible today in Budleigh Salterton High Street

Bomb 4. The Public Rooms

They were damaged by cannon and machine gun fire in the raid. It is uncertain exactly what happened here as there are some reports that it was hit by a bomb and badly damaged and demolished later. I could not find any eyewitnesses to this attack in Budleigh to confirm this bomb, but have assumed that each aircraft was carrying two bombs on an under-fuselage bomb rack. Only time will tell, if more evidence can be found.

Fatalities

FREDERICK SYMONDS

The injured were taken to the Cottage Hospital, Boucher Road. It is unclear how many injured casualties there were and how severe the injuries were as no records appear to exist.

The Exmouth Raid

The raiders approached Exmouth from the South-East, direct from the raid on Budleigh Salterton. By the time they were visible over Exmouth skies they were flying at an altitude of approx 30 meters. The remaining aircraft dropped its bombs at around 1.25 p.m. One detonated in the grounds of St Andrews Church and another detonated in the service road behind St Andrews Road. No sirens sounded in Exmouth in this raid.

Tony Smith

'During WWII, I was a Lieutenant in the Royal Marines. Part of the field course entailed a number of trips to Straight Point rifle range, for small arms courses during their field training. Straight Point had a rifle range, with no protective armoury and we only fired .303's for training. The total course was about 8 weeks and I think that I only took turns as butts officer on three or four occasions during my stay at Dalditch camp in 1941/42.'

'One day, during my time at Dalditch Camp, I was selected as the Butts Officer for duty at the Straight Point Range. This was in 1942, the butt's officer had to be on duty all day, morning and afternoon, but I can't remember what time the attack took place'.

'Whilst I was the there I witnessed a German fighter skimming over the sea and heading for Exmouth. The aircraft approached VERY low from over the sea, I thought it was a Spitfire to begin with.'

'I saw this first part of its attack and was told later that the aircraft had attacked Exmouth with a bomb that was slung underneath its belly.'

Straight Point rifle range

'After it's visit to Exmouth the aircraft then circled and returned to the area near the range butts and naturally I scrambled to safety when the aircraft appeared overhead, breaking my nose in the process! The aircraft then sprayed the range and cookhouse buildings with 20mm cannon and machine gun fire using explosive bullets. Fortunately my recruits were scattered all over the range and there were no casualties.'

Derek Rowsell

'One of our hobbies was collecting shrapnel and spent bullets. We even had some small incendiary bomb tails which were something really special, all boys collected shrapnel.'

'At around lunch time, the tide had gone down and we could walk over the sands to the old barge.'

'We walked along the cockle sands to the barge. It was the mistletoe or the mystery or something, I can't be sure. We climbed up on the boat and got into the hold. There was an old Kelvin engine still in it. Ron and I were in the pitch-black, it was like the inside of a cows guts! We looked everywhere for the bullets, with a number of our other friends.'

'Where it had been shot the day before, we could see light shining through the holes. All of a sudden there was a tremendous noise. We could hear aircraft engines and machine guns firing again. We were worried, in case the bullets came through the side of the boat and we thought they were firing at the barge again. We ducked down, frightened stiff that we would be shot. "Is anybody hurt?" I distinctly remember a cockney evacuee boy shouted, when the planes had gone over.'

'After the noise had stopped, we got out we could see smoke, there was smoke all over by the boat yard area and Ron thought it was Lavis' boatyard which had been hit. Ron had given us all a bunk up to help us get out of the hold but was left stranded. I ran off to get help and bumped into Tommy Letten who was home on leave from the Navy. Tommy went to the barge and rescued Ron.'

Ron Lavis

'We went down to the boat the day after the raid on the old barge around dinner time and wanted to dig out the bullets for our shrapnel collection. I got down into the hold of the boat with my friends, which was quite high, so we had to help each other down into the dark. We found some bullets in the wood work and dug them out. I was right down in the hold, right in the bottom of the ship when we heard fast aircraft overhead and machine gun fire, we heard explosions too.'

'My friends shouted out "Is everyone all right?" as we thought the Germans had attacked the boat again. So we decided to get out quickly. We had to give each other a leg up to get out and I was doing this when I suddenly realised there was no-one left to help me, my friends had run off and left me. After a while Tommy Letten, a family friend who was on leave from the Royal Navy came and found me and got me out.'

'Luckily the boat wasn't attacked again and when I eventually got out into daylight, I could see smoke rising over near where I thought my house was, so assumed it had been bombed, in fact it was St Andrews Church and St Andrews Road which had been hit.'

Bomb 5. St Andrews Church

This bomb completely destroyed the dwarf wall and pillars in the corner of the churchyard; the road was also badly damaged leaving a crater. Minor damage was caused to the east wall of the Church and to the Rose Window, was completely shattered by lumps of masonry from the wall.

St. Andrews Church Rose Window today

Hazel Bradford

'There was a day-time raid around lunch time. I was at home in Victoria Road, we had just had our lunch. My Dad and Brother were on leave. My sister Connie had gone to the toilet, which was in the back garden, most houses had outside toilets at the time. We heard *the planes coming over and the sound of the guns. My Dad said, "Go and get Connie, quick!" Connie and I hid in the toilet, we heard them drop the bombs and we could hear the planes were machine gunning. After the planes had gone, we rushed indoors; I was worried that our house may have been destroyed by a bomb, as the explosions were so close. When we got inside, my brother had been knocked across the room and every where was white because the ceiling had come down and the windows were broken. Dad later boarded up all the windows.'*

John Pascoe-Watson

'When I was in the Sea Scouts during the war we were called to help clear up the wreckage caused by the bombing of St Andrews Church. A bomb had landed in the road, right beside the corner of the wall. The blast had also knocked out the rose window, and big lumps of the shattered wall had gone straight through it. There was glass and stone everywhere. The Sea Scouts and others helped clear up the mess inside the church.'

Casualties

One person was injured in Exmouth Mr. Percy Norman, a Fire Guard. He lost some fingers in the explosion near the church.

Bomb 6. St Andrews Road

A bomb fell through the roof of 104 St Andrews Road, which belonged to Miss. K.A. Gray, without detonating. It badly damaged this house and also 102 the home of Mr. and Mrs. F.J. Worsell next door.

The bomb went on to detonate at the rear of No. 104 in the back garden by the service road, where it destroyed three small cottages situated opposite on

The small cottages in the service road after the raid on 17th April 1942

the service road between the backs of St Andrews Road and Victoria Road.

Hazel Bradford

'During this raid three small cottages, just at the back of where we lived were destroyed by a bomb. They were later knocked down. Mr. and Mrs Bastin lived in left hand cottage, with their children George, Frank and Samuel and in one of the other cottages lived Jenny Thompson, a cockle picker and a well known character in the town. In the other cottage lived a couple with one son, he was a Baker, I think.'

Wednesday 23 and Friday 25 April 1942 flares dropped up the river Exe and Exeter bombed

On the nights of the 23rd and 25th April 1942 some 40 aircraft, Do217's of KG/2, Ju88s of KG/106 and a few He111s of I/KG 100 targeted Exeter. The raids killed and injured several people and damage to buildings was extensive.

Bill Sleeman's Diary

23/04/42

Raid on Exeter many Planes over

25/04/42

Another raid on Exeter, Flares Dropped up the river, heavy gun fire and many bombs dropped on the city.

Friday 28 August 1942 Me 109 Shot Down Off Exmouth

Exmouth Town

No siren sounded

The Mission

Feldwebbel George Fisher from 1st Squadron / long range reconnaissance Group 123, was flying a Messerschmitt Bf 109F-4 (Call-sign White R +) on a routine reconnaissance mission around the Portland Weymouth area. At around 09.40 a.m. the raider was intercepted and shot down into the sea, by Wing Commander K. Mrazek and Squadron Leader F. Dolezal, flying Spitfires from No.310 (Czech) Squadron, R.A.F. Exeter.

During their attack, both pilots described seeing the tail section of the enemy aircraft breaking away and the aircraft crashing into the sea in a spin from around 300 ft. Both pilots claimed a half share each in the victory. The German pilot was found to have the first type of throat contact microphone attached round his neck on a leather strap. It was the first microphone of this type to be seen in Britain and it was sent for evaluation by the R.A.F.

Bill Sleeman's Diary

August 28 1942

'An Me 109 was shot down by two spitfires in the mouth of the river Exe. The plane was on fire as it flew over the town. The rescue launches went out from Exmouth and picked up the pilot who was already dead.'

Anonymous Eyewitness

'One morning a German fighter Plane was chased by two spitfires as it came along the coast. It flew out to sea to try to escape but was shot at continually by the British planes; it came down on fire in the sea, some way off'

Hazel Bradford

'Hiram Thomas was my cousin on my Mums side. He pulled up parts of a German plane over by the Warren one day when he was fishing.'

Thursday 15 October 1942
the first Focke Wulf raid

Time 17.42 Hours

Information from German sources

On the Thursday 15th October 1942 Exmouth was machine gunned by 2 Focke Wulf FW190's From 10 / JG2.

The Raid

The Aircraft flew in from the Exeter direction roughly following the line of the Exeter Road. Courtland's Cross was hit by cannon fire as were various other parts of the town. One flew over Withycombe Village and one down the Exeter Road both aircraft machine gunning in bursts as they went. A bus was attacked near Halsdown House and various buildings along the route. The aircraft then continued across the Exe estuary and attacked Dawlish Warren. The Exmouth to Starcross ferry was also shot at by cannon fire and set alight. No one was killed or injured on the boat. The aircraft then flew back out to sea, in this Typical "Hit and Run" Raid.

Bernard Greenaway

'One raid I witnessed, was when I was stood by the Highland Garage, on the Exeter Road. Two German fighters appeared, firing at the town as they came along, following the road. They had come from Exeter attacking the airfield there. I picked up some of the empty cases, which were still hot.'

Pearl Cawse

'Mary Griffiths, whose parents had owned "Griffiths" the bakers shop in Chapel Street which was destroyed by earlier bombing, was walking along Exeter Road by the Shell Garage one day. She was fired on by German Fighter planes. A man protected her from being fired at by pushing her down on the ground. She always tried to find out who he was but with no success.'

Richard Tarr was living at 102 Exeter Road, on the corner of Lawn Road during the war. He was in the garden at the time of this raid.

Richard Tarr

'I found a munitions clip in the garden, after a raid. It was day time in 1942 when plane flew down Exeter Road, I think, the Shell garage on Exeter Road was machine gunned during the same raid.'

Sunday 10 January 1943
Teignmouth and Exmouth raided

Exmouth

No Exmouth Siren Sounded

The Raiders

The raid was led by Hauptmn Heinz Shumann the new Staffel Kapitan of 10/JG 2. It was designated a "Storangriff" (nuisance) raid.

The Raid

Seven Focke Wulf 190's from 10/JG 2, took off from Caen-Carpiquet Airfield at 13.48 p.m. They crossed the channel in 40 minutes then followed the line of the coast, using Exmouth and the Exe Estuary as one of their primary point markers. From here the raiders flew on and attacked Teignmouth from the south-east.

Teignmouth

At 14.39 p.m. (German sources) the raiders dropped two SC 500 H.E. bombs into Teignmouth harbour (one into the sea) and fired machine gun and cannon at boats docked there. The remaining raiders turned their attention to Teignmouth town dropping a further 5 bombs these planes also used machine gun and cannon fire to strafe the town.

R.A.F. Exeter's Response

Two Hawker Typhoons from 266 Squadron based at R.A.F. Exeter, Exeter had taken off at 14.15 on an anti-rhubarb (low flying enemy attack) patrol.

They were flown by Flying Officer J. Small and Pilot Officer Sam J.P. Blackwell. They spotted and reported the enemy aircraft and turned to follow the intruders. Whilst approaching Teignmouth at approx 100 Metres (altitude) Flying Officer Small saw bombs hitting the water and strafing, it is at this point he selected and attacked his target, the FW 190 flown by Joachim Von Bitter.

Ivor Pike

'One day we were on the seafront and saw a plane shot down over the sea in the distance near Dawlish.'

Bill Sleeman's Diary
January 12 1943

'Jerry plane, Focke Wulf shot down between Teignmouth and Dawlish.'

The Aircraft crashed into the sea approx 500 Metres off the Dawlish side of the "Parson and The Clerk" cliffs.

The 6 remaining aircraft, of which two were damaged, returned back across the channel to land at Theville.

Launch sent from Exmouth to retrieve Airman's body

Members of the dock-side A.S.R.U. and Home Guard were sent to retrieve the body of Joachim Bitter. Some have been reticent to talk about their wartime experiences. One man who was well known in the dock community and the Home Guard mentioned that he and other Exmouth men had been sent on a launch to retrieve the body of a dead German fighter Pilot.

Anonymous Eyewitness

'We were sent out in the launch to pick up the body of a young German fighter Pilot, which had been shot down two days earlier. It had been shot down by a British fighter near Dawlish and then drifted along the coast towards the Warren. He was later buried at The Higher Cemetery Exeter.'

Joachim Von Bitter was buried at Exeter Higher Cemetery with full Military Honours. His signet ring and dented cigarette case were returned to his family in Germany via the Red Cross.

Friday February 26 1943
"Hit and Run" The Strand

The day was cold and overcast in the morning weather improved quickly throughout the day. Around lunchtime the sun was beginning to show through light clouds.

The Raiders

Were from 10 JG/2 based at Caen-Carpiquet airfield. The unit was equipped with upgraded Focke-Wulf FW 190A-4 Aircraft armed with 1 x 250kg (SC 250) bomb, cannon and machine guns.

The Raid

Derek Rowsell

'Our friend's boat was strafed when the planes attacked. It belonged to Tom Horn and Reg Searle and was called "Winifred". They were out fishing with nets near the bar in it, around the Sandy Bay to Orcombe point area, when they were attacked. The bullets were in the bow and stern in the boat and you could see the holes and later the patches which one of the local boat builders repaired. The boat nearly sank and they had to keep pumping and bailing to get the boat back to the shore, to stop it sinking.'

Bomb 1 "Treganna"
Number 7 Louisa Terrace

"Treganna" was a huge house of four storeys made from white brick. The body of a man was found a week later by workers from the Council's Demolition Squad, under the debris of "Treganna's" porch. The buildings on either side also suffered serious damage.

Fatalities

SIDNEY CLARK

The house which stands where "Treganna" was, as it is today

Ron Lavis

'I was at the Church School for part of the war. It's now called the Beacon School and my Granddaughter goes there now. The Art Master asked me to paint a picture of the school and I was sat outside near the newspaper offices, with a chair and an easel, working away.'

'My friend Derek Rowsell, part of my gang, was a school prefect and he had to open the gates before lunch time. He said "hello" to me as he opened the gates and asked me what I was doing.'

'Suddenly we heard a lot of noise and could hear planes coming over the school. There was an explosion from behind the school somewhere, I thought that the school had been hit'

Derek Rowsell

'I opened the school gates at lunchtime to get ready for the mums to come and pick up their kids. The art teacher Mr. Brown had a group of children in his art class outside on the pavement by the fountain, drawing and painting the buildings. Ron Lavis was there, he was painting the school, Suddenly there was lot of noise from the aircraft engines, bombs exploding and machine gun fire, the noise was incredible.'

Joy Penwarden aged 18 months outside the family shop with her Grandmother Mrs. Copp Circa 1937

Bomb 2 The Strand Bomb

This was the worst single bombing incident in Exmouth during WWII.

The destroyed Strand shops. Men of the Rescue Services, R.A.M.C., Royal Artillery, 477 R.A. Home Guard and Warden's clear the debris in search of the injured

John Middleton

'Mathews the Tailors, Haymes the shoe shop, Lockhart's shop which sold pencils and envelopes etc a Stationers and Pratt's the florist were all completely demolished and Boyce's, the milk-bar and a lot of other shops and buildings around Manchester Street were badly damaged in the raid. We found out later that the bomb had hit the Happy Times shop and bounced across the road, into our shop and exploded next door.'

Albert Brice's (memoires via his daughter)

'As a child during the war, my Father, Albert Brice used to go on trips into town with his Grandfather. They made regular visits to a milk parlour near to Millers Garage (now the market) in The Strand, where they used to sit and have a milk-shake.'

'One day, for some reason, My Dad did not want to go in and so he and Grandfather sat in The Strand gardens instead. They saw a bomb come down on The Strand. It hit a shop opposite the pub, bounced across The Strand destroyed the shops and the Milk Parlour that my Dad would have been in. Unfortunately he lost one of his friends in the attack.'

The Path of The Strand Bomb

This bomb actually landed on Oxford House 43 The Strand, which was then the "Happy-Times" Amusement Arcade. A bustling hive of entertainment.

The bomb entered through the Queen Street side of the roof. It penetrated through three floors, hit a steel girder, ricocheted and left the building via a lower bay window on the front of the building then continued its journey across The Strand.

After leaving the front of the building the bomb hit the corner of one of the air raid shelters and continued on, skidding across the road and into the window of Mathews the Tailors shop, where it exploded on the wall adjoining Haymes shoe shop, a total distance of around 100 Metres.

No. 21 The Strand.
Bickford's the Chemist.

The shop windows were first shattered by machine gun and cannon fire then the bombs hit.

No. 20 The Strand.
Boyce and Sons Jewellers

The right hand side of the shop was completely destroyed. The rest of the building had serious damage and was later repaired.

Fatalities

GEORGE DOMINIC PRICE

No. 19 The Strand.
J.G. Mathews Tailors

Mathews the tailors shop was completely destroyed when the bomb hit the shop next door. Mr. Percy Mathews and Mr. Percy Evans (the Cutter) were working in the shop at the time and had a lucky escape, with the aid of John Middleton, who lived with his Mother, Brother Cecil and his sister Elsie in rented accommodation above the shop.

John Middleton

'We were in out bedroom on the first floor, in bed with the flu at the time. The first thing we heard was aircraft engines and then machine gunning. We heard the windows come in downstairs. I said to my brother "we ought to get out"; we could have then gone to the air raid shelter opposite in the Strand. Cecil started his journey down the stairs with me, but decided to go back for his coat and his clothes. I stood on the stairs and waited in my pyjamas and bare feet. While he was getting his clothes the bomb struck. It went in through our building and exploded next door. There was a loud bang and I couldn't see a thing for dust. I was covered in it and could smell and even taste it.'

'As the dust cleared I looked around and could see that all that was left of the buildings where I had been standing was the stair case I was still in my pyjamas

Top: *The Rescue Squad working in the wreckage of Bickford's, Boyce's, Mathews, Haymes, Lockhart's and Pratt's Shops*

Above: *The Rescue Squad and F.A.P. working in the area around Pratt's shop and Betty's milk bar*

and surrounded by rubble. I had cuts to my hands and feet but was otherwise unhurt. All this happened in a round a minute I suppose, it was so quick, I don't think it could have been much longer.'

'My Brother Cecil was buried in the ruins, but I didn't know where he was, as the dust was everywhere. The stairs only were the only thing left and they were covered with huge pieces of debris.'

'Mr. Evans (the Cutter), Mr. Mathews (the shop owner) and Mrs. Field (who worked in the shop), were all buried in the rubble along with Cecil.'

'I walked down the stairs and over the rubble. I heard Mrs. Field was calling and went over to her, she had head injuries.

I told her I was going for help and I managed to get over the rubble and asked someone to help. I didn't have to look very far. The emergency services must have arrived very quickly.'

'As I returned to tell Mrs. Fields that help was on its way I came across Mr. Mathews and Mr. Evans their heads were showing just above the rubble and spoke *to them, I went back over the rubble to talk to the rescue services again and within a very short time, some of the rescue squad came along to dig them out. I also told them that I had been with my brother and could not find him and that he was probably buried.'*

'Our neighbours the Hancock's had a shop called Haymes shoes. I could see in the workshop at the back there was the remains of a body and the store at the back of Mathews shop, which we also rented by us, was partially demolished.'

'I could see rubble everywhere in the street and the Harts bus, which stopped outside Lockhart's was destroyed in the blast. A lot of people were killed and injured there. There were people everywhere in the street all trying to help where they could.'

Still in his pyjamas, John went off to see if he could find his Mum who had been shopping at the time. He looked around the usual places that she may have called in to on her way and eventually found her.

On Saturday October 16th 1943 John was presented with a silver watch and chain at the Y.M.C.A. on Imperial Road, by the British Legion for his courage and bravery whilst assisting the trapped people in the bomb damaged buildings. Mr. Mathews, Mr. Evans and Mrs. Fields along with the British Legion and others donated money to purchase the watch from Boyce the Jewellers.

John Middleton
'It was a silver watch, on which was engraved this on the back.'

"To John Middleton for Courage, February 26 1943"

The watch is now in the hands of his nephew for safe keeping. When I asked, John, about his feelings over the years about the incident, he said:

'I have thought about it many times, but have never felt emotional about it, I just reacted to the situation as it unfolded as I was the only one that could help in the first instance.'

'I think that the last 60-70 years of my life have been a bonus, because it could have been me that was killed. I've often thought how lucky I've been in my life, but not financially with money, just quality of my life and friendships.'

He went on to say:

'I know how they feel when I see terrorist bombings on the television and sympathise with people, I know just what it feels like.'

Fatalities
IVA CORDELIA EVELINE HOLME

Mike Heard finished work at around 12.30 for lunch and rode his bike down Victoria Road towards the town centre.

Mike Heard
'It was an awful sight, rubble and injured everywhere. The police were forming a cordon round the area and asked me to move on quickly. The clothes from the Tailor's shop were all strewn about the trees in The Strand, which made them look just like Christmas trees.'

No.18 The Strand.
W.F. Haymes Boot and Shoe Store

Haymes the shoe shop had been at 18 The Strand since December 1939. Mr Walter Hancock and his Daughter Miss. Margaret Hancock were killed as they worked at their family run business.

Mary Acton
'February 26th was a cold but bright sunny morning. I was making my way to Lloyds Bank (on The Strand) to pay in W.H. Smiths previous days cash. I made my way along the shops leading to the bank, which is on the corner. There were people waiting as usual on the opposite side of the road for the Littleham bus. I was served quite quickly in the bank that day, local shops often came in with large canvas bags of coins which needed counting.'

'I left the bank, on the way back to the bookstall and passed Boyce's Jewellers and Mathews the tailors and came to the shop of Mr Hancock, it was a shoe shop and one of my best friends was his daughter Margaret, she worked in the shop with her Dad. She had cleared the window and was re-arranging the stock, we chatted for a while and then I realised I'd better get off to W.H. Smiths. I said goodbye to Margaret and waved goodbye to her Dad who was in the back of the shop.'

'Margaret and her Dad died in the ruins of their shop and I often wondered, if I hadn't been served so quickly, whether I would have died too. I felt very guilty for a long time afterwards.'

Fatalities
MARGARET PATRICIA HANCOCK
WALTER EDWARD HANCOCK
ELSIE KATE TINDALL

No.17. The Strand.
Lockhart's the Stationers.

Mike Slater

'I remember going in to Lockhart's shop, early in the war, I was in a push chair at the time. It had Chinese lanterns hanging up on the outside and inside there was a series of small passage-ways. The shops weren't very deep and not very tall, not like they are now. They sold stationery as well as toys and games, paper chains, rubbers, and Christmas goods; it was a fantastic shop for a child.'

Fatalities

ALICE REBECCA LOCKHART
FLORENCE BERTHA PIDSLEY

The remains of the Hart's bus after the raid

The Bus Stop and Harts Bus

In The Strand people were waiting for the 12.15 Harts bus service to Budleigh Salterton and Otterton. Some passengers were already on board and others were still on the street waiting to board. When people heard the anti- aircraft fire, the aircraft firing and the report from the bomb at Louisa Terrace some ran into the shops for cover.

Elizabeth Maycock

'I had a detailed account from my mother Grace Maycock, about the bombing in The Strand. We used to catch the Harts Bus to go into the town.

'On the day The Strand was bombed, Mum and my younger sister Anne got on the bus and set off for town and did the shopping. They were about to catch the Harts bus back from the bus stop outside the shoe shop on The Strand. They had just come from Market Street, near the little shop that had the library books. They were headed along the Parade towards the bus stop and about to board the bus when she remembered she still had Granddad's library book.

She thought it best to take the book back so returned to the shop.'

'They heard a lot of noise and commotion when they were in the shop. She then retraced her footsteps with Anne back along the Parade and could see the bus was on fire. Boyce's the Jewellers was hit, along with other shops in the area. The terrace was completely destroyed.'

Mike Heard

'I remember the bus was completely destroyed outside a shop at The Strand, it belonged to Mrs. Hart of Budleigh. The driver sat in his cab to one side of the bus and it had a curved back. All the windows were broken and the body-work looked as if it had been pushed down over the chassis by a giant hand.'

Many other shops in The Strand suffered considerable damage. The whole row of shops from Manchester Street to Bickford's the Chemist was destroyed.

Fatalities

FRANCES LOUISA TOTHILL
ELIZABETH ROSAMUND WILLIAMS

Peggy Gibbins

'Miss Williams who lived at Mamhead View was killed at the bus stop in The Strand. Her sister Mrs. Tothill who was with her was killed as well. Both were well known Catholics in the town.'

Fatalities

HAZEL ANN EVANS
MARY KATHERINE MOORE HUDSON
BEATRICE LANG
HORATIO JOHN GAY LANG
OLIVE JANE LETTEN
MARY JANE MILLER
NORA DOROTHY NIGHTINGALE
ROBERT JOSEPH NIGHTINGALE
PETER GEORGE TURNER

Authors Note

The Man listed below used two names whilst he lived in Exmouth and this can sometimes lead to confusion in the total of fatalities recorded at The Strand.

HERBERT HENRY NIEBOUR
JOHN H. CLARK (second name)

Pratt's Florists and Dairy Produce

This shop was a Fruiterers and Florists shop, and was situated on the corner of Manchester Street and The Strand.

Ivor Pike

Ivor is the brother of Miss Freda Pike, who, was working in Pratt's shop at the time of the detonation.

'She said they did not hear "Moaning Minnie", the air raid siren, but they could hear shooting and aircraft engines.'

'Mrs. Pratt told Freda and another girl that worked in the shop to go through to the back of the shop and into the "Milk Room". A tiny room like a larder, to shelter from the attack. They had just made it into the milk room when they heard an explosion.'

After the explosion Freda and the others were alive and well.

'Mrs. Pratt and Freda were helped from the rubble by onlookers badly shaken, but luckily unhurt. Many people who had run into the shop for shelter were killed in the blast, as they were running through to the back of the shop.'

No. 16 The Strand. Betty's Milk Bar

Mike Slater

'The inside of Betty's Milk Bar was colourfully decorated. It had camels on the walls and paintings of desert scenes, like an oasis. I'd been taken in there for a milkshake a few times before it was bombed out.'

The F.A.P. and the Rescue Services work in the wreckage behind Pratt's shop and Betty's Milk Bar

Joy Penwarden in her Pram outside Penwarden's Tobacconist and Confectioners

No. 15 The Strand. W.R. Penwarden Tobacconist and Confectioner

Joy Penwarden

'I had just come home for lunch from Mrs. Webbers School. It was a Private School on Exeter Road. I was in the back room of the shop, playing with dolls and my dolls house when The Strand bomb dropped. Dad rushed from the shop and pushed me down on the floor and lay over the top of me. The glass from the fan-light was smashed and dolls house was broken. I still think of it now. The windows of the dolls house were broken and the curtains seemed to be tied up in knots.'

'I remember going back to school in the afternoon and wasn't all that bothered by it and apart from my dolls house, I don't remember much about it.'

No. 13 The Strand Louvil's Ladies Garments and Lingerie

Rene Ide

'At the age of 15 I was working in Louvil's shop on The Strand. I was taken on as an apprentice in the fashion trade. I was taught all aspects of the job, sales, alterations, fittings for dresses and mending clothes, sometimes I had to model clothes too!'

Rene was sent up the road to the Westminster Bank in Rolle Street to bank the money and coupons.

'After handing in the money, I came back to the shop and I noticed the sun was shining on a hat in the window which may have faded it badly, so I told my boss Mrs. Larkworthy and got her permission to get some tissue and climbed in the window to cover the hat. I was just going through the internal door from the shop, to climb in the window and suddenly heard a lot of gunfire, shouting and lots of noise. Mrs. Larkworthy grabbed me and pulled me across the shop and under the stairs. The girls from the work room above raced down the stairs and squeezed in under with us. There was a terrific explosion and dust, broken glass and the window dressings were blown in. The goods had all disappeared from the window. It suddenly went very dark and there was a very quiet, still sensation in the air.'

'The next thing I knew, the men from Millers Garage were calling in to us "Is everyone all right in there". We all answered and shouted back. We were so thankful to be alive! It only seemed to last a few minutes. There was cannon fire and the bomb it was over in a very short time.'

'I was absolutely terrified at the time, but thankful to be alive. I was shaking and absolutely stunned. I tried to pull myself my self together. Miss Villette Wreford, the owner of the business was a V.A.D. with first aid

skills, she looked outside and we could see people were hurt. She told me to go and fetch a bowl of water. The only water that we had in the shop was three floors up! I was shaking so much, but managed to get the bowl of water down the stairs without spilling too much! I took it too her. It was sheer, chaos!'

'There were lots of men everywhere trying to clear things up and rescue people. In The Strand Gardens there were bodies on the grass, which may have been laid out, or had ended up there in the blast. They were not covered by any blankets or anything, I was still shaking all the way home later.'

An American Sherman deep wading tank rolls past the cleared site in the Salute the Soldier Parade

Hazel Bradford

'We weren't married at the time, but my husband John Rowsell was an A.R.P. Warden, said he was working on a building near The Strand on this day and went to the scene of the bombing there. He had to report for duty as a Warden when there was an incident. He told me that he saw body parts and clothing in the trees outside the shops, he was only about 17 at the time. It must have been horrible."

Joy Thorn was working at Pankhurst's Engineering on the Railway Station end of the Parade, at the time of the raid on The Strand.

The rebuilt shops in The Strand as they are today

Joy Thorn

'I went on to work in Pankhurst's Engineering on the Parade, making 2 Pounder anti-Tank Gun shells. On the day of The Strand Bombing I was at work. Around midday I heard terrific bangs. Arthur Clode the Foreman, told us to get under the heavy engineering benches immediately. I then heard the Roof light window above the desk shatter and heard glass falling on to my bench and all around. When we re-emerged some bullets were embedded in some of the benches. I ran straight home to George Street to tell mum that I was all right.'

Bomb Number 3
"White Cottage" Raddenstile Lane.

This was the home of Colonel L. Thornton and was a well known and popular figure in the town. He held several voluntary posts. Colonel Thornton's wife Mrs. Leta Thornton and two other ladies, Miss Perham and Miss Down were killed in the raid.

Fatalities

LETITIA ANNA LESTOCK-THORNTON
SARAH DOWN
ALICE LOUISA PERHAM

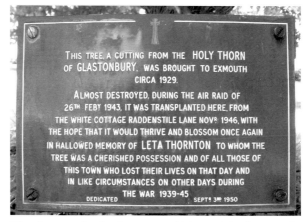

The plaque under the thorn tree, which stands in the grounds of Holy Trinity Church, as a memorial to Leta Thornton and the other victims of the raid.

Bomb Number 4 No.1 Windsor Square

The Exmouth District Nursing Association Headquarters.

This building was home to three District Nurses, who would travel out into the local community to administer medical aid to the bedridden and elderly and also supplied midwifery services.

Alfie Bolt

'The houses on the corner opposite the Gasometer had been hit by a bomb and were destroyed. There had been a pair of three storey semi-detached houses like the others in Windsor Square which are still there now.'

Pearl Cawse

'I had just finished school and had walked up to the nurses home to meet my Mum and Aunty just after 12 o'clock on the Friday. On the way I passed an old man who was struggling up the hill.'

'My Mum was in the kitchen at the back of the house with Aunt Phil who was, making a suet pudding for the nurse's lunch, deciding whether to put in all the fruit they had left or not.'

'Mum said "I won't be long." and went out to the front of the house to do something. I chatted with Aunt Phil whilst waiting for Mum to finish work. Suddenly, Mum appeared shouting and grabbed both of us and pushed us out of the back door of the building and down stone steps to the garden. She then took us over to the high garden wall to shelter.'

'I didn't fully realise what was going on at the time, but mum must have heard the sound of the planes and the gunfire from the front garden. The next thing I knew there was a rushing sound. It went dark, with dirt and dust blown all over us from a blast. It felt like strong wind. Everything happened very quickly and it took me by surprise. After the blast, all three of us were unhurt and the thing I noticed most was Mum's hair. It was standing on end, thick with dirt and dust.'

Fatalities

JOHN PONSFORD

The private house that stands on the site of the District Nursing Headquarters today

Bomb 5. The Gasometer and Allotments on Albion Hill

The Gasometer was hit by a bomb which bounced from the allotment on Albion Hill and then punctured the Gasometer without detonating, re-emerging on the other side and detonating in a house which stood in the gasworks grounds. It was also hit it in the side and on the top by cannon fire. It was set on fire and collapsed as the escaping gas burned off. Thomas Maxwell was working in his allotment on Albion Hill and was killed by cannon fire during this stage of the attack.

Jack Humphries

'This attack happened at lunch time, I was at Withycombe School and had just left school for my lunch and was cycling home. My cousin June was with me and cycling just ahead of me. I was aware that the raid had started when we reached the corner of Exeter Road and Albion Street I could hear aircraft engines and explosions. We turned off Exeter Road to cycle up Albion Street, on our usual route home. Rosie Upcott was at the bottom of Albion Street and with us by this time.'

'We were approximately three shops up from the bottom of Albion Street, outside the Milliners, called Cranes. My cousin June had rushed into the shop and shut the door tight behind her, shutting me and Rosie out on the street. June hid under the counter with the lady in the shop. We quickly lay down flat on the ground as we had been told to do by the school. We were laid on the pavement, by our bikes, with our hands over our heads, I was wearing big yellow leather gauntlets at the time, which I always wore when cycling in cold weather.

'Several planes were flying in very fast from the direction of the gasworks headed for the Parade and the Station; they were so low you could clearly see the pilots. One plane was very close to us and as it came over firing its machine guns and cannon, it released a bomb. There were more explosions and the Milliners shop window was blown out and most of it landed on Rosie, she was completely covered in glass but luckily unhurt. I kept looking up to see what was going on. I knew the planes were Focke Wulf's, as we had done a lot of aircraft recognition.'

'The combination of sounds that I can remember at the time was, machine gun and cannon fire and enormous explosions from up the road, and aircraft noise, there was a lot going on.

It was only a short attack, only a couple of minutes long! There was dust and in the air and small pieces of brick and stone rained down all over the place, landing on us, but not hurting us.'

Top left: *The entry point of the bomb*
Top right: *The exit point of the bomb*
Lower left: *The finished repair to the entry hole*
Lower right: *The finished repair to the exit hole*
Above: *The repaired gasometer still in service today*

'*Further up the road I could see the buildings were being hit by cannon fire. As quickly as it had started the machine gunning stopped and the aircraft had past and disappeared. The smell of cordite, or some type of explosive was quite strong and I could also smell gas. We stood up and brushed ourselves off and looked up Albion Street and could see that the Gasometer was badly alight with a huge amount of flame gushing out of the top of the Gasometer, like a big ball of fire. I was worried that it might explode so thought it best to get away from the area quickly. To be honest it was all very exciting from where I was.*'

Alfie Bolt now lives directly opposite the Gasometer and witnessed it burning at the time.

Alfred Bolt

'*I was asked to get some wood from the boss's house and to block up the window and remove a branch*

which had been blown down the road through the window.' I walked up Albion Street towards Albion Terrace where my boss lived and could see that the Gasometer was on fire.'

'*I saw it burning. The flames were pouring out from the side of the tank no smoke just flames. My sister was coming back from Exeter on the railway line and she could see it from there.*'

Tony Carpenter

Tony Carpenter was a gas fitter for Willey's of Exeter and was called to the scene a few days later to help with the repairs.

'*My boss was a clever man and came up with all sorts of ingenious ways of extinguishing and blocking the holes to prevent gas escaping, one of the methods used was sand bags filled with wet oats which were dumped over the holes or forced in to the holes on the sides of the tank as a temporary measure.*'

'*A few days later I had to go to the site where work had started to repair the gas holder. I was there for a total of about three months until I had to go in to the R.A.F. We used large rubber bungs with plates and threaded bolts which were forced into the cannon shell holes and then tightened up so the rubber expanded to fill the gaps. We used the oat filled sandbags where we found smaller leaks. The main holes where the bomb had entered and left by the other side, had 5 foot by 5 foot, one quarter of an inch thick steel plates welded over the top of them as a patch. The cannon holes also had smaller plates welded over them and the bungs removed. Some of the riveted seams on the gas holders sides had been knocked badly out of shape and we had to weld one and a half inch steel angle over the seams and then re-rivet the seams.*'

'*When the repair to the gas holder was near to being finished it had to be pumped up with air, to check that the seal was true. This happened several times. Eventually the gas holder was completely repaired. By this time I had been called up into the R.A.F. It took nearly six months before it was completely restored.*'

Derek Rowsell

'*One bomb hit the Gasometer. It was on the same day as The Strand was hit. The bomb went straight through a section and out the other side, exploding on an empty house on the gas company's land. People could see the Gasometer burning from all over the town. The flames were huge. The house was virtually demolished and the wreckage of the house was all piled up on the corner of Albion Hill and Montpelier Road, in the Gasometer grounds. You could also see the patches on the Gasometer quite clearly and if you look carefully, they are still there now.*'

Derek Rowsell thankfully, rescued the photographs of the Gasometer repairs executed by Willey's of Exeter when they shut down many years later. He just couldn't bear to see them thrown away. Many people thought the Gasometer was only hit by cannon fire. It was certain that at the time, the story was suppressed locally, so as not to worry the residents.

Thomas Maxwell, a retired Policeman and Licensee of the Clarence Inn, was working in his allotment approx 100 metres away from the Gasometer on Albion Hill. He was killed by 20mm cannon fire.

Fatalities

THOMAS MAXWELL

Exeter Road All Saints Hall

Brian Baker

'Our Teachers realised what was happening. They told us all to get under the tables quickly, which we did. The raid didn't last long only a couple of minutes. When it was considered safe by our teachers we came out from under our tables and then assembled in the playground.'

Halsdon Road

No. 27 Halsdon Road was hit by cannon and machine gun fire as was No.42 where Ena Ward was killed by cannon fire.

Fatalities

ENA GWENDOURA WARD

Woodville Road

Ray Challis' House 6 Woodville Road was hit:

Ray Challis

'When I got home from school I was shown where a bullet went in my gran and grandad's bedroom window, smashing the glass in the front of the house. It went between the bars of their big old cast-iron framed bed and stuck into the wall behind the headboard. My Grandad wasn't very well and spent a lot of time upstairs in his bedroom. He had a lucky escape on that day.'

Hazel Bradford

'One day my friend had to go for a medical check up. We were at school and I had to go with her, for some reason we always had to go in two's for this sort of thing. The appointment was at the school clinic, which was on Exeter Road right by where the railway arch crossed the road. Suddenly we heard a lot of noise. The sound of planes and machine guns firing.

We laid down in the gutter, we dived down, thinking we may get hurt. The planes flew right over us and were at roof-top height, it was so quick.'

Bomb 6. EXETER ROAD

This bomb detonated at the Branch of Exeter Road, Gypsy Lane and Hulham Road opposite Southlands. The house was completely destroyed. It was the home of the Southon family.

Ray Challis

'Mrs. Southon managed to get into the Morrison shelter, but her home help, Mrs. Parsons, who was following behind her still had one leg out of the steel cage and when the building collapsed on top of them, it was crushed.'

'The Rescue services managed to dig them out of the wreckage still thankfully, both alive, but the maid had a severely injured leg which she subsequently lost.'

Exmouth Grammar School

Word quickly spread in the town that the Grammar School 100 metres away had been hit. (mistakenly), by a bomb. It was hit by a few rounds of cannon fire and the pupils were badly shaken by the explosion.

Jean Acton

'I was at the Grammar school during the day at the time of the raid. I was sat in a geography lesson I could here noises, explosions which I knew was bombs going off. I could also hear the noise of aircraft. I could see the planes for a while flying very fast and low. One dropped a bomb which came in at an angle. As quick as I could I dived under the desks. After coming out from under the desk, I looked out of the window and could see feathers coming down outside which looked like snow.'

Geoff Perriam

'The inside of the School windows were covered in a fine-gauge wire net, to stop the glass being blown in. When the Exeter Road bomb dropped we heard an enormous bang and the windows did blow in but most of the big shards of glass were kept out.'

'When we eventually emerged from under our desks, everything was very quiet we couldn't see across the playground as there was a thick cloud of dust and fine debris.'

'In the mesh over the window where I was sitting, a shell splinter (shrapnel) about 3cms x 2cms across was embedded in the wire, I kept this as a souvenir for many years after the war but it eventually got thrown away.'

Bomb 7. "Oakmead" Phillipps Avenue

The bomb demolished 2 homes, sharing a common roof.

Robert Knowling lived at "Helston", Number 1 Seymour Road with his mother and father. He was off school for the day as he was ill.

Robert Knowling

'I was sent by my mother to borrow some sugar for making bread, from a family friend, Mrs. Jones who lived in Seymour Road. I went up to the leaded light front door and knocked. There was no reply (she was in but didn't hear him) so I went round the side of the house to the back door. I looked up and saw a plane I could see the pilot. It was headed south towards Phillipps Avenue, less than a quarter of a mile away. I heard an explosion and by the time I went to return home, the front door of Mrs. Seymour's house I was stood knocking at earlier was gone! Destroyed in the blast'

Fatalities

GRESHAM HUGH POWELL WILLIAMS

Bomb 8. The Signal Box and the Railway Track.

The bomb detonated by the Railway track. The track was broken and was closed on the river side of the Viaduct and Exeter Road railway bridge. It damaged the signal box and windows and roofs of the surrounding area.

The Train

Bernard Greenaway

'The Budleigh train was hit by cannon fire from Focke Wulf 190's in an air raid in 1943. The train had just left the station and was headed along the Budleigh Branch Line.'

Anonymous Eyewitness

'Machine gunning went on all over the town and the train leaving was peppered.'

The R.A.F. Response to the Raid

Two Typhoons from 266 Squadron based at Exeter were dispatched to deal with the raiders.

Air Ministry News Service

Two of the FW 190s were shot down by Squadron Leader Charles Green C/O of 266 "Rhodesia" Squadron and Flight Sergeant Richard K. Thompson.

10/JG 2 Aircraft Shot Down by 266 Rhodesia Squadron

Fw190-A4 WkNr 735.

Pilot: Feldwebbel Hermann Rohne –Missing.
Shot down 50 miles south- south east of Exmouth, by Squadron Leader C.L. Green. 12.13 p.m.

FW 190A-5 WkNr 2588.

Pilot: Unterofizzier Kurt Bressler.
Shot down by Squadron leader C.L. green and Sergeant R.K. Thompson. 12.15 p.m.

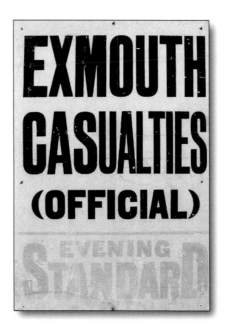

Chapter 25
The Americans

The Arrival of the Americans

America entered the war after the bombing of Pearl Harbor in Hawaii by the Japanese on December 7th 1941. The first American servicemen came to Exmouth in small numbers in 1942 and more arrived in late 1943. Finally men from the 12th Infantry Regiment rolled into town by train in early February 1944. During this period nearly 4,000 American service men and women were billeted in the community and under canvas in the town.

Winnifred Gliddon
'Around October 1943 some Americans moved in to the Burtons 50/- Tailors shop. They lived over the top of the shop. Burtons was on from the corner of Staples Buildings and the window stretched right round the corner. We made friends with Johnny Ray and other American soldiers.'

1 Engineer Special Brigade and 531 Engineer Shore Regiment

Paul O' Wood
'We arrived in Exmouth on 11 December 1943, having come to England from the Mediterranean Theatre after participating in the landings in French North Africa, Tunisia, Sicily and Italy.'

'Upon arrival in Exmouth we were told we were to be given a period of rest and relaxation, an opportunity to enjoy ourselves. This we set about with delirious

American Soldiers equipment from the 531st Shore Regiment and the 4th Infantry Division

Above left: *1st Engineer Special Brigade sleeve badge*
Above right: *531st Engineer Shore Regiment badge on M1943 jacket pocket*
Below: *U.S. First Sergeant Hackett (1st Army) and Rosalie Tarr sitting in the front garden of 102 Exeter Road in 1944*

enthusiasm- Happy to be relieved of combat duty, temporarily at least and thinking ourselves lucky to be stationed in such a lovely, friendly little town as Exmouth.'

'After 13 months of monotonous field rations, we were provided with a fully equipped kitchen and Mess Hall and able to serve foods not seen for some time, such as bread, potatoes, fresh vegetables and powdered eggs.'

'We also began to find the other pleasures available in Exmouth, such as the pubs. Fish and Chips in Forte's Café, which had speciality dishes of beans on toast and Welsh Rarebit.'

'We would also visit Clapp's Café, the Savoy Cinema and the Exmouth Pavilion. The latter provided on Saturday nights, one of the most eagerly sought pleasures that had been denied us – the company of young ladies. Moreover, we found the good people of Exmouth to be extremely friendly and most eager to invite us into their own homes, where we were always made to feel welcome.'

'As a result of this hospitality, all the G.I.s, like myself became like a group of children turned loose in Disney World and our morale reached its highest point of the war.'

Richard Tarr

'Sergeant Hackett was one of the American Engineers who was billeted with us. He was a really good man. All the Americans who stayed were very good to me. One day before they left for good, he brought home some booby trap switches.'

'There were three. One was a box that you put in a book, or could be concealed under a book or hinged lid or even fixed to a door. It was connected to a time pencil or an instantaneous fuse.'

'The next one was a rectangular plate with a tube and a fuse with a spring loaded plunger. When you trod on it you broke the fuse and it would detonate instantaneously.'

'The final one was about the size of a candle with a ring on the end to attach to a trip wire, which in turn could be placed across a road or on the back of a door handle. I would lay them under the carpet in the house loaded with caps, to fool the Americans. They had a lot of fun and said it was "good training".'

The 4 Infantry Division

On the 1 August 1943, the 4th Division's 12 Infantry Regiment was reorganized as a standard infantry regiment, converting back to its original role from a motorized infantry regiment.

On Jan 13 1944 men from the 12 Infantry Regiment, boarded H.M.S. Esperance in New York, headed for Liverpool. The Regiment along with the rest of the 4th Infantry Division arrived in England on 29th January 1944. They then travelled from Liverpool by train on to Exmouth.

The first Americans servicemen came to Exmouth in small numbers in 1942. The majority arrived in late 1943 and the 4 Infantry Division and its support troops arrived en masse in January 1943.

In WWI they had taken the symbol of the "ivy leaf" as their badge, it was a pun on the Roman numeral IV, or four.

Ray Challis

'I was on the viaduct talking to the soldiers on the ack-ack guns. We used to take them a cup of tea. I saw an extremely long train of 12 carriages pulled by two steam engines that was headed along the track from the Littleham direction. This was extremely unusual as only small trains of two carriages, or a few trucks normally used this route.'

Ray went alongside the train. It was full of American troops. The Americans shouted to him to come over which he did and saw for the first time the soldiers dressed in their different uniforms. He noticed how young they looked as most were about 18 or 19 years of age, black and white and they didn't look a lot older than him. Some of the soldiers were hanging out of the windows of the train.

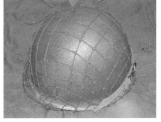

Top: *British Traps No.1 switch, Spring Detonator*

Centre: *British Traps No.2 switch. Pressure Detonator*

Above: *British Traps No.3 switch. Trip wire Detonator*

Top: *U.S. Corporal Harold Strickland*

Above: *American M1 Steel Helmet*

Above right: *Harold Strickland with Richard Tarr*

Right: *U.S. Army 4th Infantry Division (The "Ivy" boys) badge on M1943 jacket*

Above left: *U.S. Army Private Foot in the Front Garden of 102 Exeter Road*

Above right: *P.F.C. Foot, Corporal Harold Strickland, Richard Tarr and Rosalie Tarr*

Left: *American "Class A" jacket and M1943 field jacket*

'Hey kid! What's this place?' said one of the soldiers. Ray replied instantly *"Exmouth"* without thinking. They exchanged a few more words, the signal changed and the long train drew in to Exmouth Station.

' *I was anxious about saying to the troops where they were, because it was careless talk, but I was so excited, because for the first time I thought we wouldn't lose now'*

The arrival of the Americans brought with them a renewed spirit of enthusiasm, optimism and a certain

American G.I. *"Wayne" with Richard Tarr*

U.S. Army First Sergeant Hackett wearing M1943 Jacket and overseas *"Garrison" Cap with Rosalie Tarr*

George Gonzalez 12th Infantry Regiment U.S. 4th Infantry Division, wearing "Class A" uniform

"Exotic" liveliness to the town. Most of the people in Exmouth had never come into contact with Americans before the war and had only experienced their lifestyle and culture through performances on the "silver screen" at the cinema and occasional broadcasts by American musicians on the wireless.

The Americans cheerful, can-do attitude became infectious and stimulated the local residents and brought a wonderful sense of goodwill to the town.

Hazel Bradford
'George Gonzalez was from the Cannon Company. He became a very good friend of mine and I was his pen-pal for a time. He was a private in the 12 Infantry Regiment. He had served in Italy first, before coming to Exmouth.'

Billeting the Americans

Joe Radgick
'We had Americans billeted with us in 1944, we didn't know it at the time but they were destined for the Normandy landings on D-Day. One night a Sergeant came and brought two soldiers to live with us. They

shared a room at the end of the house. You had to take them, you had absolutely no choice in the matter, and he said "Let me know if they give you any trouble and I'll sort them out". We liked them immensely, they were absolutely charming. They were with us from about two months before D-Day and were very young.'

Hazel Bradford

'A lot of the American soldiers were billeted in the community in private houses, we had some staying with us. We made good friends with some of the soldiers. They were polite, friendly and very grateful for whatever we could do for them.'

'They were very young and there was only a few years difference between us really. I made friends with Otto, Clifton, Max and George. They were all from the same unit.'

Americans Under Canvas

Hazel Bradford

'Soldiers from the American 4th Infantry Division were billeted in Phear Park in tents. Some were also in the big Manor House, called Marpool Hall, which was in the Park. They were camping in six-man tents. At first there was only a dozen or so and they were set up under the trees. Later they went right the way from the bottom school to the top school. We weren't allowed in when the area got busy.'

Bernard Greenaway

'In January 1944 I used to got through Phear Park on the way to and from school. I noticed that tents were being erected. They were allocated tents six men to a tent. One man was a sergeant or senior N.C.O. and the other five were rookies.'

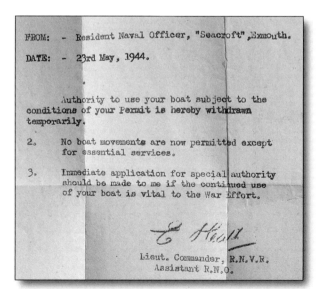

FROM: - Resident Naval Officer, "Seacroft", Exmouth.

DATE: - 23rd May, 1944.

    Authority to use your boat subject to the conditions of your Permit is hereby withdrawn temporarily.

2.   No boat movements are now permitted except for essential services.

3.   Immediate application for special authority should be made to me if the continued use of your boat is vital to the War Effort.

               Lieut. Commander, R.N.V.R. Assistant R.N.O.

Order sent to Exmouth boat owners on May 23rd 1944 withdrawing permission to use small boats, in preparation for D-Day

Joe Radgick

'The Americans Soldiers were camped in Littleham. Some in the fields in tents and also huts which were erected there. The rest were billeted in the homes of the local community. They had a lot of equipment and some anti-aircraft guns at the site, in the field.'

Training

Joe Radgick

'The Americans practised for D-Day. Loading, unloading and re-loading men and vehicles and weapons into the Duck's (D.U.K.W. amphibious G.M.C. Trucks) There were jeeps and trucks everywhere, the docks were absolutely full of L.C.M.'s (landing Craft Mechanised) and L.C.I's (Landing Craft Infantry).'

Exercise Tiger

Hazel Bradford

'One day they had to go off very early in the morning and he said to us "Don't worry about us we'll be back in a few days. Tell Mother not to make any breakfast." They did return a few days later and they were really upset. They were crying all the time and no matter what we did, we could not console them. They were in an awful state. When we asked them what the matte was, they said they couldn't tell us anything. It was a terrible weekend but there was nothing we could do to help.

'We only found out years later that a lot of the Americans based in Exmouth had gone on a practise landing where they were supposed to have landed on Slapton Sands in South Devon. Some of the boats had been torpedoed out in Lyme Bay and were sunk, killing hundreds of their men.'

Black Americans

Alfie Bolt

'There were a lot of black American troops stationed in Exmouth at one time. The white Americans didn't get on too well with them but the black soldiers were fine with us.'

John Middleton

'The Americans were everywhere, black and white, but mostly white. They wore their fatigues during the day and the smart uniforms when they went somewhere special, or out on the town during the night.'

'They helped our local economy enormously spending most of their money in the town, shops, pubs, and clubs and loved the Cinema and amusement arcades.'

From left to right: *Donut's were handed out to free to children from the American Red Cross Club-mobile, at the boxing match; U.S.A.A.F. woven badge started appearing when the Americans took over R.A.F. Exeter; American Quonset hut cook-house still on Albion Hill.*

Ray Challis

'During the war the Americans were camped under canvas on the Rugby Ground, near where the Cranford Club is now. Joe Louis the Heavy Weight Boxing Champion was stationed in Exeter for a while and was asked to come to Exmouth to put on a boxing exhibition. The Exmouth kids got wind of it from local G.I.'s and we waited outside at the gate to try and see him give his exhibition, or just to get a glimpse of him.'

John Middleton

'We watched Joe Louis box. He went to the Rugby Ground on the Salterton Road. He did an exhibition bout and then refereed some matches between servicemen.'

Alfie Bolt

Joe Louis the boxer came to fight in Exmouth during the war and we were told he was up by the American hut, but we went to the hut on Albion Hill by mistake and never got to see him fight.'

'The Americans had two large Nissan huts on the Salterton Road Salterton. Just like the one here on Albion Hill. They used to bake bread and cook food in there. It was then taken to other areas to feed the troops.'

General Eisenhower

General "Ike" Eisenhower visited the American troops in Exmouth in May 1944, just before D-Day. Ray Challis was stood on the pavement by All Saints Church on Exeter Road when he noticed a small convoy of vehicles.

Ray Challis

'First came Harley Davidson motorcycles with riders wearing, white helmets. Then a jeep with a wire cutter . T, there was about a half a dozen vehicles in total.'

'My friend Peter Lilly also saw him at The Strand Gardens. The American Military Band were opposite a shop called Griggs, next door to Thomas Tuckers outfitters. There were American troops lined up ready for inspection outside the Methodist Church on the Parade, which had recently been repaired after an earlier bombing raid.'

Exmouth People's thought's about the Americans

It should be remembered that these young Americans had come thousands of miles from across the sea leaving their families, loved ones, younger brothers and sisters and friends, to come and help us in our time of dire need. Many were home-sick, but very seldom complained. Approx 95% of Americans had never ventured out of their own state boundaries before the war, so it shows what an enormous step it must have been for the young soldiers to volunteer to fight in Europe with no guarantee of ever returning home.

Jack Humphries

'The Americans were very kind and generous to children. They gave us sweets and we always asked them for chewing gum, "Got any gum chum?" we used to say, the Wrigley's packaging was very similar to as it is now.'

Ray Challis

'As a teenager I really loved these people. They were kind, helpful, polite, good fun and were always giving the locals food and things that were difficult to get due to rationing. They would make an effort to play with the local children, make things for them, gave them toys at Christmas and birthdays and generally tried hard in every way to fit in with the community. I never had one bad experience with them.'

D-Day

Hazel Bradford

'*Shortly after the Exercise Tiger incident the Americans were due to leave. It was a few day before D-Day but we didn't know it at the time. Again we knew something was up because, they gave us all of their belongings. Probably because of their experiences earlier.*'

'*They left everything with us, photographs, address books and personal belongings too. They also gave us addresses of people in the United States for us to contact at a later date. I used to correspond with Pete's sister Betty for a while towards the end of the war.*'

Peter Mattholie was a sailor on an L.B.V. which had been moored in the estuary for 3 months before D-Day. He trained with the American troops and sailed alongside them to Omaha Beach on D-Day.

Peter Mattholie

'*I was 19 by the time D-Day arrived and quite used to living on the boat as we had been there for three months or more*'

'*We had some weapons and assault training as combined operations troops whilst in Exmouth, in case we got sunk off shore and ended up on the beach with the Rangers. We were expected to fight along side them and wore the combined ops badge of the eagle, tommy gun and anchor on the shoulder of our khaki uniforms. We bought gold bullion ones for our best dress.*'

'*We sailed from Exmouth to Poole harbour a few days before and from Poole to Omaha on the 5th of June. We arrived in the early hours of the morning at Omaha beach. We had equipment for the engineers and Rangers.*'

'*The Crossing was really rough. We weren't really bothered and I was never sea sick or even felt ill. The barges rolled a lot because of the flat bottoms, but a lot of the troops were very ill. When we were going over the channel we were surrounded by small American landing craft. A lot of them had radios blaring out swing music through loudspeakers. There was also the constant sound of aircraft flying overhead the sky was black with them.*'

'*We were holding off the coast when the big battleships and rocket ships opened up. The noise was tremendous, and we could see explosions all over the beach and cliff areas.*'

'*The battle had subsided a bit before we were moved in. The beaches were quite quiet. We made our run in. We had to go right along to the far right hand side of Omaha and thankfully never hit anything under the*

water. *We ran straight up on to the beach and dropped the ramp. They had taken the cliffs on the right and the beach by the time we got ashore and we could hear the noise of the battle moving inland. We had a near miss with a mine which was right by the front of the barge. About two feet away. A little later on a "Duck", just along the beach ran over one of these mines and the front was blown right off and up-ended the vehicle. Luckily we didn't see any casualties.*'

'*We had to wait whilst the bridging equipment and other stuff was taken off our barge and then wait for a further 12 hours for the returning high tide so we would float and could reverse off the beach.*'

Bernard Greenaway

'*I befriended an American a Private First Class called Howard Schwartz. I used to visit him and his friends in their tent in Phear Park. When I was about 14 years old I visited him one day. He knew that the invasion of France would be coming soon, although he did not say anything to me about it. He gave me a small gold plated bible (I have seen this bible) He showed it to me and asked if I would like it, I said "yes please". He wrote the date on which he gave it to me. It says 11/4/1944. He was his platoon's machine gunner and was killed on D-Day. We found this out later when some of his friends returned to Exmouth injured after D-Day.*'

At the services held in Phear Park around the 6th of June every year, we always use this bible to read from, during the service. I will always remember him he was a really good man.'

The Exmouth Memorial to the Americans

Initial approaches were made by residents of Withycombe Village, Exmouth to Lionel Howell regarding two U.S. units based in the town prior to D-Day. He agreed to investigate ways of honouring them for the huge roll they played in the Normandy landings. In 1997, after 6 months of research, both in Britain and the USA, the 531st Tribute Fund was founded. D-Day remembrance services are now an annual event and take place in Exmouth on the Sunday nearest to June 6th each year.

Above left: *British Combined Operations badge*
Above right: *French and American flag day flags, to celebrate the Liberation of Paris.*

Chapter 26
V.E. and V.J. Day

V.E. (Victory in Europe) Day

On 1 May 1945 news reached Exmouth that Hitler was dead. There were big celebrations with the children of the town that day. This was followed by Churchill's speech on 7 May 1945 announcing the unconditional surrender of the Nazis. The treaty had been signed by Field Marshall Montgomery and Admiral Doenitz.

After the unconditional surrender of the Germans was signed, a National Holiday was declared for Tuesday 8 May and Wednesday 9 May 1945. This day became known as V.E. Day or Victory in Europe Day. The nation experienced euphoria, knowing that the Third

Reich had been defeated and soon loved ones would soon be returning and life would be back to normal.

Joy Penwarden
'On V.E. Day we were living at Bradham Lane in Withycombe. About half way along the road everyone had brought long tables out and connected them up. I wore my best frock and we had sandwiches, cakes and other nice things to eat. I said to my dad in all seriousness, "What will the newspapers talk about now?" It's a thought that always stuck with me.'

Exmouth's townsfolk's spontaneous V.E. day party celebrations were on May 8 and the official celebrations were held on May 9 at various locations

The Daily Mirror V.E. news headlines May 8th 1945

The Daily Mirror V.E. news headlines May 9th 1945

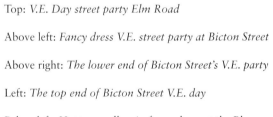

Top: *V.E. Day street party Elm Road*

Above left: *Fancy dress V.E. street party at Bicton Street*

Above right: *The lower end of Bicton Street's V.E. party*

Left: *The top end of Bicton Street V.E. day*

Below left: *Happy revellers in fancy dress at the Phear Avenue V.E. Day street party*

Below right: *V.E. Day Carter Avenue residents*

Top left: *Smiles for the camera at Point Terrace*

Top right: *Salisbury Road V.E. Day street party*

Above left: *Smiling faces and flag waving outside the corner shop at Salisbury Road V.E. Day party*

Above right: *Ivor Pike's family and friends at the Salisbury Road V.E Day party. Mrs. Pike is dressed as a maid, Emily Pike in R.M. best blues, Ivor as Mrs. Mopp and Brian Barr as Colonel Chinstrap from the radio show I.T.M.A.*

Left: *The lower end of Bicton Street's V.E. party*

Lower left: *Plenty to eat at the Salisbury Road street party*

around the town. All of the servicemen and women stationed locally and the American forces attended Special Church thanksgiving services. Exmouth was full of free street entertainment, communal lunches, tea parties and street parties were held, along with bonfire parties, a particularly large one was held at the King George V playing fields.

Salisbury Road

Roy Hole
'I don't remember any real drunkenness amongst the adults. Just a good feeling and high spirits during the day, I can't remember any bad behaviour from the children. Just everyone really happy!'

Ivor Pike
'Some Yanks (Americans) came to the party. They had their own party in a big hall somewhere nearby. With them they brought some sweets. We had sweets galore!

Robert Knowling
'On V.E. Day the 9th Battalion of the Royal Marines played concerts in the Manor Gardens, There were services of thanks giving in The Strand and virtually every house in Exmouth had bunting or flags flying on them or out of the windows. People let off fireworks, made their own bangers and were throwing them about. There was a band playing on the roof of The Strand air raid shelters, both days and nights they performed, they were really good. In The Strand enclosure it was free entertainment, a wonderful time.'

The Strand

Mike Heard
'On V.E. Day the American Big Band from the U.S. Navy Depot at Topsham, played in The Strand on the roof of one of the air raid shelters, everyone was dancing.'

Mary Ashleigh
'There were about 7 sailors climbing the street lamps in The Strand at the V.E. day celebrations. A street party was held at Madeira Villas, I wore my ankle strapped shoes and short socks. Jean Carter dressed up as Britannia, my friends Gillian and Susan Humphries and Valerie Ewings were there too.'

Ivor Pike
'We had a fantastic time. In The Strand they had loudspeakers relaying Bing Crosby singing "Don't Fence Me In" My friend Brian Barr was dressed as Colonel Chinstrap from the I.T.M.A. radio show and I was dressed as Mrs. Mopp, the cleaning lady and walked round saying, "Can I do you now sir?" We loved it! Mum was a dressed as a House-Maid; sister

Young marksmen at the Madeira Villas V.E. party

Bunting, flags and paper hats on May 8th at Madeira Villas

Freda was dressed as a Royal Marine wearing her Boyfriends Best Blues.'

Dennis Pratt (from his unpublished memoirs)
'At 7.00p.m a large crowd gathered in The Strand enclosure to witness a spectacle organised by the army cadets who were camped in the town. Following this, music was relayed for community singing and hundreds of voices blended in boisterous song.'

'Then they danced and danced, in circles and long lines. The whole crowd swayed and bobbed along in unflagging energy. In and around the enclosure they danced and sang, while an orchestra played. The musicians being perched on top of an air raid shelter. The square ugliness of which was relieved in fairy lights.'

'Of the many changes of scene that took place during the day, the one that came at 9.p.m. was the most striking. As the strains of the National Anthem peeled from loud speakers, a sudden hush descended on the milling crowd.'

'People fell into silence as the voice of the King came over the air, thanking people for their courage and endurance and associating himself with their rejoicing, calling them to "build on the old wastes and restore peace-time fullness of life.'

'When the voice ceased the National Anthem sounded again and the crowd turned once more to rejoicing and, apparently inexhaustible, they continued to sing and dance for hours.'

'As night fell a gigantic blaze broke the darkness on the site of the King George V Grounds. A great bonfire, "as high as a house", crackled into life and orange, yellow and red flames sent up great showers of brilliant sparks.'

'Another bonfire blazed up in Windsor Square and yet another in New North Road. In each case the hilarious scenes were re-enacted on a smaller scale.'

'From the King George grounds a big blaze could also be seen on Dawlish Warren. The wavering flames lighting up the ripples on the water. Once again the river reflected the mood of the moment-the mood of a joyful people celebrating the peace, for which they had worked, fought and waited so long.'

'A loud-speaker relayed music in the square behind the now former A.R.P. Headquarters and here again the local residents enjoyed amusing dances. They too carried on until one o' clock in the morning.'

'As the night drew on, however the noise diminished and the shouting and the tumult died. The crowds slowly dispersed, wending their way wearily but joyfully back home to bed.'

'The service men, gaily bedecked in national colours, many of whom were far from their own homes, also quietly disappeared from the streets. The dancers vanished and once again the town wrapped itself in slumber. This time the sleep of happy exhaustion.'

V.J. (Victory over Japan) Day

The unconditional surrender of the Japanese forces took place on Wednesday 14 August 1945. The British Government declared public holidays for parties for August 15 and 16.

Robert Knowling
'For V.J. day there were not such big celebrations in Exmouth. They were held on the 15 and 16 August and were both declared public holidays in Exmouth.'

Roy Hole
'On our final Scout camp to Buckfastleigh we went on a 16 mile hike. When we reached Buckland in the Moor, the locals told us that the war with Japan was over and they invited us to go to their village V.J. day celebrations. It was great. Real country entertainment, with the greasy pole, pillow fights whilst sitting on poles, apple dunking and lots of food.'

John Middleton
'We lived in Albion Street during the war. On V.J. day me and some of my friends, went for a swim by the slipway, we then cycled to Kentisbeare to see my Gran. It was lovely weather, Gran gave us a slice of cake each, and then we cycled back again. We went passed Exeter airport and had a look at all the planes. There was all sorts of planes there. It was a really good day.'

The Daily Herald *headlines August 16th 1945*

V.E. Day party Manchester Street just off The Strand

The Strand

Dennis Pratt

'Among the throng was an American officer. Spontaneously he suggested that there should be an act of thanksgiving. With no religious person present the crowd, to a person, sang "Abide with Me", as well as saying the Lord's Prayer.'

'In procession the crowd then paraded the streets, letting the whole town know by way of their happy cheering and singing that final hostilities had ceased.'

'It was a day to remember!'

Ray Challis

'I always think when I am at the War Memorial, in The Strand on Remembrance Sunday. You'd never realise it now, but this too was once a front line war zone, so many people were killed and injured right here by enemy action.'

Above: *The Battle of Britain Memorial on the seafront*

Right: *The seafront War Memorial and the inscription on the seafront War Memorial*

SECOND WORLD WAR
1939 - 1945

THIS FLAGPOLE MEMORIAL
WAS DEDICATED ON 20TH AUGUST 1995
TO MARK THE 50TH ANNIVERSARY OF
THE END OF WORLD WAR II
AND TO OFFER THANKSGIVING FOR ALL THOSE MEN,
WOMEN AND CHILDREN FROM ALL NATIONS
WHO SUFFERED AND MADE THE SUPREME SACRIFICE

"WE WILL REMEMBER THEM"

"NOW LET US ALL LIVE IN PEACE"
1995

The inscription on the Strand War Memorial where the civilian casualties names and the servicemen and women's names are commemorated.

Select Bibliography

Aircraft Verses Aircraft Illustrated
By Norman Franks, Published by Bantam Press.

Battle Of Britain
By Len Deighton, Published by Book Club Associates.

Blackshirts In Devon
By Todd Gray, Published By The Mint Press.

Britains Air Defences 1939-45
By Dr. Alfred Price, Illustrations by Darko Pavlovic.
Published by Osprey Publishing.

Britain At War
By Roger A. Freeman, Published by The Daily Express.

Britain Tip and Run 42-43
By L.F. Bover

British Homefront 1939-45
By Martin J. Bradley
Illustrated by Malcomb Mc.Gregor
Published by Osprey Publishing.

British Home Defences 1940-45
By Bernard Lowry.
Illustrated by C.Taylor and V.Boulanger.
Published by Osprey Publishing.

British Society 1914-45
"The Social History of Britain".
By Joe Stevenson, Published by Pelican.

British Women's Uniforms in Colour Photographs.
By Martin Brayley and Richard Ingram.
Published by Crowood.

Churchills Secret Army
A History of the Auxilliary Units in WWII.
By John Warwicker, Published by Frontline books.

Devon Within Living Memory.
Published by The Devon Federation of Women's
Institutes.

Devon and Cornwall Airfields In The Second World War
By Graham Smith, Published by Countryside Books.

East Devon At War
By Ted Gosling and Ray Chapple.
Published by Alan Sutton Publishing.

Exercise Tiger
"The D-Day Practise Landing Tragedies Uncovered"
By Richard Bass, Published By Tommies Guides.

Exeter Airport In Peace And War
By Geoff Worrall, Published by Devon Books.

Exeter a Shattered City
The Exeter Blitz Illustrated.
By Peter Thomas, Published by Halsgrove.

Exeter In The 1940's
By Todd Gray, Published by The Mint press.

Exeter Remembers The War
By Todd Gray, Published ByThe Mint Press.

Exmouth and Budleigh Salterton
Britain In Old Photographs.
By Ted Gosling, Published by Budding Books.

Exmouth and Budleigh Salterton People
By George Pridmore, Published by Obelisk Publications.

Exmouth Century – Part One
By George Pridmore, Published by Obelisk Publications.

Exmouth Century – Part Two
By George Pridmore, Published by Obelisk Publications.

Exmouth Evacuee 1939-1945
By Dennis Cozens, Published By Shaldon Burnham Books

Exmouth Lifeboats 1803 – 2003
By Jeff Morris
Published by Exmouth Station Branch. R.N.L.I.

Exmouth Milestones
A History.
By Eric R. Delderfield, Published by E.R.D.Books 1948

Exmouth Photographic Memories
By John BainBridge.
Published by Francis Friths Photographic memories.

Exmouth Postcards
By Maurice Southwell, Christopher Long, Elizabeth
Gardner and Sally Stocker,
Published by Tempus Books.

Fighter
"The True Story Of The Battle Of Britain"
By Len Deighton, Published By Book Club Associates.

Final Touchdown
Compiled by Grahame Holloway.
Published by The East Devon Aircrew Association.

F.U.B.A.R.
Soldiers slang of WW2.
By Gordon L. Rottman, Published by Osprey Publishing.

Home Front Recall Exmouth
Published by the Exmouth 531st tribute fund.

Kampfflieger
Bomber Crewman of the Luftwaffe 1939-45
By Robert Stedman. Illustrated by Adam Hook.
Published by Osprey.

Keep Smiling Through
The Home Front 1939-45
By Susan Briggs, Published by Book Club Associates.

Living Through The Blitz
By Tom Harrison, Published By Collins 1976.

Make Do and Mend
"Keeping family and home afloat on war rations"
Forward by Jill Norman.
Published y Michael O'Mara Books.

Make Your Own Crystal Set.
By R.H. Warring illustrated by Andrew Calder.
Published by Wolfe Publishing Ltd.

Old Telephones
By Andrew Emmerson.
Published by Shire publications Ltd.

Picking Up The Pieces
Women In Wonford 1939-1945 (special Edition).
Written by the Women of Wonford Exeter.
Published By Exeter and Devon Arts Centre.

R.A.F. Squadrons
A Comprehensive Record Of The Movement And
Equipment Of All R.A.F. Squadrons And Their
Antecedents Since 1912.
By. Wing Commander C.G.Jefford M.B.E., R.A.F.
Published by. Airlife Publishing Ltd.

Make Do and Mend
Keeping the family afloat on war rations.
Reproductions of official secondworld war instructiin
leaflets. Foreword by Jill Norman.

Modern Small Arms
An Illustrated Encyclopeadia Of Famous Military
Firearms. By Major Frederick Myatt M.C.
Published By Salamander Books.

Sidmouth The War Years
By John Adkins.

Somerset Verses Hitler
Secret Operations In The Mendips 1939-1945.
By Donald Brown, Published by Countryside Books.

St. Peters Church Budleigh Salterton 1893-1993
Published by St.Peters Church (Centenary Publication)

Take Cover
The Memories Of A Devon Policeman, 1938-1946.
Written by Edward Trist.
Compiled by Simon Dell, M.B.E.

Target Exeter
By Geoff Worrall, Published By Geoff Worrall

The 1940's House
By Julliet Gardiner, Published by. Channel 4 Books.

The 1940's Look
Recreating The Fashions, Hairstyles And Make-up
Of The Second World War.
By Mike Brown, Published by. Sabrestorm Publishing.

The Battle of Hurtgen Forest
By Charles Whiting, Published by Pan.

The British Home Front 1939-45
By Martin J. Bradley
Illustrated by Malcomb Mc.Gregor
Published by Osprey Publishing.

The British Red Cross
A pictorial history of 125 years of the British Red Cross
By Emily Wood.
Published By Dorling Kindersley Books.

The Few
Summer 1940 and the Battle of Britain.
By Phillip Kaplan and Richard Collier.
Published by Geenwich Editions / Orchard.

The Home Front
British Wartime Memorabilia 1939-45
By Peter Doyle and Paul Evans.
Published By. The Crowood Press.

The Home Guard
By S.P. Mackenzie, Published by Oxford Press.

The Typhoon and Tempest Story
By Chris Thomas and Christopher Shores.
Published by Arms and Armour Press.

The Way 'Twas
A Devon Country Boy's Memories
By Walter Isaac, Published by P.W. Isaac.

Touchdown East Devon.
Compiled by Grahame Holloway.
Published by The East Devon Aircrew Association.

War Over The West
By Eddie Walford, Published by Amigo Books.

When the Siren Wailed
By Crystal Elizabeth Nicholson.
Published by. C.E. Nicholson 2005
An account of her life in Exmouth during WWII.

Winston Churchill's Toyshop
By Colonel Stuart Mc Crae.
Published by Kineton: The Roundwood Press. 1971.

Women At War In Uniform 1939-45
By Carol Harris, Published By Sutton Publishing

The People's War
By Juliet Gardiner, Published By Select Editions.

Wartime Publications

14th (Moorside) Devon Home Guard
No Author Named. No Publisher Named.
Book number W356-1.

Air Raid Precautions
Home Office official Publication
Published By H.M.S.O. 1938.
Foreword by Samuel Hoare.
(A Facsimile of this book is now available from Tempus
Publishing) ISBN-7524-4470-3

Civil Defence
A Practical Manual.
By C.W. Glover, Published (1942) by Chapman and Hall
Ltd.

Devon W.I. Cookery Book.
(wartime edition) Edited by Mrs. Blackmore. Published by
Devon Federation of Women's Institutes.

"Forever Faithful"
The Story of the 1st (Loyal) Battalion of the Exeter Home
Guard. By Lt. Col. H.J. Wiltsher O.B.E.

On Guard! 10th Battalion Of
The Devonshire Home Guard.
Edited By G.H. Lidstone.
Published By The Battalion Publication Commitee.

The 5th (Bideford) Battalion Of The Devon Home Guard
By Colonel D.C. Crombie C.B.E.

The Home Guard of Britian
By Charles Graves
Published by Hutchinson and Co. London / New York /
Melbourne. 1943.

The Home Guard Manual 1941
Published by H.M.S.O.

The Home Guard Pocket-Book 1942 (Second Edition)
By Brigadeer General. A.F.U. Green, C.M.G,D.S.O., p.s.c.
A reprint of this book is now available.
Published by Conway Books.

The "New" Rapid Pocket Ready Reckoner.
By J. Gall-Inglis, F.R.S.E.
Published (1941) by Gall and Inglis.

The Picture Post
Volume 8 Number 12. September 21st 1940.
"The Home Guard Can Fight"
By Tom Wintringham.

The Story of the Exeter Blitz
By S.M. Green, Published by Wheaton of Exeter

Appendices

APPENDIX I - ROLL OF HONOUR

NAME	RANK AND ARM OF SERVICE	APPROXIMATE DATE
Percy Acton	Royal Navy	May. 1941
William Barclay	Captain. Army Air Corps	January. 1945
Dennis Barnes	Sergeant Bombardier R.A.F.	May. 1944
William George Bedwell	Royal Engineers	January. 1941
Ralph Bennett	Airborne Unit	July. 1944
J.P. Boddington	Sergeant R.A.F.	June. 1940
Kenneth H. Bonner	Flying Officer R.A.F.	November. 1944
William H. Boundy	Pilot Officer R.A.F.	June. 1943
Leslie R. Bowmer.	Lance Corporal Royal Engineers	September. 1944
Joyce F. Bowmer	A.I.D (?) (Possibly V.A.D.)?	April. 1943
E.T. Bradford	Pilot Officer R.A.F.	December. 1941
William H.T. Breading	Leading Signaller Royal Navy	June. 1940
Leslie W.C. Bricknell	Royal Artillery	November. 1942
Gerald E. Brown	Sergeant R.A.F.	March.1944
Charles E. Burch	Chief Petty Officer Royal Navy	June. 1940
Peter Cable	Royal Tank Regiment (?)	March.1943
E.J.L. Carpenter	Flying Officer R.A.F.	August.1944
Charles Carter	Royal Tank Regiment (?)	May. 1943
Frederick J. Carter	Sergeant Army (?)	October. 1942
Stanley A. Carter	Sergeant R.A.F.	August. 1942
Gear E. Chapman	Herefordshire Regiment	April. 1945
William Chown	Leading Stoker Royal Navy	December. 1942
J.A. Chudley	Army	November. 1944
Charles Clare	Royal Engineers	December. 1941
Cyril Cockerton	Infantry Regiment	March. 1945
Leslie Collins	Leading Air Craftsman R.A.F.	May.1944
Dudley S. Cooper	Sub. Lieutenant Royal Naval Volunteer Reserve	May. 1943
George Cornish	Royal Marines	17th September. 1939
John F.R. Crane	Flying Officer R.A.F.	May. 1940
E.S.C. Cross	Flight Lieutenant R.A.F.	November. 1944
William K. Daniel	Royal Tank Regiment	July. 1941
Jack Daveyv	Sergeant R.A.F.	December. 1942
Raymond Davey	R.A.F.	October. 1945
Leonard E. Davies	Devonshire Regiment	August. 1945
W.A.L. Davidson	Sergeant R.A.F.	March. 1941
William Denner D.S.M.	Chief Petty Officer Royal Navy	June. 1941
W.J. Dunster	Cook Royal Navy	September. 1943
Sidney Edwards	Army	April. 1942
Cecil Fowler	Royal Engineers	June. 1940
Ronald Fowler	Merchant Navy	March.1942
William H. Gard	Pilot Officer R.A.F.	June. 1944
Alf Gatter	Devonshire Regiment	May. 1944
Eddie Gillard	Army	June. 1943
Dennis Glover	R.A.F.	July.1940
John Godliman	Bugler Royal Navy	July. 1940
William J.Gooding	Chief Petty Officer Royal Navy	June.1940
Robert R. Graham	Commander Royal Navy	December. 1940
Tony Greenaway	Sergeant R.A.F.	June. 1941
James Hall	Royal Navy	December. 1944
Kenneth Hancock	Chief Engineer Artificer Royal Navy	February. 1944
Clifford R. Harris	Major. Royal Engineers	September. 1944
Frank R. Hartnell	Airborne Division	March. 1945
William R. Hawkins	R.A.F.	September. 1944
J. Hayman	Petty Officer Royal Navy	April. 1941
W.J. Heard	Lance Corporal Royal Engineers	May.1944
J.F. Heimsath	Sergeant Pilot R.A.F.	May. 1945
Ted Hewitt	Petty Officer Royal Navy	February. 1942
S.A. Hillman	Flight Sergeant R.A.F.	May. 1940
Richard Holloway	Telegraphist Royal Navy	17th September. 1939
C.J. Holman	Electrician Artificer Royal Navy	June. 1940
R.A. Holmes	Royal Armoured Corps.	October. 1944
John D. (Jackie) Hough	Second Officer Merchant Navy	April. 1943
Phillip E. Humphries	Sergeant R.A.F.	February. 1945
Kenneth Hunt	Flight Engineer Sergeant R.A.F.	September. 1942
W.W. Hutchinson	Leading Aircraftsman R.A.F.	July. 1941

Geoffrey H. James	Sergeant R.A.F.	April. 1940
Dick Jarvis	Corporal the Devonshire Regiment	July. 1944
James F. Jefferies	Telegraphist R.A.F.	May. 1941
Ronald G. Jewell	Sergeant Pilot R.A.F.	March. 1943
Harold Jones	Lance Bombardier Royal Artillery	June. 1940
Walter B. Kemeys-Jenkin	Lieutenant the Devonshire Regiment	September. 1944
John N.W. Kerr	Squadron Leader R.A.F.	July. 1943
O.J. Lander	Flying Officer R.A.F.	September. 1944
S.C. Lane	Anti-Aircraft	October. 1942
Gordon Langdon	Sergeant Observer R.A.F.	December. 1941
Henry J. Lewis	Sergeant Royal Artillery	May. 1940
John G. Llewwelyn	Wing Commander R.A.F.	May. 1940
Robert Lomax	Pilot Officer R.A.F.	July. 1941
D. Loving	Electrician Artificer Royal Navy	December. 1941
Ernest G. Ludgate	Regimental Sergeant Major, Devonshire Regiment	August. 1943
Martin H. Macpherson	Captain Royal Navy	November. 1939
Harry G. Manning	Merchant Navy	January. 1943
Lawrence R. Marshall	Pilot Officer R.A.F.	September. 1941
Roy Marston	Flight Sergeant R.A.F.	March. 1944
John Paul Telford Martin	Sub. Lieutenant Royal Naval Volunteer Reserve	December. 1942
William H. Martin	Royal Naval Submarine Service	August. 1941
William D. Minor	Petty Officer Royal Navy	March.1943
Harold Mock	Flying Officer R.A.F.	February. 1945
C.A.C. Montgomery	Lieutenant Commander Royal Navy	December. 1941
Francis D. Norton D.F.C.	Flying Officer R.A.F.	December. 1943
Ivor Norton	Telegraphist Royal Navy	17th September. 1939
Bernard Palfrey	Army	June. 1944
Herbert Palmer	Corporal Royal Signals	February. 1943
Jack Pannell	Corporal	December. 1943
William Pannell	Petty Officer Royal Navy	May. 1941
Maurice Paver	Royal Navy	June. 1942
H.P. Payne	Lieutenant Nigerian Rgt. Indian Commission	May. 1944
Charles A. Penaluna	Corporal Royal Engineers	May. 1943
Norman C. Perry	Royal Navy	December. 1941
F.C. Piesse	Band Master Royal Marine Band	October. 1943
Frank H. Pitman	Wireless Operator (Royal Navy)	January. 1943
George Pyne	The Devonshire Regiment	February. 1944
W.H. Robjohns	Sergeant R.A.F.	February. 1944
Peter H. Rodwell	Flight Sergeant R.A.F.	January. 1945
William Salter	Army	November. 1944
Jack Sedgemoor	Royal Navy	November. 1939
Neil Shapley	R.A.F.	September. 1943
Edward J. Skinner	Petty Officer Royal Navy	November. 1939
H.J. Skinner	Royal Artillery	September. 1944
Ivor Skinner	Telegraphist Royal Navy	17th September. 1939
Roy Skinner	Royal Navy	December. 1941
Harry Smith	Sergeant Army (?)	August. 1944
S. "Syd" Smith	R.A.F.	August. 1943
Leonard Soper	Royal Engineers	May. 1942
Charles P. Southcott	Sergeant / Flight Engineer R.A.F.	August. 1943
Cecil J. Southwell	R.A.F.	August. 1943
Eustace Stamp	Sub. Lieutenant Royal Naval	March. 1943
Henry F. Stone	Army	October. 1942
William F.G. Strawbridge	Merchant Navy	May. 1940
Dick Street	Army	August. 1944
F. Surridge	The Devonshire Regiment	December. 1944
Douglas E. Taylor	Flight Lieutenant R.A.F.	May. 1944
D.E. Thomas	Lieutenant Royal Army Service Corps	September. 1942
Michael Tickell	Army	May. 1941
James H. Tolman	Pilot Officer R.A.F.	December. 1941
Gilbert Venner	Lance Corporal Army	June. 1944
Frederick Vincent	Petty Officer Royal Navy	June. 1940
Gordon R. Webb	Major The Indian Army	July. 1944
Albert E. West	Royal Navy	September. 1944
William F. Whatmore	Duke of Cornwall's Light Infantry	June. 1945
E.H. Williams	Pilot Officer R.A.F.	March. 1944
George Willis	Flight Sergeant R.A.F.	March. 1944
Stan Wills	Corporal Army	March. 1940
Robert F.J. Wiltshire	Leading Aircraftsman R.A.F.	March. 1940
Harry B. Wood	Flight Sergeant R.A.F.	May. 1940
Charles F. Worsley	Second Lieutenant Royal Armoured Corps	July. 1942
Edward J. Wright	Lieutenant Royal Engineers	February. 1945
Robert A. Wright	Flight Lieutenant R.A.F.	December. 1941

APPENDIX II
KEYS TO HOME GUARD PHOTOGRAPHS

Key to photograph on page 23: *477 Royal Artillery Home Guard Coastal Battery.* This photograph was taken in front of the Imperial Hotel September 24th 1944 by a local Photographer called John Puddicombe.

Back Row. From Left to Right 1. Gunner W.G. Andrews. 2. Gunner A.V. Bolt. 3. Gunner W.J. Doderell. 4. Gunner J.W. Fasey. 5. Gunner H. Long. 6. Gunner. A.L. Skinner. 7. Gunner W.J. Richards. 8. Gunner S.W. Martin. 9. Gunner L.H. Farrant. 10. Gunner A. Pemberton. 11. Gunner Raymond A. Steer.

Third Row. From Left to Right 12. Gunner Percy W. Gatter. 13. Gunner W.B. Luxon. 14. Gunner C. Thomas. 15. Gunner G. Hitchcock. 16. Gunner J.R.G. Thorn. 17. Gunner W.T. Morrish. 18. Gunner A. Edwards. 19. Gunner Edward J. Derrick. 20. Gunner J. Hyde. 21. Gunner A.J.R. Seager. 22. Gunner C. Dudley. 23. Gunner B. Eley. 24. Gunner Michael A.G. Heard. The only man wearing his Royal Artillery gunner's white lanyard.

Second Row. From Left to Right 25. Lance Bombardier. R.C. Smith. 26. Gunner E.T. Pannell. 27. Gunner T. Western. 28. Gunner E. Williams. 29. Lance Bombardier. J.W.M. Denford. 30. Gunner H. Stowell. 31. Gunner G.H. Slocombe. 32. Gunner A.G. Brailey. 33. Gunner E. McIntosh. 34. Gunner P.L. Harris. 35. Gunner C. Nichol. 36. Gunner P. Sedgemore. 37. Lance Bombardier. A.A.G. Searle.

Front Row. From Left to Right 38. Bombardier Arthur J. Clode. 39. Sergeant G.M. Walburn. 40. Sergeant T.C.V. Burnhill. 41. Second Lieutenant G.R.W. Glanville. 42. Captain A.E. Jones. M.C. (seated with stick). 43. Major A.S. Archdale. D.S.O. (seated with stick). 44. Second Lieutenant S.J.G. Southon. 45. Company Sergeant Major C.H. Havill. 46. Sergeant H. Swinnerton. 47. Sergeant E. C. Raven. 48. Bombardier Wilf Lowton. 49. Bombardier E. Charlie Bond.

Key to photograph on page 24: *N.C.O.'s of Exmouth Company 2nd (Clyst) Battalion Home Guard*

Back Row. From Left to Right 1. Sergeant G. Seldon. 2. Sergeant T. Mathews. 3. Sergeant W. Croft. 4. ? 5. Sergeant. W. Pascoe. 6. Sergeant H. Lawes. 7. Sergeant ?

Middle Row. From Left to Right 1. Sergeant C. Tindall. 2. Sergeant W. Holman. 3. Sergeant J. Brock. 4. Sergeant W. Clarke. 5. Sergeant W. Bryant. 6. Sergeant Reginald Dixon. 7. Sergeant Frank Troulan. 8. Sergeant Roy. Fairchild. 9. Sergeant R. Haydon.

Front Row. From Left to Right 1. Sergeant L. Hyde. 2. Sergeant W. Pope. 3. Quarter Master Sergeant. P. Mc Larin. 4. Company Sergeant Major. Charlie Havill. 5. Sergeant F. Havill. 6. Sergeant A.E.D. Pollard. 7. Sergeant C. Axon.

APPENDIX III
EXMOUTH MEN KNOWN TO HAVE SERVED IN THE HOME GUARD

Southern Command

The Exmouth men served under Southern Command, the Clyst Battalion. Listed below are the combined members of 2nd Clyst Battalion Exmouth Company and the 477 Royal Artillery Coastal Battery.

There are no official records held to give all of the names of these men. This list had been put together with the aid of photographs and the last surviving members of the Exmouth Home Guard.

There are approximately 700 Guardsman's names missing from this list, who served during the war years. I am keen to complete this information if possible. Please forward any names to my e-mail address given at the front of the book.

Exmouth Guardsman's names listed by rank first then alphabetical order.

OFFICERS:
Majors
1. Major A.S. Archdale D.S.O. 2. Major. J.W. Palmer.

Captains

1. Captain. T.C.C. Evans. D.S.O. 2. Captain A.E. Jones, M.C. 3. Captain. A.C.G. Roberts. M.C.

Lieutenants

1. Lieutenant. A. Beach. 2. Lieutenant. R.T. Anderson. 3. Lieutenant. S.C. Cassyn. 4. Lieutenant. W.A. Ingham. 5. Lieutenant. J.M. Pavey. 6. Lieutenant. J.F.R. Richards. 7. Lieutenant. C.R. Rickeard. 8. Lieutenant H.W. Sharp. 9. Lieutenant. A.R. Smith. 10. Lieutenant. H.S. Sutherland.

Second Lieutenants

1. 2nd Lieutenant. W.A. Britton. 2. 2nd Lieutenant. K.H. Coxe. M.C. 3. 2nd Lieutenant G.R.W. Glanville. Owned a Drapers shop in The Strand. 4. 2nd Lieutenant. A.F. Pratt. Second Lieutenant. 5. S.J.G. Southon. An Accountant. His house was destroyed on 26th February 1943 at 12.15 in the German "Hit and Run" Raid. 9. Mr. Anstey? (Was based at the Seaman's Mission)

SERGEANTS AND OTHER N.C.O.S

Company Sergeant Major

1. Company Sergeant Major Charlie H. Havill. He owned a boot and shoe repair business, a very popular man locally. He was also a musician and played the trumpet in a band.

Quartermaster sergeant

1. Quarter Master Sergeant. P. Mc Larin. Nicknamed "Spuddy". He owned the Hardware shop on the corner of Albion Street and George Street, a very popular and helpful Man.

Sergeants

1. Sergeant. C. Axon. 2. Sergeant. J. Brock. John Owned "Brocks" Furniture shop in Exeter. 3. Sergeant. W. Bryant. (2nd Platoon B Company Lympstone). Sergeant T.C.V. Burnhill. Worked in Norrington's on the Parade and later the Landlord of the Ship Inn. 4. Sergeant. W. Clarke. 5. Sergeant. W. Croft. (2nd Platoon B Company Lympstone) 6. Sergeant. Reginald Dixon. Owned "Dixon's" Boat Yard. 7. Sergeant. Roy. Fairchild. He was a Solicitor. 8. Sergeant F. Havill. (Charlie Havill's Brother). 9. Sergeant. R. Haydon. (2nd Platoon B Company Lympstone). 10. Sergeant. W. Holman. A Plumber by trade. 11. Sergeant. L. Hyde. 12. Sergeant. Harry Lawes. He worked as a carpenter. 13. Sergeant. T. Mathews. 14. Sergeant. W. Pascoe. 15. Sergeant. A.E.D. Pollard. Edward Pollard, worked for Derry's the Chemists in Rolle Street. Joe Radgick's father in law. He kept show canaries. 16. Sergeant. W. Pope. 17. Sergeant. J. Pover. 18. Sergeant E.C. Raven. He was a Gas Company Foreman. 19. Sergeant. F.J. Rendle. 20. Sergeant. G. Seldon. A Shoe repairer in Albion Street. 21. Sergeant H. Swinnerton. Was the owner of the Devon Court Hotel. 22. Sergeant. C. Tindall. 23. Sergeant. Frank Troulan. He was an Optician. 24. Sergeant G.M. Walburn

Corporals and Bombardiers

1. Bombardier E. Charlie Bond. A Private Hackney Cab Driver. 2. Bombardier Arthur J. Clode. He was a trained Engineer and worked for Pankhurst's engineering on the Parade. 3. Corporal. K. Ford. 4. Corporal. F.R. Grimes. 5. Corporal. D.E. Hamson. 6. Corporal. C. Harding. 7. Corporal. H. Lavis. 8. Bombardier Wilf Lowton. He was a gasfitter and ex professional footballer. 9. Corporal. D.C.A. Miller. 10. Corporal. Archie E. Sandcraft. He was Mike Heard's best friend. 11. Corporal. C. Young.

Lance Corporals and Lance Bombadiers

1. Lance Corporal. A. Axon. 2. Lance Corporal. E.T. Bradford. 3. Lance Corporal. R.D. Bradford. 4. Lance Corporal. H.G. Carder. 5. Lance Bombardier J.W.M. Denford. He worked for a wet fish shop in Chapel Street. 6. Lance Corporal. D.B. Mear. 7. Lance Bombardier A.A.G. Searle. 8. Lance Corporal Bill Sleeman. 9. Lance Corporal. D.H. Smalldon. 10. Lance Bombardier. R.C. Smith 11. Lance Corporal. C.J. Tolman.

Privates and Gunners

1. Private. C.W. Andrews. 2. Gunner W.G. Andrews. 3. Private. J. Bain. 4. Private. F. Basgleoppo. 5. Private. S.G. Bastin. 6. Private. S.G. Bastone. 7. Private. F.E. Beach. 8. Private. A.H. Beer. 9. Gunner A.V. Bolt. 10. Private. M.T. Bowden. 11. Private. Bernard J. Bradford. 12. Private. W.L. Bradford. 13. Gunner. A.G. Brailey. Had a second hand shop in Chapel Street. 14. Private. S.C. Bronsdon. 15. Private. C. Brown. 16. Private. H.W. Clarke. 17. Private. A.G. Coles. 18. Private. T. Coles. 19. Private. A.W. Crispin. 20. Private Dennis Davey. was in C Company 3rd platoon. 21. Gunner Edward J. Derrick. Worked for Carters brick works. 22. Gunner W.J. Doderell. 23. Private. H.G. Down. 24. Gunner C. Dudley. A Local

character and man of private means! 25. Gunner A. Edwards. Worked for the Urban District Council. 26. Private. W.G. Edwards. 27. Gunner B. Eley. Worked for the Urban District Council. 28. Gunner L.H. Farrant. 29. Gunner J.W. Fasey. 30. Private. L.J. Franks. 31. Gunner Percy W. Gatter. Worked for Carters Brick Works. 32. Private. A.E. Grant. 33. Private. W.E. German. 34. Private. S. Hall. 35. Gunner P.L. Harris. Owned a bakers shop in St. Andrews Road. 36. Private. C. Harrison. 37. Gunner Michael A.G. Heard. He worked building lifeboats at Dixon's Boat Yard. The only man wearing his Royal Artillery gunners white lanyard in the 477 photograph. A very knowledgeable man. 38. Private. P. Hellier. 39. Private. S.P. Helson. 40. Gunner G. Hitchcock. 41. Private. H. Hitchcock. 42. Private. R. Horn. 43. Gunner J. Hyde. 44. Private. G.A. Islip. 45. Gunner H. Long. 46. Gunner W.B. Luxon. Owned a Haberdashery Shop in The Strand. 47. Private. T. Maden 48. Private. H.D.M. Edwards. 49. Private. L.K. Yardley. 50. Private. W.E.C. Slocombe. 52. Private. H.W. Marshall. 53. Private. A.L. Martin. 54. Gunner S.W. Martin. 55. Gunner E. McIntosh. 56. Private. S.E. Morris. 57. Gunner W.T. Morrish. 58. Private. P.L.S. Mortimer. 59. Gunner C. Nichol. 60. Private. W. Osborne. 61. Private. R.A. Palmer. 62. Gunner E.T. Pannell. Worked for the G.W.R. 63. Private Ken Parker. 64. Private. A. Parkhouse. 65. Private. Percy J.R. Parsons. A well known and popular man. 66. Private. G.R. Parsons. 67. Private. G.W. Parsons. 68. Private. W.J. Payne. 69. Gunner A. Pemberton. 70. Private. E. Perry. 71. Private. R.S. Peters. 72. Private. R.E. Piners. 73. Private. A.G. Pike. 74. Private. G.A. Pike. 75. Private. L.S. Pike. (Ivor Pike's Father) 76. Private. P.G. Richards. 77. Gunner W.J. Richards. 78. Private. W.F. Rockey. 79. Private. W.G. Salter. 80. Gunner A.J.R. Seager. Was the Manager the Forum cinema. 81. Gunner P. Sedgemore. Worked for the Electricity Board. 82. Gunner A.L. Skinner. 83. Private. P.C. Skinner. 84. Gunner G.H. Slocombe. Independent Coal Merchant. 85. Private. G. Smale. 86. Gunner Raymond A. Steer. 87. Private. F.G. Stone. 88. Gunner H. Stowell. Worked at the Point Iron Works. He was killed in an accident with an American truck. 89. Private. J. Street. 90. Private. A.R. Stuart. 91. Gunner C. Thomas. Was a Dust-Cart Driver for the Urban 92. District Council. 93. Gunner J.R.G. Thorn. 94. Private. W.G. Tolman. 95. Private Ray Towill. 96. Private. C.C. Turl. 97. Private. A.H. Weekes. 98. Private. R.T. Weller. 99. Gunner T. Western. Worked in Norringtons on the Parade. 100. Private W.A. Westwood. 101. Private. R.E. Whiddon. 102. Gunner E. Williams. 103. Private. L.M.O. Wills.

Women's Home Guard Auxiliaries
No names have come forward for the Women Auxiliaries except possibly Miss Whiteway. The Home Guard's Secretary, who worked at the Sailors Rest.

APPENDIX IV

EXMOUTH POLICE

Devon Constabulary "D" Division, Exmouth Force Members

Inspector. W. Abrahams. Sergeant. Donald Charles Buckingham. P.C. Blamey. P.C. "Ossie" Boyd. P.C. Fogwill. P.C. Leach. P.C. Ron Lee. P.C. Mc Sweeney. P.C. "Ollie" Oliver. P.C. Pester. P.C. Ronald Rendell.

Key to Photograph on page 36: *Exmouth's War Reserve Constables 1943*

Back Row (Standing) Left to Right 1. W.R.C. E.G. Manning. 2. W.R.C. C. H. Avery. (Charlie) 3. W.R.C. William E. Ackland. (Bill) 4. W.R.C. R.H. Parker. (Roy) 5. W.R.C. R.J. Blewett. 6. W.R.C. P.R.B. Bradford, (Percy) 7. W.R.C. S. Rees.

Front Row (Sitting) Left to Right 8. W.R.C. .H. West. 9. Inspector W. Abrahams. 10. Superintendent W.C. Johnson. 11. Sergeant R. Lee. 12. W.R.C. L.G.G. Langdon. (George)

APPENDIX V

THE A.R.P. / CIVIL DEFENCE

Authors Note. Senior Wardens were also known as Sector Wardens.

Key to photograph on page 76: *Exmouth Corps of Air Raid Wardens, Sector 16-18 1944*
Back Row Left to Right. 1. Mr. H.W. Bastin. 2. Mr. F.W. King. 3. Mr. W.J.K. Harris. 4. Mr. F. Patch. 5. Mr. R.G. Brinnicombe. 6. Mr. A.C.T. Saunders. 7. Mr. F. L. Davey.
Front Row Left to Right. 8. Mr. R. Pocock. 9. Mrs. E.K. Perriam. 10. Mr. B. Rusling. 11. Mr. A. Moore. 12. Miss. D.H. Mann. 13. Mr. W. Box.

Sector 15 photograph on page 76:
People recognised in the photograph, but positions unknown. H.W. Stocker Sector Warden (Harry) white helmet in the front centre wearing glasses. Franks, Burrows, Harris, Miss Stocker, Sheppard, Reverend Carey, Wotton, Flook, Mrs. Sheppard, Mrs, Batchelor, Mitchell, "Suzy" Copp, Fairchild, Goodman.

The Decontamination Squad
A photograph is known to have been taken of the Decontamination Squad during WW II. No copies were available to publish.

Officers in Charge
Mr. Campbell-Dudley (Chemist), Mr. H.W. Bastin.
Known Members.
1. Mr. L.H. Bastin. 2. Mr. J.A. Nelson. 3. Mrs. Vi. Mellish. 4. Miss A. Spink. 5. Mrs. I.E Bacon. 6. Mrs. M.T. Macmillan. 7. Mr. C.A. Shute. 8. Mr. G.H. Croft. 9. Mrs. Katherine R. Basgleppo. 10. Mr. W.H. Cox. 11. Mr. F.R. Mathews. 12. Lt. Colonel. E. Clayton. 13. Mr. E.F. Bastin. 14. Mr. W. German. 15. Mrs. Ivy F. Gale. 16. Lou Gage.

Exmothians that served in the A.R.P.

Exmouth Group 2 Wardens
Group Warden
Captain A. Dixon. Royal Navy (retired).

Sector 4
Senior Warden
Mr. William G. Morris.
Wardens
Mr. S.E. Knowling. Mr. A.W. Spencer. Colonel. P.H. Campbell. Mr. J.E. Denham. Mr. E.T. Bond.
Supernumeraries
Mr. J.H. Jarman. Mr. O.A. Guy.

Sector 5
Senior Warden
Mr. T.A. Raikes.
Wardens
Mrs. ? Raikes. Mr. C.W. Cardell. Mr. E.A. Nichols. Mr. M. Tucker. Mr. W.T. Doble.

Sector 7
Senior Warden
Mr. C.H. Whitehouse.
Wardens
Mr. H.T. Marchant. Mr. J.W. Hayman. Mr. A.C. Strang. Mr. J. Ley. Mrs. W. Butcher.
Supernumerary
Mr. L.N. Cloke.

Sector 8
Senior Warden
Mr. H.M. Tickell.

Wardens
Mr. E. Kenyon. Mr. C.H. Roper. Mr. F. Dunsford. Mrs. W.L. Hillman. Mrs. E.F.C. Caton.

Sector 9
Senior Warden
Mr. A.J.T. Ogden.
Wardens
Mr. H.J. Stoneman. Mr. E. Jeffs. Mr. F.C. Wetherill. Mr. D.F. Civil. Mr. W.J. Langdon.

Sector 10
Senior Warden
Rev. E.C. Mortimer.
Wardens
Mr. J. Chudley. Mr. T.J. Marks.
Special Warden
Mr. D.A.W.A. Hughes, M.A. (Headmaster)

Sectors 16-18
Deputy Head Warden
Mr. B. Rusling. Deputy Head Warden
Senior Wardens
Mrs. E.K. Perriam. Sector Warden Mr. A. Moore. Sector Warden Miss. D.H. Mann. Sector Warden
Wardens
Mr. H.W. Bastin. Mr. F.W. King. Mr. W.J.K. Harris. Mr. F. Patch. Mr. R.G. Brinnicombe. Mr. A.C.T. Saunders. Mr. F. L. Davey. Mr. R. Pocock. Mr. W. Box.

APPENDIX VI

THE FIRE GUARD

Key to photograph on page 91: *Sector 104/c Fire Guards at All Saints Church 1941*
The group which were responsible for the Waverly Road area are pictured with their stirrup pumps and hose supports/shields and Fire Buckets.

Back Row Left to Right 1. Mrs. Pile. 2. Mrs. Mc Cabe. 3. Mrs. Peters. 4. Mrs. Corbyn. 5. Mrs. Handy. 6. Mrs. Gorfin.
Second Row Left to Right 7. Mr. Gage. 8. Miss. Bower. 9. Miss Hart. 10. Mrs. Davis. 11. Mrs. Bragg. 12. Miss Copp. 13. Miss Bradbeer. 14. Miss. Owens. 15. Mr. Gorfin.
Front Row Left to Right 16. Miss. Hart. 17. Mr. Clements. 18. Mrs. Smith. 19. Mrs. White. 20. Mr. Bragg. 21. Mr. Hart. 22. Mrs. Norton. 22. Miss Langdon. 23. Miss Lawes.

Key to photograph on page 91: *Sector 109 Fire Guards at All Saints Church 1944*

Back Row left to right 1. H. Bond. (B.E.M. Medal Recipient) 2. A. Backhouse. 3. M. Bond.
Third Row left to right 4. M. Tucker. 5. D. Seagratt. 6. E. Richards. 7. E. Pidgeon. 8. D. Salmon. 9. L. Bell. 10. E. Williams. 11. M. Oxford. 12. K. Maers. 13. D. Southwell. 14. M. Ridley. 15. F. Humphries.
Second Row left to right 16. D. Dymond. 17. E. Madge. 18. E. Letten, 19. E. Smith. 20. I. Tozer. 21. L. Stubbington. 22. M. Fryer. 23. A. Roach. 24. L. Underwood. 25. A. Thompson. 26. V. Dobel.
Front Row left to right
27. G. Howe-Hayson. 28. W. Hall. 29. A. Dommett. 30. J. Southwell. (Supplementary Fire Party Leader) 31. H. Hayward. (Supplementary Fire Party Leader) 32. W. Bond. (Supplementary Fire Party Leader) 33. G. Hall. (Supplementary Fire Party Leader) 34. B.H. Avery. (Sector Captain) 35. R. Milford. (Supplementary Fire Party Leader) 36. R. Ridley. (Supplementary Fire Party Leader) 37. A. Carpenter. (Supplementary Fire Party Leader) 38. L. Bradford. (Supplementary Fire Party Leader) 39. Miss. Moist. 40. A. Moist. 41. H. A. Johnson.

Typical structure of a Supplementary Fire Party Mr. W.D. Wilson. (Sector Controller). No. 1 Mr. Davey. axe, whistle, torch). No. 2 Mr. Peachey. (stirrup pump).No. 3 Mr. Madge. (2 buckets). No. 1 Mrs. Davey. (axe, whistle, torch). No. 2 Mrs. Madge. (stirrup pump). No. 3 Mrs. Street. (2 buckets)

Exmouth Fire Guards recorded in newspaper reports
42. Mr. Dennis Cozens. 43. Mrs. Cozens, 44. Miss. Davey. 45. Mrs. Kathy Evans. 46. Mr. Percy Norman. 47. Mrs. Tuck.

APPENDIX VII

THE FIRE SERVICES

Key to photograph on page 88: *Exmouth A.F.S. members photographed in the bandstand in Manor Gardens 1941*

Back Row Left to Right 1. A.F. F. Priddis. 2. A.F. C. Thomas. 3. A.F. A.C. Harrison. 4. A.F. R. Perry. 5. Messenger. H. Salter. 6. A.F. H.W. Tucker. 7. L.F. T.D. Priest. 8. A.F. W. Godsland. 9. A.F. C. Young. 10. Messenger. F. Wilson. 11. L.F. E.J. Westcott.
Fourth Row Left to Right 11. L.F. B.W. Dymond. 12. A.F. D.H. Willsman. 13. A.F. J.R. Burch. 14. A.F. J. Mitchell. 15. A.F. L. Perkins. 16. A.F. W. Seager. 17. A.F. J. Osman. 18. L.F. W. Doran. 19. L.F. C. A. Hazell. 20. L.F. R. Smith. 21. L.F. W.T. Comstock.
Third Row Left to Right 22. A.F. C.R. Lovell. 23. A.F. A.V. Perry. 24. A.F. H. Gooding. 25. A.F. D.C. Roberts. 26. Telephonist. M. Bowerman. 27. Telephonist. O. Haines. 28. Telephonist. J. Symes. 29. A.F. C.T. Martin. 30. A.F. W.H. Rogers. 31. L.F. T. Mead. 32. L.F. H.J. Litton. 33. L.F. R.T. Skinner
Second Row Left to Right 34. A.F. W.R. Penwarden. 35. A.F. H.E. Pithers. 36. A.F. F.C. Searle. 37. A.F. W.L. Prior. 38. Telephonist. M. Morris. 39. Lady Driver. J.M. Hazell. 40. Lady Driver. S.L. Brown. 41. Telephonist. E. Saunders. 42. A.F. J.M. Proctor. 43. A.F. W.E. Knight. 44. A.F. S.J. Lugger. 45. A.F. W.B. Bone.
Front Row Seated Left to Right 46. Patrol Officer. E.E. Kendell. 47. Section Officer. G.M. Thompson. 48. Chief Officer. F.W. Bindon. 49. Engineer and Surveyor. B.H. Holden 50. Divisional Officer. G. Piggott. 51. Patrol Officer. A.J. Hedgethorn. 52. Patrol Officer. H.H. Letten.
Boy sitting on the floor 53. Mascot. D. Bindon.

Exmouth Firemen known to have been in the Exmouth Fire Brigade and the A.F.S. in April 1941.

Exmouth Fire Brigade (Full Time)
Officers
Divisional Officer. G. Piggot. Chief Officer. F.W. Bindon. Deputy Chief Officer. G. Rendell. 2nd Officer. J.J.C. Phillips. 3rd Officer. H. Hanger.
Firemen
Fireman. F. Grace. Fireman. R. Pengelly. Fireman. G. Doble. Fireman. H. Pyne. Fireman. J. Deem. Fireman. S.R. Batten. Fireman. A. Sydenham. Fireman. B.M. Brownjohn. Fireman. C. Mortimer. Fireman. W. Bush. Fireman. J. Strawbridge. Fireman. L. West.

The Auxiliary Fire Service
Officers
Section Officer. G. Murray Thompson.
Patrol Officer. Crook.
Patrol Officer. A.J. Hedgethorn.
Patrol Officer. E.E. Kendell.
Patrol Officer. H.H. Letten.
Firemen
Leading Fireman. W.T. Comstock. Leading Fireman. B.W. Dymond. Leading Fireman. W. Doran. Leading Fireman. C. A. Hazell. Leading Fireman. H.J. Litton. Leading Fireman. T. Mead. Leading Fireman. Pricat. Leading Fireman. T.D. Priest. Leading Fireman. R.T. Skinner Leading Fireman. R. Smith. Leading Fireman. H.W. Tucker. Leading Fireman. E.J. Westcott. Leading Fireman. G. Willatts
Auxiliary Firemen
W.B. Bone. J.R. Burch. Davis. Dixon. Escott. W. Godsland. H. Gooding. A.C. Harrison. W.E. Knight. Lavis. C.R. Lovell. Lucas. S.J. Lugger. C.T. Martin. Milford. J. Mitchell. J. Osman. W.R. Penwarden. E. Parsons. L. Perkins. A.V. Perry. R. Perry. F. Priddis. H.E. Pithers. Prior. J.M. Proctor. D.C. Roberts. W.H. Rogers. Rose. W. Seager R. Skinner. Smith. J. Symes. Tanton. C. Thomas. C. Ware. Wills. Wood.
Women Staff
Section Officer. Mrs. S.L. Brown
Drivers
Lady Driver. Mrs. Cosford. Lady Driver. M. Hazell. Lady Driver. Mrs. Lockwood.
Telephonists
Miss. North. Miss. Saunders. Miss. Haynes. Miss. Brockman. Miss. Mary Evans. Mrs. M. Bowerman. Mrs. O. Haines. J. Symes. M. Morris.

APPENDIX VIII

EXMOUTH MEN KNOWN TO HAVE SERVED IN THE OBSERVER CORPS

The men listed are known to have served during the war, prior to it becoming known as the Royal Observer Corps. A photograph is known to have been taken outside "Fox Four" post during WW II but a copy could not be located for publication.

Chief Observer
1. Mr. C.P. Oswin.

Observers
2. Mr. Bragg. 3. Mr. Bulley. 4. Mr. Butler. 5. Mr. Carter. 6. Mr. Crump. 7. Mr. Dearen, 8. Mr. Ellis. 9. Mr. Escott. 10. Mr. Fogarty. 11. Mr. Galsworthy. 12. Mr. Greenaway. 13. Mr. Hemeys-Jenkin. 14. Mr. Hill. 15. Mr. Lake. 16, Mr. Langdon. 17. Mr. Mead. 18. Mr. C.P. Oswin. 19. Mr. Parker. 20. Mr. Reader.

APPENDIX IX

EXMOUTH URBAN DISTRICT COUNCIL 1941

The members of Exmouth Urban District Council during the early part of WW II were as follows.

1. Chairman. Mr. W.E. Dean. 2. Vice Chairman. Mr. W.E. Down. 3. Chairman of the Roads Committee. Mr. F.L. Edwards. 4. Chairman of the Finance Committee. Mr. H.A. Blackmore. 5. Chairman of the Public Health Committee. A.S. Belsher. 6. Chairman of the A.R.P. Committee. A.L.E. Berlyn. 7. Chairman of the Foreshore Committee. J.J. Summers. 8. Town Clerk. R.S. Rainsford. 9. Rating Officer. A.G. Beazely. 10. Surveyor. B.F. Holden. 11. Treasurer. R.J. Cochrane. 12. Sanitary Inspector. E.A.C. Long. 13. Water Works Foreman. S. Jones. 14. Water Inspector. W. Somerton.

APPENDIX XIV

PERSONS KILLED BY ENEMY ACTION IN EXMOUTH IN WW II

18 JANUARY 1941 **Frederick Place:** 1. EMMA MARY DOMMETT. 2. JOHN ALBERT JEFFERY. 3. PATRICIA JEFFERY **The Cross:** 4. MADGE WALKDEN-GOODALL. 5. IVY MAY BATTEN . 6. EDITH MARY MASON. 7. EDWIN DAVID MASON. 8. BERYL MASON. 9. NORMAN MASON. 10. RAYMOND MASON **Chapel Street:** 11. PRIMROSE MAY BROOKS. 12. DOROTHY ETHEL COLES. *25 FEBRUARY 1941* **114 St Andrews Road:** 13. ARTHUR JOHN HARDING HILL. *1 MARCH 1941* **The Upper Parade:** 14. GLADYS GWENDOLINE JACKMAN . 15. LILIAN IRENE TAYLOR. 16. VICTOR JOHN DAVIE 17. JOHN PATCH. *28 MAY 1941* **7 Carter Avenue:** 18. CHARLES HENRY MORTIMER. **18 Woodville Road:** 19. DORIS MAY PANNELL. **20 Woodville Road:** 20. PERCY BRADFORD. 21. EVELYN WINIFRED GRIFFITHS. 22. MAUREEN ANNE GRIFFITHS. **22 Woodville Road:** 23. JANIE BRYANT. 24. ANNE PEMBERTHY. 25. JOYCE HEATH. **24 Woodville Road:** 26. RONALD R. FEAGAN. **11 JUNE 1941** 27. DONALD WALKER. 28. FRANK PERRY. *12 FEBRUARY 1942* **1 Bicton Place:** 29. EDITH LOUISA NICKOLS. 30. ELLEN MARGARET HAMILTON. 31. KATHERINE ANNE HAMILTON. 32. ELIZABETH ANN DENMEAD. 33. FLORENCE ELIZABETH GULLIVER. **Louisa Cottage:** 34. EDITH MAUD PULFORD. **26 FEBRUARY 1943** "Treganna" Louisa Terrace: 35. SIDNEY CLARK **The Strand:** 36. HAZEL ANN EVANS. 37. MARY KATHERINE MOORE HUDSON. 38. BEATRICE LANG. 39. HORATIO JOHN GAY LANG. 40. OLIVE JANE LETTEN . 41. MARY JANE MILLER . 42. NORA DOROTHY NIGHTINGALE. 43. ROBERT JOSEPH NIGHTINGALE. 44. PETER GEORGE TURNER. 45. FRANCES LOUISA TOTHILL. 46. ELIZABETH ROSAMUND WILLIAMS. 47. ALICE REBECCA LOCKHART. 48. FLORENCE BERTHA PIDSLEY. 49. MARGARET PATRICIA HANCOCK. 50. WALTER EDWARD HANCOCK. 51. ELSIE KATE TINDALL. 52. IVA CORDELIA EVELINE HOLME . 53. GEORGE DOMINIC PRICE. 54. HERBERT HENRY NIEBOUR - JOHN H. CLARK (second name). **White Cottage:** 55. LETITIA ANNA LESTOCK-THORNTON. 56. SARAH DOWN. 57. ALICE LOUISA PERHAM. **The Gasometer:** 58. THOMAS MAXWELL. **Windsor Square:** 59. JOHN PONSFORD. **Halsdon Road:** 60. ENA GWENDOURA WARD. **"Oakmead" Phillipps Avenue:** 61. GRESHAM HUGH POWELL WILLIAMS.